"With their new co-edited book, *A Vision of Justice: Engaging Catholic Social Teaching on the College Campus*, Susan Crawford Sullivan and Ron Pagnucco have provided an important service for all of us interested in assisting both students and faculty in learning more about the ideas and values from the rich body of teachings and practices that we call CST. Whether the CST stands for Catholic social teachings, Catholic social thought, or Catholic social tradition, it is the case that not many faculty or students on our Catholic college and university campuses have more than a cursory familiarity with this essential resource. That will change when they delve into this collection of intellectually stimulating, historically rooted, and empirically grounded essays. While not all will agree with every interpretation of the authors, all will benefit from reading and using this significant book in addressing the challenge we all face: to make CST no longer the 'best-kept secret.' We are in debt to the editors and authors of this book for their critical contributions to that task."

> Kathleen Maas Weigert, PhD
> Carolyn Farrell, BVM Professor of Women and Leadership
> Assistant to the Provost for Social Justice Initiatives
> Loyola University Chicago

A Vision of Justice

Engaging Catholic Social Teaching on the College Campus

Edited by Susan Crawford Sullivan and
Ron Pagnucco

Foreword by
Michael Galligan-Stierle

A Michael Glazier Book

LITURGICAL PRESS
Collegeville, Minnesota

www.litpress.org

A Michael Glazier Book published by Liturgical Press

Cover design by Jodi Hendrickson. Photo: Dreamstime.

	2	3	4	5	6	7	8	9

Library of Congress Cataloging-in-Publication Data

    A vision of justice : engaging Catholic social teaching on the college campus / edited by Susan Crawford Sullivan and Ron Pagnucco.

       pages   cm
    "A Michael Glazier book."
    ISBN 978-0-8146-8216-6 — ISBN 978-0-8146-8241-8 (ebook)
    1. Christian sociology—Catholic Church.   2. Universities and colleges—United States.   3. Universities and colleges—Religion.   I. Sullivan, Susan Crawford, editor of compilation.

BX1753.V58   2014
261.8088'282—dc23   2013050526

Contents

Acknowledgments

We would like to thank Michael Galligan-Stierle and Lindsay Weldon of ACCU for all of their support for this book as well as the ACCU Peace and Justice Advisory Committee for their companionship and efforts in bringing CST to college campuses over the years.

We would also like to thank Kate E. Ritger for all of her editorial assistance; we wish her success with her book, *Benedictine Living*. And we are grateful to Sheila Hellermann, peace studies office manager at the College of Saint Benedict and Saint John's University, for all of her help with preparation of the book manuscript.

Foreword

Catholic Social Teaching is central to our faith. It is rooted in the human dignity of all, especially the poor and vulnerable, and is founded on the life and words of Jesus Christ. Catholic Social Teaching is about building a society based on justice and living lives of holiness amid the challenges of society.

In 1998 the U.S. Conference of Catholic Bishops published *Sharing Catholic Social Teaching: Challenges and Directions*. It was the bishops' response to what they described as an urgent need to bring together the church's remarkable commitment to Catholic education and its rich tradition of Catholic Social Teaching. "Far too many Catholics are not familiar with the basic content of Catholic Social Teaching. More fundamentally, many Catholics do not adequately understand that the social teaching of the Church is an essential part of Catholic faith," they wrote.

It was an important moment in the relationship between the church and Catholic colleges and universities, for it demonstrated clearly how well we walk together on this issue. The Association of Catholic Colleges and Universities (ACCU) was honored to be a contributor to this effort, conducting research and submitting a report on the state of Catholic higher education and the social mission of the church.

For the ten-year anniversary of the document's publication in 2008, the bishops' conference gathered many Catholic higher education leaders to highlight the good work being accomplished and to encourage us to continue. The ACCU Peace and Justice Advisory Committee took that occasion to take the pulse of Catholic Social Teaching and Catholic higher education. Our findings were distilled into *Catholic Higher Education and Catholic Social Teaching: A Vision Statement*. This document aimed to help those in Catholic higher education continue to communicate and use the concepts and values of Catholic Social Teaching across the curriculum.

What strikes me most about retracing this history is the continuum—of activity, of commitment, and of faith. At our Peace and Justice Gatherings in 2009, 2010, 2012, and 2013, ACCU reached out to the more than two hundred participants and asked them to offer us their best thinking on the vision statement. They came forward enthusiastically to offer their insights on institutional culture, the dignity of work, education and formation, and other important topics addressed within the document. Their input has enabled us to keep the content fresh and in step with modern campus issues. We published the newest version of the vision statement in 2012. A copy is found in appendix 1 of this book.

Now, with this fine volume, we move the conversation even further. This book is the most recent effort to listen to the world and respond to what we hear. It invites our students, faculty, staff, and leaders of our institutions to consider how they can advance their commitment to Catholic Social Teaching and social justice and to learn from the examples of their peers. Clearly, we all can discover more of the rich history of the church's commitment to social justice and the possibilities that exist to build upon that history, one of our deepest obligations as Catholic educators. This is our prophetic voice at work.

What this book also demonstrates is that, just as the good work of the bishops more than two decades ago drew in those of us with a deep connection to Catholic campuses, Catholic Social Teaching is clearly a bottom-up enterprise, not a top-down initiative. It is that model that keeps the Catholic Social Tradition from being more than just a tradition but rather a living example of the model that Christ gave us. It is what keeps us engaged with issues like immigration, climate change, and peace building.

As we celebrate the fiftieth anniversary of the Second Vatican Council, let us appreciate the opportunity to look back and reflect on how far the church and Catholic higher education have come, together, in their commitment to Catholic Social Teaching. Let us also look forward. With the help of this volume, we can indeed look ahead to a renewed commitment to social justice, to a church that remains vitally alive in the world today.

Michael Galligan-Stierle, PhD
President, Association of Catholic Colleges and Universities

Introduction

Susan Crawford Sullivan and
Ron Pagnucco

Catholic Social Teaching and the College Campus

This volume aims to introduce Catholic Social Teaching (CST) to a new generation of students. In *A Vision of Justice* we explore what CST says on a number of pressing issues of our times *and* provide concrete examples of students, faculty, and staff at Catholic colleges and universities putting teaching into action. *A Vision of Justice* speaks both to formal CST—the body of official church encyclicals and other documents on social issues—and the broader Catholic social tradition of Catholic organizations and individuals working for justice. The essays included in this volume explore the key principles underlying CST, such as notions of the common good, the dignity of the human person, and solidarity with others, and show what is being done at Catholic colleges and universities.[1]

The Catholic Social Tradition and Modern Catholic Social Teaching

The Catholic social tradition is long and broad, encompassing the work and witness of exemplary individuals, the work of Catholic organizations

1. For a good comprehensive basic overview of Catholic Social Teaching, see Thomas Massaro, SJ, *Living Justice: Catholic Social Teaching in Action*, 2nd ed. (Lanham, MD: Rowman & Littlefield Publishers, 2012); and Elias Omondi Opongo and Agbonkhian-meghe E. Orobator, *Faith Doing Justice: A Manual for Social Analysis, Catholic Social Teachings and Social Justice* (Nairobi, Kenya: Paulines Publications Africa, 2007).

that work for peace and justice, and the actions of ordinary parishes and their members as they seek to serve the communities around them. As part of the Catholic social tradition, consider, for example, the life of Dorothy Day (1897–1980), who founded the Catholic Worker Movement in the 1930s which continues today. Day's Catholic Worker houses stress hospitality toward and solidarity with the poor and living lives of nonviolence and peace. Blessed Mother Teresa of Calcutta (1910–1997) turned away from a relatively comfortable life as a schoolteacher to live among the poorest of the poor in India. Winner of the 1979 Nobel Peace Prize, she founded a religious order, the Missionaries of Charity, which works among the poor.

The broad Catholic social tradition includes the work of many Catholic organizations at the international, national, and local levels. We briefly note here some of the largest ones. Catholic Relief Services (CRS) is the official international humanitarian organization of the U.S. Catholic Church. Founded in 1943, it now reaches over one hundred million people in ninety-one countries. Catholic Relief Services aims to foster charity, justice, and peace by working in the spirit of the Catholic social tradition to alleviate poverty and suffering and to build peace and protect human rights in the countries in which it works, serving people only on the basis of need, not religion or other factors. Within the United States, CRS partners with parishes, colleges, and other organizations to connect and encourage Catholics to live out their faith in solidarity with the world's poorest people.[2]

Catholic Charities USA and its local affiliates serve as the largest private network of social service provision in the United States. Local Catholic Charities agencies serve over ten million people every year, regardless of religious background. In addition to its direct service provision to the poor and needy, Catholic Charities is a national advocate for the most vulnerable, advocating in areas such as economic security, health care, housing, and hunger.[3]

The Catholic Campaign for Human Development (CCHD) is the official domestic antipoverty agency of the U.S. Catholic bishops, working to break the cycle of poverty by working in partnership with community

2. http://www.crs.org.
3. http://www.catholiccharitiesusa.org.

organizations and educating on poverty and its causes. These agencies are but a few examples of the largest, most prominent official Catholic organizations trying to live out the Catholic social tradition of charity and justice, but there are many, many smaller ones operating in parishes and communities everywhere.[4]

Within the broad Catholic social tradition of which these agencies and individuals are shining examples, there exists a set of official documents relating the church's ideas on social issues such as poverty, peace, and globalization. Taken together, these documents are referred to as Catholic Social Teaching (CST). Modern CST began when Pope Leo XIII issued the encyclical *Rerum Novarum* (On the Condition of Labor) in 1891. This document emphasizes the rights of workers to receive just pay, to have humane working and living conditions, and to organize into workers' associations. Similar issues continue to be as relevant today as in the time of *Rerum Novarum*, especially in an economy in which inequality has grown and many people's livelihoods have become insecure. The body of official CST includes subsequent papal social encyclicals on the gap between rich and poor countries, war and peace, urbanization, and consumerism, among other topics.[5] Several of these documents are discussed in the following essays.[6] In addition to official Vatican documents, local bishops' conferences translate concepts into their own local contexts. In the United States, the U.S. Conference of Catholic Bishops (USCCB) has issued letters and statements on issues such as economic justice, war and peace, racism, and immigration (see appendix 2 for a list of both Vatican and U.S. bishops' documents).

For those new to CST, it is helpful to think of CST in terms of the key themes that run through the documents and underpin CST. Different scholars and organizations use slightly differing lists of key themes, but below is the list of themes compiled by the USCCB in their 1998

---

4. http://www.usccb.org/about/catholic-campaign-for-human-development/.

5. Massaro, 46–47.

6. There are also a number of good resources that provide commentary and summary (and in some cases, the entire text) of the major CST documents. See, for example, David O'Brien and Thomas A. Shannon, eds., *Catholic Social Thought: The Documentary Heritage: Expanded Edition* (Maryknoll, NY: Orbis Books, 2010).

document, "Sharing Catholic Social Teaching" and abbreviated versions of the themes' descriptions.[7]

- *Life and Dignity of the Human Person*: Life is sacred and the dignity of the human person is the foundation of a moral vision for society. Every person is precious, people are more important than things, and the measure of every institution is whether it threatens or enhances the life and dignity of the human person.
- *Call to Family, Community, and Participation*: The human person is not only sacred but also social. Marriage and the family are the central social institutions in society and must be supported. People have a right and a duty to participate in society, seeking the common good and well-being of all, especially the poorest.
- *Rights and Responsibilities:* Human dignity can be protected and a healthy community can be achieved only if human rights are protected and responsibilities are met. Every person has the right to life and the right to those things required to live in dignity. Corresponding to rights are responsibilities—to one another, our families, and the larger society.
- *Option for the Poor and Vulnerable*: A basic moral test is how the poorest and the most vulnerable are faring. In a world characterized by growing prosperity for some and pervasive poverty for many, we must put the needs of the poor and vulnerable first.
- *The Dignity of Work and the Rights of Workers:* The economy must serve people, not the other way around. Work is not just a way to make a living but is a form of participating in God's creation. The basic rights of workers must be respected—the right to productive work, decent and fair wages, the organization of unions, private property, and economic initiative.
- *Solidarity:* We are one human family, whatever our national, racial, ethnic, economic, and ideological differences. We are our brothers' and sisters' keepers, and loving our neighbor has global implications

7. U.S. Conference of Catholic Bishops, "Sharing Catholic Social Teaching: Challenges and Directions," 1998. http://www.usccb.org/beliefs-and-teachings/what-we-believe/catholic-social-teaching/sharing-catholic-social-teaching-challenges-and-directions.cfm.

in today's world. Love for our brothers and sisters demands that we work to promote peace and justice.

- *Care for God's Creation:* Care and stewardship of the earth shows our respect for the Creator. We are called to protect people and the planet. We cannot ignore the environmental challenge and its moral and ethical dimensions.

As Massaro notes, Catholic Social Teaching derives from four basic sources.[8] One source is Scripture: in the Old Testament we can see prophets who cry out for justice and care of the vulnerable in their societies, and in the gospels we can see Jesus reaching out to the marginalized, healing the sick, and showing love and compassion.

Another source is Reason, which includes things such as rational analysis, philosophy, and use of Natural Law reasoning. In the Catholic Intellectual Tradition, faith and reason are complementary, and one finds in CST much use of philosophy, including the philosophy of non-Christian thinkers such as Aristotle and others.

The third source of CST is Tradition, which includes the writings of theologians and leaders of the church such as Augustine of Hippo and Thomas Aquinas, and the magisterial documents of the church.

The fourth source of CST is Experience, learning from history, from social scientific analysis, and from the lives of the faithful.

One popular way of putting CST into practice is a process summarized as "See, Judge, Act." The first step, seeing, means that putting CST into practice starts with trying to really see and understand the social issue of interest. In the case of poverty, for instance, one would want to gather relevant information—data and statistics, relevant public policies, the faces and stories of people affected by poverty—as well as trying to understand why poverty exists; what structural factors might contribute to its persistence. "Seeing" means true deep social analysis, not just impressions or ideas. Social science and sometimes other sciences can be of great help in doing deep social analysis.

After "seeing," the next step is "judging"—that is, reflecting on what you see and interpreting it. The principles of CST can aid in the judging

8. We draw on Massaro's very helpful discussion of sources of CST in Massaro, 55–75.

step, as you examine a social reality, for example, through the lens of solidarity or preferential option for the poor.

The final step in this model, "act," is just that—after you have seen, and interpreted, then it is time to act. "See, Judge, Act" is actually a cycle, for after action comes looking anew, reflecting, and acting again.

The essays in this book generally follow a "see, judge, act" model in describing a social issue or problem, examining it through the lens of CST, and providing examples of actions taken at our Catholic colleges and universities.[9]

CST and Reflective Action

Consider the following findings for reflection. In a recent book on social justice and the millennial generation, Helen Fox of the University of Michigan discusses important patterns among college students that readers might find familiar. Drawing on studies and observations of the millennial generation (as the current generation of college students and young adults is called), Fox describes a paradox: many millennials are, on the one hand, eager to please, compliant, overscheduled, and anxious about grades, while at the same time confidently believing they can make a difference in the world. In large numbers, college students engage in social service or go on short immersion trips to impoverished areas, tutoring, building houses, and doing many other charitable good works.[10] In short, millennials want to make a positive difference in the world and want to contribute to the common good. But what happens if volunteering is done without much social analysis or reflection? When this happens, one may end up seeing oneself in a "rescuer" role to the "unfortunate others," an attitude that can increase power imbalances and be divisive.

9. See Erin M. Brigham's excellent new volume, *See, Judge, Act: Catholic Social Teaching and Service Learning* (Winona, MN: Anselm Academic, 2013), for a fuller discussion of the see, judge, act process and its application to community-based learning.

10. Helen Fox, *Their Highest Vocation: Social Justice and the Millennial Generation* (Pieterlen, Switzerland: Peter Lang Publishing, 2011), 7–14. Fox notes that these are of course overgeneralizations and not meant to characterize every member of the millennial generation.

Without reflection, do we grapple with the structural reasons behind the situations we encounter? While for some students community service is merely some kind of requirement or a resumé-builder, for most students community service is well-intentioned and students are trying to do good. The question is: how can one see beyond charity and good deeds and come to understand the social and political realities which have shaped social problems? How can one come to see oneself as working in solidarity with the poor, as working *with*, not *for*, them?

To engage in community service or domestic or international immersion trips uncritically can be highly problematic, leading middle-class people to believe that they can come into poor communities as outsiders and "solve" their problems—creating an "us and them" elitist mentality, which, however unintentional, can be experienced by community members as arrogant and condescending.[11] Catholic Social Teaching, with its emphasis on solidarity, participation and empowerment, the dignity of the human person, and the common good, can serve to counterbalance these tendencies, providing the moral and intellectual tools to unpack complex social problems and interactions in a more nuanced way, and to act with, not for, the community. We invite students, faculty, and staff to reflect on their experiences with volunteering and service in the United States and on study abroad/immersion trips. Is it done in true solidarity, to be with and to empower people?

Consider also for reflection: psychologists find that college students and young adults are in a key life stage for developing their identities. With the increased length of schooling and career preparation, "emerging adults" (approximately age eighteen until the mid-twenties) are in the most important developmental period for exploring personal, social, and professional options.[12] In college, students try to figure out a sense of who they are and discern how they want to direct their strengths and interests in terms of a future career. What should I major in? How should I spend my extracurricular time? What do I want to do when I graduate? Both academic coursework and nonacademic experiences, such as volunteer work or campus leadership roles, can have a strong impact in helping to

11. Ibid., 38–39.
12. Jeffery Arnett, "Emerging Adulthood: A Theory of Development from the Late Teens through the Twenties," *American Psychologist* 55 (2000): 469–80.

develop citizens engaged in their communities.[13] Catholic Social Teaching fosters a view of participation in local and global societal life as a moral endeavor.

"How then shall we live?" Tolstoy famously asked. We believe that an introduction to CST can help foster a sense of vocation as you discern how to best use your talents and education when answering this question—a use of your talents and education that goes beyond a narrow focus on wealth and status to what you can contribute toward the common good of your society.[14] Catholic Social Teaching can help you prepare for dealing with the moral and ethical dimensions of your future professions and roles as family members and citizens.

Looking Ahead

This volume grew from a collaboration of scholars working to incorporate CST in their work on their respective campuses. Many of these scholars are current or former members of the Association of Catholic Colleges and Universities Advisory Committee on Peace and Justice, which works to better integrate CST on Catholic college campuses. Most are not theologians but scholars from a variety of disciplines endeavoring to bring CST into their work.

Chapter 1, by noted historian of American Catholicism David O'Brien, looks at the historical trajectory of American Catholicism, in trying to unpack how CST developed for the universal church is applied in the American context. O'Brien looks at the situation of the contemporary American church using a metaphor of "center and edge"—that is, American Catholics are found at the very pinnacles of power and influence in society but are also found in large numbers in our poorest and most vulnerable communities. His essay explains and distinguishes between formal CST found in papal encyclicals and bishops' letters; Catholic social action in organizing for justice; and the Catholic social gospel, fuel-

13. Scott Seider, "Catalyzing a Commitment to Community Service in Emerging Adults," *Journal of Adolescent Research* 22 (2007): 612–39.

14. Also see Susan Crawford Sullivan and Margaret A. Post, "Combining Community-Based Learning and Catholic Social Teaching in Educating for Democratic Citizenship," *Journal of Catholic Higher Education* 30, no. 1 (2011): 113–31.

ing charity and justice toward the poor, peace efforts, and other movements toward a more just and humane society.

Following O'Brien's essay, sociologist Tom Landy takes a step back from CST to look at the broader Catholic Intellectual Tradition. As Landy explains it, the Catholic Intellectual Tradition includes Catholic teaching on justice but also broadly encompasses intellectual and artistic contributions of Catholic thinkers and artists in a wide variety of fields. While modern CST began in 1891 under Pope Leo XIII, the broader Catholic Intellectual Tradition spans two millennia. Landy provides examples from literature, art, architecture, science, philosophy, music, and others. He considers how the Catholic Intellectual Tradition is a tradition in process, continually learning from new knowledge.

Finally, religion scholar David Coleman rounds out the introductory essays with a chapter on religion, state, and civil society in CST. He discusses the forms of church and individual Catholic engagement with society and state. Coleman further examines the role of civil society and the state in CST, and the central importance of the common good in CST.

The book then turns from the more theoretical to the more concrete, looking at how CST addresses some critical issues confronting contemporary society. As CST calls for a preferential option for the poor, this section of the book opens with a chapter on poverty by social work professor Linda Plitt Donaldson and sociologist Susan Crawford Sullivan. Chapter 4 provides a statistical overview of poverty and related issues in the United States and globally, then moves to a discussion of key CST principles which assess how we are to deal with these issues. In his early papacy, Pope Francis has repeatedly stressed the importance of solidarity, service, and justice with regard to the poor. This chapter highlights CST principles such as the dignity of the human person, interdependence and solidarity, and rights and responsibilities, and looks at what CST has to say about the economy and economic justice. Donaldson and Sullivan conclude by providing examples of how students at a number of Catholic colleges are trying to live out the gospel imperative to walk with the poor, alleviate poverty, and bring about more just social structures.

Following this chapter, Fr. Daniel Groody and Colleen Cross take up one of the "hottest" topics of our time—immigration. They discuss how extreme poverty, violent conflicts, natural disasters, human rights violations, and imbalanced international trade agreements, remain the primary reasons people uproot from their homelands and risk their lives and search for better lives. Guided by CST, Catholic institutions and organizations work to stand in solidarity with migrants, regardless of their immigration status. Groody and Cross conclude with examples drawn from Catholic colleges and universities. Through education, advocacy, and direct service, and by providing scholarships and educational opportunities that open doors to the marginalized and excluded, Catholic colleges and universities seek to foster right relationships that promote diversity in the human family and human dignity among those who are most vulnerable in our society.

In chapter 6, theologian Bernard Evans tackles another pressing issue of our times—the environment. Evans discusses how environmental degradation and global climate change pose fundamental challenges to our contemporary form of life. Evans claims that just as care for the sick and respect for the sanctity of life have made Catholic universities centers of research on bioethics, our era desperately needs a similar combination of ethical reflection and scientific research grounded in care for God's creation. To address these global moral challenges, the Catholic community needs education on resource consumption and climate issues in tandem with a rich moral formation. Evans explains how CST calls upon us to help the world see and justly respond to the fact that environmental degradation will adversely affect the world's poor in profound ways. He provides examples from Saint John's University and the College of Saint Benedict of sustainability, community-supported agriculture, and a vast arboretum that fosters environmental respect, education, and stewardship of the land.

The last section of the book turns to issues of peacemaking, human rights, and solidarity. First, Gerard Powers, director of Catholic Peacebuilding Studies at University of Notre Dame's Kroc Institute and coordinator of the Catholic Peacebuilding Network, discusses CST's rich tradition of reflection and action on peace. This tradition includes both the ethics of war and peace (just war and nonviolence) and the spirituality, theology, ethics, and praxis of peacebuilding (conflict prevention, conflict management, and post-conflict reconciliation). Since peace is not just the absence of war, but the result of justice motivated by love, peace calls for the development of just institutions at all levels of society, including international institutions that can address questions that individual nations cannot address alone. Powers provides an example of how Notre Dame lacrosse players worked with the men's basketball team, student government, and other groups at Notre Dame, St. Mary's, and Holy Cross, and with sponsorship by Adidas, to host a major rally for peace in Sudan. Led by the assistant lacrosse coach, a delegation of Notre Dame students then went to Washington, DC, to meet with senior leaders at the White House, State Department, and Congress, as well as with executives at Catholic Relief Services. The campaign concluded with an ESPN half-time segment about the Playing for Peace campaign during a nationally televised lacrosse game.

In chapter 8, sociologist Ron Pagnucco and political scientist Mark Ensalaco look at human rights theory and practice. They show the long history of human rights thought in the Catholic Church and how the church has become a leading advocate of human rights since the late 1960s. They explore the basic tensions between underlying assumptions of CST and underlying assumptions of the secular Liberal Rights Theory that informs much of the secular human rights movement. Pagnucco and Ensalaco also describe the human rights major at the University of Dayton, where students preparing for careers with human rights organizations learn about navigating these tensions. They conclude with an inspiring example of how activism by University of Dayton students helped lead to the passage of anti-trafficking legislation in their state.

In the next chapter, Pagnucco and Kenyan theology professor Fr. Peter Gichure unpack the concept of solidarity, an often-used word in CST. They provide the theoretical underpinnings for understanding what solidarity is and show where CST fits among the models of solidarity. They give an example of the Catholic University of Eastern Africa, the University of Notre Dame, and a local Kenyan parish working together in solidarity on a vexing environmental and social problem. Finally, Susan Crawford Sullivan and Pagnucco conclude the volume with reflections on future directions in CST of Catholic colleges and universities.

We end this introduction by borrowing a concept from the former Jesuit Superior General Fr. Peter-Hans Kolvenbach, SJ, that is, that the measure of Catholic colleges and universities is not what students do but the people they become and how they exercise their adult responsibility for their neighbor and the wider world.[15] Students cannot become what

15. Peter-Hans Kolvenbach, "The Service of Faith and the Promotion of Justice in American Jesuit Higher Education," Keynote Address to 'Commitment to Justice

they do not know and what they do not see. *A Vision of Justice* will provide the tools to *know* the Catholic social tradition—what it is, what is says—but more importantly, allow us to see CST in action in the work of our Catholic colleges and universities as they engage CST principles in building a more just society.

in Jesuit Higher Education," Santa Clara University, October 6, 2000, reprinted in *A Jesuit Education Reader: Contemporary Writings in the Jesuit Mission in Education, Principles, the Issue of Catholic Identity, Practical Applications of the Ignatian Way, and More,* ed. George W. Traub (Chicago: Loyola University Press, 2008), 144–62.

Chapter 1

David O'Brien

The United States' Historical Engagement with Catholic Social Teaching

There is of course a wide diversity among the situations in which Christians—willingly or unwillingly—find themselves according to regions, sociopolitical systems, and cultures. . . . In the face of such widely varying situations it is difficult for us to utter a unified message and to put forward a solution that has universal validity. Such is not our intention, nor is it our mission. It is up to the Christian communities to analyze with objectivity the situation which is proper to their own country, to shed on it the light of the Gospel's unalterable words, and to draw principles of reflection, norms of judgment and directives for action from the social teaching of the church. This social teaching has been worked out in the course of history. It is up to these communities with the help of the Holy Spirit, in communion with the bishops and in dialogue with other Christian brethren and all men of good will, to discern the options and commitments which are called for in order to bring about the social, economic and political changes seen in many cases to be urgently needed.[1]

Part 1: The Historical Trajectory of U.S. Catholicism

As Pope Paul VI made clear, efforts to understand, develop, and apply Catholic Social Teaching (CST) require careful attention to historical

1. Pope Paul VI, *Octogesima Adveniens*, 1971.

1

circumstances, in our case to the social, cultural, and political experience of the people of the United States and the people of the American Catholic Church. Social action leaders have always known they must apply Catholic teaching, developed for the international church, to the particular require-ments of American society.[2] Similarly, teachers and pastoral ministers take into consideration the experience of the people among whom they live and work. In the case of social thought and imagination, as in most Catholic work, Americanization is simply a pastoral as well as an intel-lectual imperative.[3]

So as we begin incorporating Catholic social thought into our research and teaching, what do we make of American Catholicism? Unfortunately there is no widely accepted narrative of the history of Catholicism in the United States. Like everything else in U.S. Catholic life, history is contested, and the contest makes a difference in social thought and imagination.

One way of looking at the contemporary situation of the Catholic Church in the United States is with a metaphor of center and edge: Catho-lics and their church are located in national centers of power and privilege. But Catholics are also found, in large numbers, among the nation's poorest and most vulnerable communities. Descendants of European Catholic immigrants are now spread across the social and cultural landscape; many are now insiders, shaping American institutions, and have a full share of responsibility for public life. At the same time, many African Americans, Latinos, and new immigrants and more than a few descendants of earlier immigrant groups, are economically and socially insecure—unorganized outsiders with limited opportunities and less power.

Catholic pastoral and educational ministries at their best seek to em-power the poor and inspire those who are not poor to use their newly

---

2. This is the central theme of every serious history of CST in the United States. See, for example, Charles Curran, *The Social Mission of the U.S. Catholic Church: A Theological Perspective* (Washington, DC: Georgetown University Press, 2012).

3. Of course, social action often goes further, seeking to develop issues, judgments, and strategies from the bottom up, for example, in faith-based community organizing. See Richard L. Wood, *Faith in Action: Religion, Race and Democratic Organizing in America* (Chicago: University of Chicago, 2002) and Jeffrey Stout, *Blessed Are the Organized: Grassroots Democracy in America* (Princeton, NJ: Princeton University Press, 2010).

acquired resources to secure greater justice for the poor and for society as a whole. Similarly, Catholic social thought and imagination encourages Catholics everywhere to make their own both the option for the poor and dedication to the common good through personal and community-wide efforts to share responsibility for public life. This sounds easy enough but is in fact complex. For example, what does care for the common good require when we think of Christian nonviolence and just war, or getting a good job and "go sell what you have and give it to the poor"? Doing the right thing is one challenge, figuring out the right thing to do is another. That is what we try to think about in programs of education for justice and peace. And that is why, as Pope Paul indicated, social ethics is inseparable from social and historical studies.

Part 2: Catholics at the Center

Some educators work to affirm the quest of outsiders for economic advancement and social respect, and others work to support middle- and upper-class ideals of social service and shared historical responsibility. Presence among both groups, and deep care for them—throughout the history of the United States—is perhaps the great gift Catholic ministry offers U.S. society as a whole.

At one level at least the historical experience of European immigrants and their descendants in the United States is a success story.

Step one in this history was the self-construction of multiple Catholic subcultures among groups who came to the United States in successive waves between 1820 and 1920. Of enormous importance is the fact that many churches and church-related ministries arose from lay initiative, as communities of commitment and mutual assistance grounded in common language, tradition, and experience. While they appeared to some as enclaves of doomed resistance to modernity, in fact they blended "folk memories and new aspirations," their histories shaped by dynamic interaction of family and communal loyalties and the attractions of new-world opportunities for economic, social, and political improvement.[4]

4. Jay P. Dolan's *The American Catholic Experience* (New York: Doubleday, 1985) is an immigrant-centered, bottom-up history of the Catholic people. The link of memory and aspiration comes from the work of Timothy L. Smith, especially

Step two of the Center story was the consolidation of a wider Catholic subculture formed around the journey of families up, out, and into:

- up the social and economic ladder and into managerial and professional jobs with secure income, a well-documented story of social mobility
- out of the tight ethnic neighborhoods and into the automobile suburbs with their thinner relationships and more segmented Catholic practice
- out of embattled ethno-cultural, working-class enclaves and into the many centers of American political, economic, social, and cultural life from the margins once occupied by working-class immigrants

The church for the most part encouraged this ascent; only a few pastoral leaders raised serious questions about the impact of this ascent on national life. When it was starting, back in the late nineteenth century, some bishops, pastors, and lay leaders explored ways to give Catholic meaning to this "Americanizing" experience, but their effort was smothered by the papal condemnation of "Americanism" and the arrival of masses of new Catholic immigrants from southern and eastern Europe. As a result, few people asked about the theological and spiritual meaning of these experiences of social, economic, and cultural transformation.[5] This process reached its climax in the highly organized American church of the period between 1945 and 1965, when the Catholic population doubled, financial support soared to record levels, vocations to the priesthood and religious life kept pace, four million children attended self-financed Catholic ele-

---

"Religion and Ethnicity in America" (*American Historical Review*, December, 1978, 83). I have long argued that failure to appreciate aspirations as well as memories has led to serious misunderstandings of later social history.

5. The condemnation of Americanism in 1899 and subsequent subcultural pastoral strategies tended to locate religious meaning in church and family with work, popular culture, and civic life—secular experience deprived of religious meaning. Americanist ideas revived between 1945 and 1965 and once again sparked a reassertion of Catholic-over-public priorities. On Americanism, see Isaac Hecker, *An American Catholic* (Mahwah, NJ: Paulist Press, 1994), 376–403, and *Public Catholicism* (New York: Macmillan, 1989), chapter 3.

mentary schools, and almost all Catholics attended church regularly. This was the Catholic Church that experienced Vatican II (1962–1965) and the social and moral challenges of the 1960s.

Step three came after Vatican II when dramatic changes in social location and religious self-understanding brought about what some have called the "disintegration" of this remarkable U.S. Catholic subculture. After a generation of dramatic changes the Catholic community no longer seemed "certain and set apart," "happily in but not really of American society."[6] Catholics at the center for the most part still affirmed their Catholic affiliation, at least until recently, and institutions proved remarkably resilient, but church attendance gradually went down, vocations became scarce, identity seemed less certain, conflict and scandal damaged morale, and lay and clerical passivity limited internal reforms and missionary renewal.

Thus many American Catholics of European origin can tell family stories of success while expressing uncertainty about Catholic identity seen in reduced participation by children and grandchildren, reflecting the shallowness, if not the absence, of post-ethnic Catholic culture. These same stories often conclude with testimonies of personal faith, moral seriousness, experiences of intense, if temporary and fragile community, and spiritual hunger. The institutional counterpart of Americanized lay Catholics, found everywhere from Congress and the Supreme Court to positions of power on Wall Street and Hollywood, is evident in the vast reach of Catholic educational, medical, and social service institutions. There too one often finds remarkable work combined with an uneasy blend of religious, professional and public purposes, and uncertainty about Catholic identity.[7]

Education in Catholic social thought and imagination, now firmly embedded in church teaching, even as "doctrine," is often addressed to Catholics at the center. In each country and region Catholics try to understand the meaning of faith and the requirements of discipleship in their historic

6. For disintegration, see Philip Gleason, "In Search of Unity: American Catholic Thought 1920–1960," *Catholic Historical Review* (April 1979): 65. The certain and set apart, in but not of phrases come from James Hennesey, *American Catholics: A History of the Roman Catholic Community in the United States* (New York: Oxford University Press, USA, 1981), chapter 17.

7. See Philip Gleason's Marianist Award Lecture "What Made Catholic Identity a Problem?" (University of Dayton, 1994).

circumstances. In the United States and elsewhere, the church directs pastoral attention and social services to Catholics at the edges but has less success inspiring and educating Catholics at the center. Perhaps the reason for that in the United States is cultural as well as ecclesiastical reluctance to think deeply about one's own social location and responsibility. As a result, American Catholics, like other Americans, often seem like fish in fresh water streams, carried by the flow, doing what the flow allows, hardly aware that they live, after all, in a flowing stream that has been, and is going, somewhere. Social education may begin best with historical self-consciousness.

Part 3: Catholics at the Edge

There are many American Catholics—Native Americans, Mexican Americans, and Puerto Ricans among them—who have always been present on land they knew as their own. Some found freedom and success, but, in the aftermath of conquest, they were perceived, with their communities, as outsiders in civic and at times religious life. As large numbers of newcomers arrive in the United States, many of them Catholics, renewed energies and great pastoral challenges come from the social edges of the American people. Once again one finds in those communities, especially among those who take the initiative to join or form communities of faith, the familiar combination of "folk memories" and "new aspirations." The growing numbers of Catholics who are either recent immigrants or newly organized Latinos and African Americans together may already constitute a majority of baptized Catholics in the United States. Pastoral development and institutional self-construction varies, and there are vigorous competitors for their religious loyalty.

Each group experiences conflicting attractions of memory and hope, determination to preserve and win respect for traditional culture, and fierce commitment to a better life for the next generation. Each struggles too with those burdens of poverty, discrimination, and class conflict that accompany immigration at a time when the increasingly undemocratic political economy places enormous burdens on workers, educated or not, and limits their capacity to organize. The result is that people at the edge face enormous and fairly obvious injustices. Thus it is that the most common theme of CST is the "option for the poor," discussed by Sullivan and Donaldson in their chapter 4 on poverty. So too the acknowledgment by the vast majority of self-professed Christians that caring for poor people is one of the most important markers of faith.

Signs are everywhere of American Catholics at the edge, as are efforts by their fellow Catholics to assist them to express folk memories and realize new aspirations. The bishops, speaking and acting on the community's behalf, strongly support immigration reform respectful of persons and families. They regularly champion safety-net programs for the poor and, persistently if less forcefully than in the past, public policies aimed at full employment and an equitable distribution of the burdens and benefits of economic development. Local churches work hard to support educational opportunities for communities with limited resources, both by seeking creative ways to support parochial schools and initiating creative educational alternatives. College and university mission statements and financial aid policies acknowledge responsibility to assist people at the edge. Catholics at the center and edge together maintain the vast network of Catholic agencies of medical care and social service, from neighborhood soup kitchens and settlement houses to complicated public partnerships for the delivery of social services to huge hospitals embedded in the country's vast, generous, and enormously costly system for health care.

Perhaps most remarkable has been the forty-year-old effort by the American Catholic Church to support grassroots organizing efforts among those at the edges of the American political economy. The Catholic Campaign for Human Development (CCHD) is the best known but far from the only Catholic effort to support community organizing, the process by which so many Catholic families and communities earlier negotiated their way from edge to center. Across the country, Catholic Charities, religious orders of men and women, and local parish networks have done this work, as pastoral care and social action converge around democratic methods of grassroots organizing, regarded by some very prominent scholars as the most important movement for social reform in the country.[8]

In the church's work at and for the edge, there are also major, and not unfamiliar, questions of resources, relationships, and respect. Religion in

---

8. See, in addition to Wood and Stout cited above, Mark R. Warren, *Dry Bones Rattling: Community Building to Realize American Democracy* (Princeton, NJ: Princeton University Press, 2001) and more broadly Kristin E. Heyer, *Prophetic & Public: The Social Witness of U.S. Catholicism* (Washington, DC: Georgetown University Press, 2006).

America remains heavily dependent on what a major theologian fifty years ago called "personal decisions constantly renewed amid perilous surroundings."[9] Commitments to social justice are not always an obvious component of these personal decisions. Furthermore, long experience suggests that American religion also tends toward community support in the local church—congregationalism—that may inhibit wider collaborative efforts to bring about social and cultural change. When social services are professionalized and centralized for greater efficiency, parishes at the centers may have little relationship with parishes at the edges. The absence of relationships between people at the center and those at the edge may also reinforce other factors leading to disrespect in both directions, especially when there are perceptions of injustice or irresponsibility.[10]

Thus the multicultural and class challenges associated with increasing inequality of wealth and income facing the country as a whole are present within the church as well. That poses problems, especially when the church resists serious pastoral research and planning of any kind, much less the socio-pastoral planning once common in Latin America. In its absence, institutions and even persons, including bishops, priests, and other ministers, parishes, and educational and social institutions find themselves on their own. Parish shopping among the laity, decentralized pastoral ministry in parishes, and continuing "mission and identity" discussions, and self-centered strategic planning in institutions reflect the limited ability of the community as a whole to share a common story and engage in internal dialogue, much less develop coherent and collaborative approaches to social education and action.

Part 4: Reflections on the Historical Trajectory of American Catholicism

Three brief comments about this historical sketch as it influences Catholic social thought and imagination.

9. Karl Rahner, *The Christian Commitment: Essays in Pastoral Theology* (New York: Sheed &Ward, 1963), 34.

10. I participated in many dialogues about these matters in the period between 1970 and 1989.

First, the single most important theme of recent American social history is that of historical agency: even in the most oppressive circumstances, like southern slavery, people make decisions, form relationships, and express their experience in song and story. Thus the use of the active voice in speaking of immigrant Catholic projects of subcultural construction. The same is to be said of subcultural disintegration: change came because people sought education, economic opportunity, cultural respect, and political power. At each stage, at center and edge, people have been and remain to some degree architects of their own history. For example, in dealing with elementary and secondary education, U.S. Catholics made separatist choices, while in health care, human services, and higher education they chose to work closely with non-Catholic agencies and to enter into formal relationships with governmental bodies. Important arguments took place about these matters. There were and remain important strategic arguments, a politics of the church, if you will, that requires constant critical examination. In its absence Catholic social thought and imagination may have little impact in church and society. In teaching it should be clear that all are invited to take part in that process of observation, reflection, and action.

Second, the harsh divisions in the U.S. church in recent years turn in part over the question whether the historical journey of European immigrants from edge to center is good news, and constitutes an appropriate direction for families and communities now at the edge. Or was Americanization, and the ideas that affirmed it, Americanism, a huge mistake, as so much contemporary Catholic discourse suggests? Once, ideas of Americanism gave meaning and purpose to the experience of assimilation. That position has recently given ground to contentions that personal and institutional success has been purchased at the cost of religious identity, even integrity, leading to efforts by the hierarchy to reemphasize Catholic identity in theology, pastoral practice, higher education, and more recently social services. Confessional institutions dependent entirely on private funds, such as Catholic elementary and secondary schools, are honorable participants in American civil society and culture.

I have argued elsewhere for a choice which would locate Catholic social thought and imagination more firmly at the center of American life and culture, where so many Catholics live and work and so many hope to live and work. Whether either Americanism or countercultural resistance is the right choice, or the only choice, is the question. On its answer depends the future form and expression of Catholic social thought and imagination, and of Catholic studies of all sorts in our colleges and universities.[11] These disagreements and dialogue about them should be part of any serious program of Catholic social education.

Third, and closely related to this point, is the challenge of dealing with the relationship of the center and edge, the politics of difference within the church. Pastoral and ministerial collaboration within the United States, or its absence, necessarily influences the quality of social ministry and the quality of CST, thought, and imagination. At times the Catholic community has shown a remarkable capacity to convene people across barriers of race, class, and culture. Lizabeth Cohen has recently recalled the participation of the church of Boston in that city's economic renewal in the 1950s and many can recall similar experiences of Catholic leadership in local conflicts over the last fifty years.[12] But Boston Catholics failed in their effort to help overcome bitter divisions during the crisis over "forced busing" in the 1970s, and many Catholics have memories of similar failures in the past. In most cases Catholics would applaud efforts to overcome injustice and serve the common good and would regret absences and failures in that regard. For programs dealing with Catholic social education in colleges and universities, the question of trajectory is very important. Participants in such programs all want to assist students and their families to find secure and respected places in American society. Once social and economic advancement has been achieved, what then? Do we hope to help form leaders like Leon Panetta, a faithful Catholic graduate of Catholic higher education serving at the center of American power? Or do we wish to help form Catholic Workers like peacemaker Christopher Doucot, recently honored by Yale Divinity School? Most would reject an either-or formulation of the question, but the question

11. For one development of this argument, see my Marianist Lecture "The Missing Piece: The Renewal of Catholic Americanism" (University of Dayton, 2005). See also "God's Kingdom Lies Ahead: American Catholicism in Historical Perspective," *American Catholic Studies Newsletter* (Notre Dame, Fall 2007): 1, 6–9.

12. See her chapter in R. Scott Appleby and Kathleen Sprows Cummings, eds., *Catholics in the American Century: Recasting Narratives of U.S. History* (Ithaca, NY: Cornell University Press, 2013).

is real, embedded in American Catholic history and responsibility: trajectory, into the centers of power and responsibility, or out to the prophetic edges of society and history? Here is a central challenge facing Catholic pastoral, social, and educational ministries.

Part 5: In Catholic Social History, Many Traditions, Not One

Finally, confusion is inevitable in trying to assess the historical record and current situation of Catholic movements for social justice in the United States. A little light can be found by distinguishing between CST, expressed in papal encyclicals, bishops' statements and positions on public policy, Catholic social action, as Catholics communities try to deal with issues of justice, and a less noticed Catholic social gospel, the marvelous impulse to service evident in soup kitchens, communities of witness, and advocacy networks in many varieties.[13]

CST arises from the social thought and imagination of Catholics, and that in turn arises from the need for Catholics since the earliest days to form communities committed to a church with universal, exclusive claims, and at the same time to share with others responsibility for the common life of their communities and their countries. Through much of history in the United States, this led to a contentious social and religious pluralism, still evident among Catholics at the edge, where winning basic rights and a share of power often overshadows the claims of the public interest and the common good. Catholics, if they were to claim a place in their communities, needed to develop a language for public discourse that allowed room for faith-based commitments but required in public life no direct reference to their specifically Catholic traditions or Christian beliefs.

Thus the church developed what the bishops in 1983 called two styles of teaching: one for use within the church as Catholics form their conscience on the basis of their shared faith in the risen Christ, and one for

13. This is a revision of "Social Teaching, Social Action, Social Gospel," *U.S. Catholic Historian* 5 (1986): 195–225. See also *Public Catholicism* cited above and "Catholics and American Politics: An Historical Perspective" in *We Hold These Truths: Catholicism and American Political Life*, ed. Richard Miller (Liguori, MO: Liguori Publications, 2008).

engagement in the civic task of shaping a moral dimension to public policy and the common life.

This combination of Catholic commitment and shared responsibility for public life defines the tradition associated with John A. Ryan, John Courtney Murray, and J. Bryan Hehir, and it informed until recently the pastoral letters and policy statements of the U.S. bishops. What distinguishes that voice since Vatican II is the acknowledgment of genuine shared responsibility consequent on arrival at the center. The pastoral consequence of this approach is the formation of the church as a community of conscience, with citizens left free to apply the principles learned in the community of faith to the complex problems and projects that arise in public and professional life. Thus serious, faithful Catholics lead each political party in the House of Representatives and two more served as candidates for the vice presidency of each party in the 2012 election. At times, as in the 1980s on nuclear weapons and on the economy, this allows bishops and other pastoral leaders to convene people across political boundaries and foster dialogue about serious moral questions before the public. But often this leaves Catholics feeling "politically homeless," as one party respects Catholic views on economic and social justice, and the other on moral issues at the beginning and end of life.

This dualism of teaching helps explain the sometimes bewildering self-presentation of Catholic agencies of social ministry, which seek to locate themselves solidly within the community of faith, collaborate with other private and public agencies in the delivery of needed services, and share in public funds and the accountability that accompanies them. Collaboration with agencies that disagree with one or another church teaching, and participation in public programs which may include segments that violate Catholic teaching can be regarded with suspicion. Demands for the renewal of Catholic identity through accountability to church authorities place such institutions and programs at great risk. They are simply one expression of a growing uneasiness with the construction of CST in the United States around themes of shared responsibility for the common life.

Catholic social action, as distinct from CST, deals less with responsibility than with participation. It is characterized historically by skillful accommodation to the multiple marketplaces of American society. Parishes were self-help organizations, and the skills learned in their construction easily transferred to the organization of ethnic societies, political party work at the grassroots, and the peculiar trade unionism that developed in the United States. And, of course, the influence of secular experience in workplace and neighborhood could influence approaches to congregational life as well. Machines, unions, and ethnic societies were non-ideological, somewhat amoral, interest groups bent upon achieving power as a capacity to act on behalf of their members. Shared responsibility and the common good were less significant values than equal justice and genuine participation.

In the mid-1930s almost every leader of Catholic social ministry in the United States signed a manifesto on social responsibility entitled "Organized Social Justice." In recent years the bishops once used the phrase "justice as participation," expressed in widespread support for community organization, often supported by the CCHD. Organization remains the most widely understood method of moving from charity to justice, and it has many attractions to Catholic communities at the edge. And it at once expresses and creatively forwards American democratic themes of liberty and justice for all. As a growing number of scholars recognize, labor, neighborhood, and community organizing has been, and remains, remarkably effective.

This has been and remains a kind of Catholic realism learned from the many conflicts which confronted working-class immigrants in American history. Here, at least, justice could not be securely achieved through governmental action or the goodwill of others but only through organization. This tradition accepted conflict and often created it, rubbing raw the sores of discontent, in order to mobilize people and bring about change. Its self-interest focus created tension with the natural law rationalism of Catholic social thought and the generosity of the gospel, while its democratic spirit often worried bishops and bureaucrats. Its appeal has been to immigrants, outsiders, and workers at the bottom of the class ladder; no one has ever been able to adapt its realism to people at the center, who remain remarkably innocent about political and social questions that involve matters of power.

Finally, there are increasing expressions of a Catholic social gospel as Americanized Catholics become more evangelical in their religious piety and practice. For Christians awakened to the gospel, the moderation of CST and the realism of Catholic social action seem equally compromised.

The sometimes radical demands and countercultural rhetoric of the Catholic Worker movement, the Catholic peace movement, and the pro-life movement draw on this turn toward a social and political gospel.

Serious, not just rhetorical, versions of the social gospel have long been spawned by the Catholic Worker and the Catholic peace movement, but the historical movement of Catholics to the center has popularized evangelical, and usually less than radical, forms of piety and social reflection. Indeed, it can be argued that the combination of religious liberty and religious diversity, and the decline of strong ethnic and regional subcultures, necessarily produces evangelical styles of piety and practice. By this is meant the authority of the Scriptures, emphasis on interior religious experience and personal conversion, and voluntary community and primarily personal insertion of Christian qualities into public life. Unquestionably such qualities are multiplying among American Catholics. On social and on other questions "what would Jesus do?" is a more compelling question for many Catholics than "what does the church teach?"

That question does not close conscience to the appeal of social responsibility; quite the contrary. But it dramatically changes the language of internal church discussion and poses problems for those who would encourage study of CST and serious academic study of social questions. In the see-judge-act method, the evangelical approach encourages simplistic judgments and modest, often personal, forms of action. In their more radical form they give rise to sectarian positions that challenge the tendency to accommodation and call into question the restraint required by acceptance, or achievement, of citizenship as shared public responsibility. But at their best, as in the ever-developing teaching on nonviolence and Pope Benedict XVI's reflections on an economy of gift, social gospel ideas and witness introduce a utopian vision that can inspire, inform, and critique Christian strategies arising from shared historical responsibility.

That point should be emphasized. One characteristic of American versions of social Catholicism is the sharp separation in theory and practice of peace and justice. Activists of the last generation, particularly in religious orders, tried to overcome that separation by adopting without too much analysis slogans like "if you want peace, work for justice" and "development is the new name for peace." At the national level, during the era dominated by Cardinal Joseph Bernardin, much was done to build on these ideas of an integral justice and peace movement. In practice, diocesan agencies dealing with domestic policy were well established and helped shape and publicize programs for social justice, but few comparable agencies for peacemaking existed. Religious orders tried to fill the vacuum with freestanding justice and peace centers, but those faded as the resources of the religious orders declined. Peace studies never caught on in Catholic higher education. But community service and service learning flourished, including programs of overseas service. Focused on poverty and marginalization, these projects and the theology supporting them tended toward a social gospel direction, with limited reference to questions of power and the demands of politics.

Yet Catholic imagination, thought, and teaching on peace has changed dramatically over the last generation, offering signals of new directions for Catholic social education. In 1983 the bishops optimistically argued that nonviolence and just war were distinct but complementary approaches to peacemaking, but many scholars argued that in fact they arose from very different theological and ecclesiological ideas. In recent years, Vatican officials and global peace leaders have narrowed the gap by placing the church solidly behind gospel-based nonviolence while applying just-war categories with far more rigor than in the past.

This was evident in the United States when the bishops in 1993 published a remarkable letter on the tenth anniversary of the widely discussed letter on nuclear weapons published a decade earlier. In the 1993 letter they placed nonviolence at the center of Catholic teaching, argued for pastoral approaches to turn peace into action, peacemaking, and urged efforts to develop less violent and nonviolent approaches to global conflicts. On the one hand this showed a remarkable creativity in holding in creative—not paralyzing—tension the ideal of nonviolence and the responsibilities of civic engagement, a stance often missing in discussion of issues of life and social justice. A similar opening of CST took place with Pope Benedict XVI's *Caritas in Veritate,* where long-standing teachings on economic justice were placed alongside a "social gospel" argument for an economy of love based on a theology of gift.

Perhaps these three quite different understandings of social Catholicism might blend into a coherent whole, even inspire a wide-ranging movement for social change and social responsibility within the church, as seemed possible two decades ago. But there are few steps being taken at the moment to encourage dialogue among multiplying factions, build relationships, or face political questions in and out of the church. Two of those political questions are how to face extremely divisive problems within the church, such as the status of women, and how to face honestly the long-standing "political homelessness," at least in national politics of Catholics committed to life, justice, and peace. If and when all choices are inadequate, new options must be opened. Thus the challenges facing Catholic social education are linked to equally compelling challenges in church and society.

Chapter 2

Thomas M. Landy

Catholic Social Teaching
in the Catholic Intellectual Tradition

The task of this chapter is to explore connections between Catholic Social Teaching (CST) and the larger Catholic Intellectual Tradition (CIT). This exploration should help to answer some questions readers might have about how and why that tradition developed (and continues to develop), how it may contain competing perspectives held in tension, and indeed, about whether true Christian faith, a faith grounded in concern for the poor and love for others, requires intellectual exploration at all.

Formal CST generally traces its origin back only to 1891, a relatively recent moment in the history of a church whose intellectual tradition is nearly two thousand years old. As we shall see, though, CST is a logical outcome of the CIT—a powerful continuation of that older tradition of reflection in the light of changing societal situations and new ways of thinking about how humans can live together in a just society that mirrors God's hope for creation. Many of the questions raised by modern CST are as ancient as those raised by Christian thinkers like Irenaeus (d. AD 202), Augustine (d. AD 430), Thomas Aquinas (d. AD 1274), and thousands of unnamed persons of all faiths and none, who help us ponder more clearly and carefully what a just social order would look like.

Catholic Social Teaching is a modern attempt to systematize and explicate church teaching in new social situations, and plays an essential role in helping us to better live out some of the most important requirements of the gospel. As this chapter will make clear, the CIT encompasses reflection on a very wide range of issues, not all of which are taken up by Catholic social thought. The CIT provides a deep historical grounding for Catholic social thought—a pool of ideas and habits that gave weight and authority to CST and bring a range of perspectives from the past into dialogue with problems today.

The Catholic Intellectual Tradition

When imagining what Catholic intellectual life is about, I suspect that most Catholics would think first of theology and philosophy. They would focus on scholars who trade in ideas and express them in the written word. While the CIT includes those realms of learning in an essential way, however, it is not limited to them, by any means. Rather, the tradition embraces forms of imagination and creativity, and work in disciplines often labeled "secular," insofar as all those forms provide ways to help us understand human nature, God, and God's creation.

The broader CIT includes "theological thought; philosophizing; devotional practices; works of literature, visual art, music, and drama; styles of architecture; legal reasoning; social and political theorizing."[1] One can and should extend that list to include work in science, like the pioneering work of the Augustinian monk Gregor Mendel, whose observations of plants led him to be regarded as the father of modern genetics, or the Jesuit paleontologist Pierre Teilhard de Chardin, who helped us to think about the implications of evolution for Christian theology.

In terms of form, the CIT includes autobiography (think of Augustine's *Confessions* or Dorothy Day's *The Long Loneliness*), poetry (Dante's *Divine Comedy* or Denise Levertov's "Ascension"), novels (Flannery O'Connor's *Wise Blood* or Shusaku Endo's *Silence*), sculpture (Bernini's *Theresa in Ecstasy* or Jaume Busquets' nativity portal), architecture (Michelangelo's Saint Peter's Basilica or Antoni Gaudí's Sagrada Familia), painting (Giotto's Assisi frescoes or Caravaggio's "Call of Saint Matthew"), philosophical works (Erasmus' *Enchiridion* or Edith Stein's *On the Problem of Empathy*), various musical forms (Olivier Messaien's *Saint François d'Assise* or James

---

1. The Catholic Intellectual Tradition: A Conversation at Boston College. http://www.bc.edu/church21.

MacMillan's *Veni, Veni Emmanuel*), and political works (Thomas More's *Utopia* or Francisco de Vitoria's *De potestate civili*).

Some questions in the tradition are older than the tradition itself, stretching back before Christianity: What does it mean to be human? What does it mean to live a good life? The first question—What does it mean to be human?—must be asked in new ways in light of the gospel, but the questions posed by older and newer philosophies also led thinkers to ask new questions of the gospel that might not have occurred to the Evangelists.

All of the writing and works of art that find a place in the heritage of the CIT share in common that they increase our understanding of what it means to be human, or our understanding of creation as a whole. They ask questions or provide new insights in the light of faith, sometimes bringing old questions to the surface in ways that make sense to a new age, or other times helping us to confront questions or issues that never occurred to us before. All of them—even explicitly fictional accounts—share the capacity to increase our insight into God's relation to creation. At its core, the tradition is the work of Catholics reflecting on their faith and the world, but the tradition has always been enriched by other persons who had interesting questions to bring to the table and who have shaped the conversation by virtue of their questions and insights.

In their discussion of the CIT, Anthony Cernera and Oliver Morgan assert that we should think of the CIT in terms of "themes and habits" and "concerns and sensitivities."[2] These pairings provide a good organizational framework for our discussion.

A Tradition Very Much in Process

One helpful way of thinking about the CIT is to think of it not simply as a thing—a *heritage*, a set of consistent themes or sources—but also to think of it as an *activity*, a process, a set of habits. The same holds true for CST. Theologians in the past often spoke of the "deposit of faith" in

2. Anthony J. Cernera and Oliver J. Morgan, "The Catholic Intellectual Tradition: Some Characteristics, Implications, and Future Directions," in *Examining the Catholic Intellectual Tradition*, ed. Anthony J. Cernera and Oliver J. Morgan (Fairfield, CT: Sacred Heart University Press, 2000), 203.

such terms, as if it were a physical thing to be kept in a vault. Sometimes people who speak of the Catholic intellectual life speak of it in similar terms, as if it were a finished, fixed body of thought.

The phrase "Catholic Intellectual Tradition" is misleading if it is used to represent a supposedly unified and uniform tradition that is passed down to us in settled form. The value of a "heritage" understanding is the recognition that we do stand on the backs of giants. There are many great thinkers in the past who help us to reimagine the world in ways few of us could possibly do on our own. Their insights can radically enrich human understanding about a range of questions.

But heritage metaphors are wholly inadequate if they communicate a sense that the CIT—or CST—are static bodies of past knowledge to which we turn. As Monika Hellwig put it, the CIT "cannot be reduced to a treasury of deposits from the past, though it certainly contains such a treasury."[3]

If I were to ask most readers of this book to reflect on family traditions or cultural traditions, they would tell me about things that their families or people of a particular culture *do*. They would tell me about activities that may be passed down from generation to generation, or at least have endured over time. I think it is helpful to think of CIT as a set of habits that have endured over time—as an effort by thinkers in every generation to bring elements of that heritage into dialogue with new ideas, questions, and issues, or at least to try to elaborate those ideas in ways that speak freshly to new situations.

The CIT as activity entails bringing an inherited body of ideas and reflection to bear in dialogue with new forms of knowledge. Such a conception of the CIT fits Jesus' own description of the educated person in his own time: "every scribe who has been trained for the kingdom of heaven is like the master of a household who brings out of his treasure what is new and what is old" (Matt 13:52).

The second reason why a "heritage" definition is inadequate is that the tradition itself is pluralistic. It includes an array of answers to the questions it looks at. On war, to take just one example, it includes an array of important and perfectly orthodox thinkers who embraced either paci-

---

3. Monika K. Hellwig, "The Tradition in the Catholic University," in Cernera and Morgan, *Examining the Catholic Intellectual Tradition*, 3.

fism or just war theory. Both traditions have a firm place within the CIT, but each can lead to a very different conclusion about the justice of going to war. A "heritage" conception of the tradition can be pluralistic, of course, but it always runs a strong risk of being reductionistic.

Learning from New Knowledge

The notion that the church might have to learn its way through new situations and knowledge may not come as a surprise to students living in an information age that they perceive as a time of massive change. But the fact is that throughout its history the church has needed to learn and adapt—and has done so, though sometimes in fits and starts. We could say that the CIT was born essentially as an attempt by Christians to engage with new questions that were posed by the world around them, despite—and sometimes because of—the Scriptures.

The earliest Christians expected that Jesus would return quickly, bringing the end times. They lived and shared resources freely in anticipation of that. In an empire and culture that was often starkly anti-Christian, Jesus' claim that "my kingdom is not from this world" (John 18:36) made early Christian communities encourage people to sell what they had, share it with others, and await the inevitable return of Jesus.

As time went by, they had to ask questions about how to live in the world, and about what their tradition had to say in answer to important questions raised by Greek and Roman philosophy. Eventually, when Christianity became the official religion of the empire, they had to ask how Christians could govern justly, and when it was legitimate to go to war. Christians in those first centuries never lived in isolation from other religious people and ideas. They lived in a mobile society that saw traders bringing ideas and beliefs from all over the world.

The CIT, and with it, CST, arise from a this-worldly spirituality that has precedents in Scripture, but also has to do with the situation that the church found itself in once its persecuted status was over. It is a vision of church that suggests that the church's role is not to huddle away in a corner but to take responsibility for shaping the world God asks us to shape. Catholic theology has long understood the world to be a place where God is present and acting through all of creation, and where God expects us to participate in that creation. This includes using our talents to create what is beautiful and to express what we might not otherwise be fully able to grasp.

Therefore, in an important sense, distinctions between the sacred and secular are not entirely or necessarily satisfactory. If the whole world is God's creation, then the study of geology or astronomy, while each has its own methods distinct from theology or philosophy, will still reveal something that is important to the Christian believer, precisely because it is a study of creation. Great paintings, sculpture, music, novels, and the like are not simply distractions to pass the time while we wait for heaven.

When Christianity was an outsider, a persecuted religion, the questions about how to live were much different than after Christianity became the official religion of the empire. Is it just to go to war? How should the state defend itself? Are Christians supposed to be pacifists? Can a pacifist state survive in a world of enemies? Those sorts of questions gave rise to one of the oldest strands of the CIT—just war theory. It asks questions about what conditions make it appropriate to go to war (*jus ad bellum*) and what obligations or limits combatants should face during war (*jus in bello*).

The tradition has always learned from encounter with new situations, but also with new knowledge. That encounter has sometimes been halting and conflicted, but at its best the tradition has also been quick to absorb new ideas. Because the created world is the realm of God's activity, the tradition embraces, if at times awkwardly, the idea that God speaks to other peoples and traditions in ways that enlighten Christians. Otherwise, a theologian like Thomas Aquinas would have been in trouble for relying so heavily on the pagan Greek philosopher Aristotle, Muslims like Averroës and Avicenna, or a Jew like Moses Maimonedes.

Today, the CIT continues to grapple with new issues in science—increasing knowledge about the vastness of the universe, about the evolution of life on earth, about human sexuality and reproduction. The field of bioethics, which grew in important ways out of the CIT,[4] confronts issues around cloning, artificial birth control, stem cells, the beginning

---

4. See M. Therese Lysaught, "The Seamless Garment of the Intellectual Life: Reflections from Bioethics and the Consistent Ethic of Life," in Thomas M. Landy, ed., *As Leaven in the World: Essays on Faith, Vocation and the Intellectual Life* (Franklin, WI: Sheed & Ward, 2001), 180–81.

and end of human life, and respirators and other tools that can artificially prolong life, among other issues.

Catholic Social Teaching has had to learn how to adjust or respond to a wide variety of changes and developments in the world. Many of the themes present in CST documents, such as migration, nuclear weapons, and the environment, were not considered even one hundred years ago, or were inchoate at best. Though some important Catholic thinkers had done so earlier, all forms of slavery were not definitively condemned by the church until three years before *Rerum Novarum*. Issues surrounding social class, race and gender, child labor, and more were overlooked in the past, with terrible consequences for human beings. That should make us cautious about thinking that our own age has already adequately identified and begun to address all the forms of injustice that face us.

The Holy See recognizes all of this when it regularly convenes organizations like the Pontifical Academy of Sciences and the Pontifical Academy of Social Sciences. These organizations exist not to tell scientists or social scientists where they have it wrong, but to keep the church's leaders apprised of what scientists are learning about the world and how that learning raises new challenges. These academics are interreligious and include thinkers of no faith.[5]

It seems fitting that the first document in the modern tradition of CST was titled *Rerum Novarum*, Latin for "new things." Among the "new things" Pope Leo XIII felt compelled to consider and address were "in the vast expansion of industrial pursuits and the marvelous discoveries of science; in the changed relations between masters and workmen; in the enormous fortunes of some few individuals, and the utter poverty of the masses."[6]

Even where the tradition is well-developed and has spoken influentially to the contemporary world, it can still include very different ideas held in tension. Catholic thinking about war includes pacifist and just-war

---

5. The statutes of appointment read: "Candidates for a seat in the Academy are chosen by the Academy on the basis of their eminent original scientific studies and of their acknowledged moral personality, without any ethnical or religious discrimination, and are appointed for life by sovereign act of the Holy Father." http://www.casinapioiv.va/content/accademia/en/academicians/ordinary.html. Accessed Feb. 19, 2013.

6. *Rerum Novarum* 1, http://www.vatican.va/holy_father/leo_xiii/encyclicals/documents/hf_l-xiii_enc_15051891_rerum-novarum_en.html.

traditions which are in a number of ways in conflict with one another. Theologically we think of a world that is created by God and hence is good, but still marred by sin. In generations these tensions will likely still be in place, and it will be up to us to consider how these perspectives apply to new situations.

Whatever its shortcomings, we are fortunate to have such a tradition as a foundation. As Hellwig argues, some elements of the tradition have risen to "classic" status, "not to prevent later developments, but to form a touchstone against which later developments were to be seen and judged."[7]

The CIT is global in scope and reaches into the past; as a Christian vision, it is always grounded in hope for the future. As such, it gives us some opportunity to look past the current situation in our local place, so that we do not always assume that the social systems and structures that surround us are necessary and unchangeable.

Concerns and Sensibilities

While much of CST deals directly or indirectly with issues affecting the poor, the broader CIT is still justifiably concerned with questions that don't directly put the poor at the center. For example, it is legitimate and important to ask how one thinks of the traditional Jewish and Christian narratives in light of knowledge that the universe is billions of years old, or the possibility that there are many billions of planets in the universe capable of supporting life. It asks questions about the meaning of life, about questions of bioethics and human sexuality. All of these questions often have implications for the poor and powerless, but it is CST that most puts front and center concern about the poor and powerless and about kinds of human flourishing. Catholic Social Teaching is that part of the CIT which most demands a preferential option for the poor.

Catholic Social Teaching benefits directly from the longer and broader tradition of the CIT because the latter helps us to see who we are as human beings. The CIT ultimately grounds its account of mutual obligation in a notion of what it means to be human, and indeed in an account that simply *as* persons, we have certain rights. If one were to change those

7. Hellwig, 4.

foundational assumptions, one would come to a very different ethical conclusion about our mutual obligations to one another.

Scripture argues that humans are created in the image and likeness of God and that the Incarnation itself is the willingness of God to take on the realities of human existences. "The doctrine of the Incarnation invests the human person with a particular dignity and status insofar as it holds that God became human in the person of Jesus of Nazareth"[8] That insight alone leads to some of the most profound and important questions of the CIT, and especially to a core concern of CST: what we owe to one another if we are creatures created in God's image. Our concern is not only about how we treat each other face-to-face as individuals, but necessarily needs to extend to how the social structures that humans create make it more or less possible to live in as fully human a way as we believe God intended.

The fact that the Christian notion of God is trinitarian ought to help us to see that to be like God is not to be alone and independent but to be in relation. In the Trinity, a God who is One is also a relationship of Father, Son, and Holy Spirit, and indeed, through creation and the Incarnation, now exists in relationship to us. As Catherine Mowry LaCugna wrote, "living as persons in communion, in right relationship, is the meaning of salvation and the ideal of the Christian faith. God is interactive, neither solitary nor isolated."[9] The Trinity, then, "is a doctrine that tells Christians that they must live their lives not individualistically but relationally."[10]

As I attempted to show earlier, both CST and the broader CIT are built from a variety of other traditions and embodied in a number of forms. Particularly since the Second Vatican Council, CST has tried to speak to all of the world in two languages—one more scriptural and distinctly theological, that draws explicitly on Catholic traditions, images, and precedents—and a second more philosophical that aims to convince all people, even those who do not accept Scripture and Catholic tradition as an authority. A tradition born only out of scriptural study might have

8. Brian F. Linnane, "The Dignity of Persons and the Catholic Intellectual Tradition," in Landy, 194.

9. Catherine Mowry LaCugna, *God for Us: The Trinity and the Intellectual Life* (San Francisco: HarperCollins, 1991), 292.

10. Dennis M. Doyle, "The Trinity and Catholic Intellectual Life," in Landy, 145.

trouble speaking to persons who do not perceive the Scripture as authoritative. But a tradition of long reflection based on Scripture and reason is well-suited to do this.

This dual effort is built upon the conviction in Catholic theology that God speaks through both creation and Scripture, and that the two do not conflict. Indeed, it is a conviction that, unique and important as the Incarnation is, God has been speaking to the whole world since before the Incarnation. The whole of creation, because it comes from God, says something important about God. Likewise, it sees humans' capacity to think and reason as a gift from God. The Catholic tradition has long been convinced that the search for truth, whether explored through Scripture or through reason, leads us towards the one Source of both, even if our understanding of Scripture or use of reason is always imperfect.

In light of this, CST can have a very different feel from some Protestant churches' efforts to speak about ethical questions. Catholic Intellectual Tradition is not the equivalent or extension of Bible commentary. It seeks to build upon the insight of Scripture—particularly the gospel—but also depends very much upon human reason.

Conclusion: Reflection and Action

The CIT is grounded, as Monika Hellwig has argued, in "a conviction that human life has meaning and that the meaning can be known."[11] The same holds true for CST. This is a deeply important grounding for people who have tried to work in situations of extreme or persistent suffering or privation. In such situations, we all have to encounter moments when such suffering and privation seems to suggest a lack of meaning or justice in the universe. The CIT does not suggest that we resort to simple formulations about God's will to impose meaning on situations that derive from sin. It gives us a much richer, more complex, and nuanced resource to return to during the times when we might otherwise burn out or just turn away from because our own capacity to bring about change seems too limited.

One interesting difference between CST and the CIT is that the content and agenda of CST has primarily been determined by popes and bishops,

11. Hellwig, 6.

while the CIT has been much more of a lay and priestly phenomenon. Lay Catholics have long made important intellectual contributions to the official CST tradition,[12] and many theologians continue to develop that tradition. In encyclicals these contributions are unacknowledged because the documents are issued as papal documents. In the 1980s, the U.S. Conference of Catholic Bishops was particularly adept at drawing in lay expertise for its documents on Peace[13] and the Economy,[14] but even these documents were voted on and issued as bishops' documents.

No *imprimatur* (formal approval by bishops) exists to say that Graham Greene's *The Power and the Glory*, Ron Hansen's *Mariette in Ecstasy*, or any number of works one might take as part of the CIT, are "official." Any "*imprimatur*" for what belongs to the CIT is more broadly and informally bestowed. Artists, musicians, poets, and novelists can make their way in, even unintentionally. There is room for all of us to make a contribution.

At the same time, that is not to suggest that ordinary Catholics have no role in helping to shape CST into the future. We all have much to learn from it, but many of us can and should work to contribute to it, to ask fresh questions based on what we know about what it means to be human and to find ways to address the new questions we will inevitably encounter in the future.

One of the most problematic dichotomies in American culture is a perceived gulf between thinking and doing. Some students I encounter often want to get out and "do something" and can be impatient with what they might learn in college. Many people may perceive a gulf between some of the philosophizing questions about the human person that run throughout the CIT. Many Americans tend to be a bit suspicious of what we call the "ivory tower" and in their own pragmatic way often prefer to get out and do something.

---

12. For a few examples, see Thomas Massaro, *Living Justice: Catholic Social Teaching in Action* (Lanham, MD: Rowman & Littlefield Publishers, 2012), 43–46.

13. U.S. Conference of Catholic Bishops, *The Challenge of Peace: God's Promise and Our Response* (Washington, DC: U.S. Conference of Catholic Bishops, 1983).

14. U.S. Conference of Catholic Bishops, *Economic Justice for All: Pastoral Letter on Catholic Social Teaching and the U.S. Economy* (Washington, DC: U.S. Conference of Catholic Bishops, 1986).

Nonetheless, the most successful and enduring social action any of us can achieve depends on our willingness to think through the origins, causes, and best solutions for social problems. As David O'Brien discusses in chapter 1, lay Catholics have a strong role to play in broad Catholic social action and social gospel work, whether through organizations such as Catholic Charities and Catholic Relief Services, or through other forms of participation through parishes and communities. Catholic Intellectual Tradition, and CST together stress the importance of thought *and* reflection, and then connect thought and action, aiming to be a "catalyst for a 'way of thinking' with distinctive themes and tones . . . deeply connected to a way of living."[15] Such connection helps us not only to do "something" but to find the *right* thing to do.

15. The Catholic Intellectual Tradition: A Conversation at Boston College. http://www.bc.edu/church21.

Chapter 3

David L. Coleman

The State and Civil Society in Catholic Social Teaching

In this chapter we will explore Catholic Social Teaching's (CST) understanding of politics, civil society, and the common good, and the secular traditions out of which these concepts arose. At the center of this exposition will be the *Compendium of the Social Doctrine of the Church*.[1] Throughout the chapter we will show how the Catholic community became an effective partner in the public discourse of a highly secular, pluralistic civil society. We will explore the ways that the Catholic Church engages and critiques the secular understanding of political community, civil society, and the common good. The church's teaching seeks to enrich our secular political theory and institutions with its experience of God's unfailing love, challenging our structural disregard for the least among us, and providing hope when cynicism suggests inevitable chaotic failure.

The civil society, state, and the common good are concepts that have both secular origins and specific theological interpretations within CST. The concept of civil society, as we shall discuss later, has a long developmental history in Western political thought. For our purposes, we will restrict its *political* definition to that network of more or less interdependent voluntary institutions and nongovernmental organizations that work

---

1. See Pontifical Council for Justice and Peace, *Compendium of the Social Doctrine of the Church*, sixth printing (Washington, DC: United States Conference of Catholic Bishops Communications, 2011).

independently of the state and that mediate, collaborates with, and restrains the power of the state. Within civil society we belong to voluntary groups that help to organize how the society works, plays, educates its members, advocates for those in need and for those who are not, and identifies, maintains, and sometimes creates cultural traditions. Ideally, within this network, each citizen can reflect on and advocate for policies that benefit the society as a whole. For the civil society to thrive, the state must protect the basic freedoms of speech, association, press, and religion and must create structures and processes (such as voting, representation, and access to an independent judiciary) to form policy and address abuses by the state itself. This conventional secular portrayal of civil society that I present here is overly idealized and positive. In reality, organizations in civil society, such as the Red Cross, can make positive contributions, but other organizations, such as the Ku Klux Klan, can be detrimental to the common good.[2] Many discussions of civil society focus on its ideal, positive dimension, and I will do so too, bearing in mind that there is a dark side to civil society as well. Sometimes, for the common good, the state must protect citizens from civil society organizations, such as hate groups.

While implied in this secular definition, CST makes explicit the principle that (ideally) the institutions and organizations that make up the structural network of civil society are themselves committed to the common good of all who make up the civil and political community. The *Compendium* asserts that the civil society is prior to the political community (that is, the state); it calls civil society the "third sector," separate from the state and the economy.[3] It defines civil society positively as "the sum of the relationships and resources, cultural and associative, that are relatively independent from the political sphere and the economic sector."[4] The major distinction between these two understandings of civil society is that the secular tradition assumes that civil society arose out of a rational contract between individuals to protect individual interests that established the civil society and the forms of the government that structures the com-

---

2. See Clifford Bob, "Civil and Uncivil Society," in *The Oxford Handbook of Civil Society*, ed. Michael Edwards (New York: Oxford University Press, 2011), 209–19.

3. Pontifical Council for Justice and Peace, *Compendium of the Social Doctrine of the Church*, 180, para. 419.

4. Ibid., 179, para. 417.

monwealth itself. The CST view is that civil society, the "third sector," is an organic community arising from and required by the social nature of the human person. "The activities of civil society . . . represent the most appropriate ways to develop the social dimension of the person, who finds in these activities the necessary space to express [her- or] himself."[5] It is not a product of a "social contract." The CST portrayal of civil society is also an idealized positive view. Both the secular and CST depictions of civil society presented above don't adequately account for its dark side. When we speak of the ideal role of civil society, we nevertheless must be careful not to romanticize it and ignore its shortcomings.

The state in the contemporary secular political context is defined as the governmental structures associated with a given people and a specific territory—commonly known as a "nation-state." Generally the state has the right and responsibility to protect the community from external threats and internal chaos through the legitimate use of force. The history of the state is associated with the culture of cities in the sense that it develops bureaucracies through which the power and presence of the state can be exercised. Within the culture of cities, the state becomes possible because the civic culture allows for the division of labor, some of whom can devote their lives to serving the emerging bureaucracies of the state. In Western political history the civil society came about as a form of critique and, ultimately, resistance to the power of the state embodied in the absolute monarch. Catholic Social Teaching contends that the state first and foremost originates in the human person.[6] It arises from the civil society and "is established to be of service to civil society."[7] Its exercise of authority and use of power is legitimate when it is guided by subsidiarity, that political virtue that seeks to respect the relative capacity of each level of civil and political society (national and local institutions and organizations) to realize the common good. "Civil society, therefore, cannot be considered an extension or a changing component of the political community [i.e., the state]; rather it has priority because it is in civil society itself that the political community finds its justification."[8]

5. Ibid., 180, para. 419.
6. Ibid., 166, para. 384.
7. Ibid., 179, para. 417.
8. Ibid., 179, para. 418.

The common good, the central responsibility of our vocation as social beings, is defined by the *Compendium* as "the sum total of social conditions which allow people, either as groups or as individuals, to reach their fulfillment more fully and more easily."[9] As we will discuss later, the common good is the responsibility of each person and the end of the civil society and the reason for activities of the state rightly understood. The common good, however, extends to the whole of humanity and in recent CST is ultimately inclusive of all God's creation, on which the sustainability of the human community depends. In this assertion, the common good is an expression of the ultimate end of the human person, which is God. "God is the ultimate end of his creatures and for no reason may the common good be deprived of its transcendent dimension, which moves beyond the historical dimension while at the same time fulfilling it."[10]

Cooperation for the common good requires the organization of people and resources needed for the human family to flourish. The Christian vision of human nature ("Christian anthropology") assumes that we have both temporal and spiritual ends. We are physical human beings, born in a specific time and place working out our destiny within this temporal world structured by space and time. We also have a spiritual end, an "eternal destiny" that we work out in response to God who calls us into being and into the return journey to loving union with God. Obviously, while conceived of as two separate dimensions of existence (temporal and spiritual), we prioritize choices to be true to God's call in our lives within the context of our everyday temporal world. My personal responses to God's movement in my life obviously impact my everyday world. Our social nature draws us into communities that foster shared responses to God among us through commonly held beliefs, rituals, ethical worldviews, values, and institutions. We also engage with others in political, social, economic, and cultural communities within the nation-state, and through globalization and global solidarity, in the world community as well. As social and political animals we naturally organize ourselves into communities to achieve our personal and communal good. "The state is a 'natural' institution in the sense that it assists human beings to achieve

9. Ibid., 72, para. 164.
10. Ibid., 75, para. 170. See note 359: John Paul II, *Centisimus Annus*, 41.

their proper fulfillment in the order of nature, just as the church enables humans to attain their fulfillment in the supernatural order."[11]

Depending on our understanding of human condition, the character and role of the state will be perceived quite differently. If, with St. Augustine, we believe that the human beings are for the most part motivated by their selfish desires, irrational passions, and hatreds, then the state arises out of sin, a necessity to protect us from one another, to prevent anarchy, to secure at least rudimentary justice for all, and to defend the people from outside aggression. From a current perspective, Augustine's view of the state and civil society was not very positive. On the other hand, if with St. Thomas Aquinas, we believe that while we are sinners, we have a degree of natural goodness and are given reason that enables us to see and act toward our true ends in the temporal order, then the state is part of "God's plan for creation," which will protect us from injustice, and will itself attempt to nurture justice in service to the common good. From a current perspective, Aquinas has a more positive view of the state and civil society than does Augustine.

The church is a divine institution living in the world. Responding to the Spirit, it is a community of men and women who are the Body of Christ, sustained by Christ in unfailing love, love even unto death on a cross. The mystery of the church manifests itself in this truth: it is God become present in and through the lives of the people of God. Its imperfections arise from our sins, our brokenness founded in our incessant desires and fears. And yet God becomes present to us as we participate in God's ongoing reconciliation with all creation through God's choice to love us first.

The church is itself a sign of the truth that each of us finds our happiness in communion with God who is with us. We respond to God's gift through our own gift of love to our brothers and sisters creating the communities that sustain us. First in the family, then in the variety of organizations to which we belong, be they religious, economic, political, educational, cultural, or social, we express the reality that we are social beings. Our individual dignity flourishes in relationships that respect the dignity of others. Our survival as a species depends on this fundamental drive for community and collaboration for the good of others. This common good

11. Kenneth R. Himes, *Christianity and the Political Order: Conflict, Cooptation, and Cooperation* (Maryknoll, NY: Orbis Books, 2013), 101.

sustains all and when we pay attention, the mystery of God-with-us irrupts within, transforming us in the love we receive and give. We can read this social reality within which we live with the eyes of faith, hope and love. This vision is articulated in Catholic Social Teaching.

Questions about the Advocacy and Action of the Church in Civil Society

The debate on the relationship between the church and the state has continued throughout Western history. At various points, they were seen as relatively equal partners for the common good, and at other times one claimed superiority over the other. The contests for power between them underlie the evolution of their mutual relationship within Western culture. In the United States today, we have the most radical division of church and state that has evolved in the Western liberal democracies. This of course impacts the issue of participation of religious communities of all sorts in the public discourse of American society.

You will hear some argue that the church should stay out of public discourse, that its concerns are best stated only within the confines of its own structures among Catholics. They argue that faith-based values do not have a place in secular society. The church has responded with a carefully thought-out tradition of social thought that speaks to our shared nature and the sort of society that will help human beings flourish in justice and love. The contributions the church brings to public discourse assume the dignity of each person and that we are social beings whose welfare depends on relationships of loving service to one another. Therefore the priorities we set within our societies as to economic, political, social, and cultural policies and institutions make a profound difference to both our personal lives and the life we share in the communities within which we live. Seen in this light, it not only permissible for the church and all of its members to participate in the public discourse on the common good as Catholics, it is a moral imperative to do so. Based on the principles and values of CST,[12] the mode of argumentation used by church

---

12. For a discussion of the four sources of Catholic Social Teaching—Revelation, Reason, Tradition and Experience, see Thomas Massaro, *Living Justice: Catholic Social Teaching in Action* (Lanham, MD: Rowman & Littlefield Publishers, 2012), 56–78.

organizations advocating specific policies—the church never supports political candidates—is a secular mode, using facts and reasoned arguments open to reasoned debate. For example, church organizations will take a position on poverty policy because of CST's gospel-based principle of the preferential option for the poor, but the policy they advocate is based on data and reasoned argument. Such participation in public discourse is, as the bishops remind us, a part of the church's fundamental obligation to proclaim the gospel in our world. "This is not a marginal interest or activity, or one that is tacked on to the Church's mission, rather it is at the very heart of the Church's ministry of service. . . . This is a ministry that stems not only from proclamation but also from witness."[13]

Does the church's advocacy extend to telling us to vote for a specific candidate? No, it calls us to carefully evaluate the policy positions of all candidates according to this standard of the common good and dignity of each person, as we will discuss later in this chapter. This is derived from reasoned reflection on the nature of the human person and human well-being. When John F. Kennedy, the first Catholic president of the United States, ran for the office, many attacked his candidacy by claiming that he would simply support those policies that the pope commanded him to support. His own response came out of the constitutional tradition of his country that he swore to protect: "I believe in an America where the separation of church and state is absolute, where no Catholic prelate would tell the president (should he be Catholic) how to act, and no Protestant minister would tell his parishioners for whom to vote."[14] The bishops indeed resist the notion that the separation of church and state is "absolute," if by absolute one means that religion is a totally private affair. Of course, Kennedy recognized this in that he was addressing a conference of Protestant ministers, who, like the bishops, argued for both the right and the duty to participate in the nation's public discourse.

As indicated earlier, the bishops, often with partners from across the religious and secular spectrums, engage the society on a variety of social

13. Pontifical Council for Justice and Peace, *Compendium of the Social Doctrine of the Church*, 30, para. 67.

14. John F. Kennedy, "Transcript: JFK's Speech on His Religion," Greater Houston Ministerial Association (September 12, 1960), http://www.npr.org/templates/story/story.php?storyId=16920600. Accessed August 2, 2013.

justice policy positions: going to the site of the United States Conference of Catholic Bishops (USCCB; www.usccb.org), one is almost overwhelmed by the volumes of materials on the issues flowing from our faith and social convictions that articulate our church's commitment to the welfare of the human family, not only in our nation but across the whole world. Among the issues and areas of concern: protecting life from conception through natural death; protecting and fostering religious liberty for all peoples and religious institutions; responsible citizenship; promotion and defense of marriage; immigration reform; the blessing of cultural diversity in the church; cloning; contraception; restorative justice; national policies on global issues facing the people of other nations; human trafficking; hunger; just and unjust war; sexuality; torture; violence; and myriad other issues.

In looking at the USCCB website, one finds policy statements formulated by policy experts working for USCCB guided by principles of CST. Among important CST principles are the following: First, the foundational principle that our social nature requires a "communitarian vocation"[15] in our personal and ethical worldview. This vocation is our response to God's call to live a productive and sustainable relationship with the entire community of being that includes God, all humanity, and the entire ecosystem (creation) of which we are a part. "For by his innermost nature man is a social being, and unless he relates himself to others he can neither live nor develop his potential."[16]

Second, this communitarian vocation requires that authentic human development recognize the dignity of each person who will flourish only by recognizing that this dignity calls one into relationship with God and with the entire human family. In a reciprocal manner this communitarian vocation requires social institutions to organize and act in order that "the subject and the goal of all social institutions is and must be the human person which for its part and by its very nature stands completely in need of social life."[17]

---

15. In their chapter on human rights, my colleagues Ron Panucco and Mark Ensalaco discuss Catholic Social Teaching as a "communitarian liberal" or "solidarity" ethic because it includes the liberal rights emphasis on autonomy, freedom, and equality, which is understood within the context of community and the common good.

16. Vatican II, *Gaudium et spes*, para. 12. Translations of Vatican II documents in this chapter are from *The Documents of Vatican II*, ed. Walter M. Abbott (New York: The America Press, 1966).

17. Ibid., 25.

Third, as argued by Oliver F. Williams, CSC, in his exposition on John Paul II's *Centisimus Annus*, this communitarian vocation affects how the church understands contemporary human rights, the free market, the state, and the importance of social institutions in forming human character for better or worse. The communitarian context of CST reminds us that each of these is a means to promoting first and foremost the dignity of the human person within the context of the varieties of communities within which each person lives. As my colleagues will further discuss in this book, human rights are always understood within "the context of their role of promoting and protecting human dignity in community."[18] Williams argues that the market, as envisioned by Adam Smith, assumes that the self-interest out of which each of us acts must be "shaped by moral forces in the community so that economic self-interest would not always degenerate into a crass selfishness."[19] The bishops assert that the role of the state is "to be *in the service of society*," interacting with the various communities and institutions to achieve the common good in respect of subsidiarity.[20] Finally, Williams observes that the contemporary social reality is formed in a dynamic interplay of large and small institutions that hold values that either corrupt the individual human person or reinforce those values and priorities that nurture our fundamental humanity. This reality requires that we understand how these institutions form our personal values and how solutions for many social problems require that we transform this social reality in order to assist the development of each person. Bringing these concerns together, Williams concludes that a "communitarian democratic capitalism could blossom from a vision that respects both individual rights and a virtuous community, values an essential but not all-powerful role for the state and the market, and supports a conscious effort to sustain and enhance those institutions that develop and support character."[21]

18. Oliver F. Williams, "Catholic Social Teaching: a Communitarian Democratic Capitalism for the New World Order," in *Catholic Social Thought and the New World Order: Building on One Hundred Years*, ed. Oliver F. Williams and John W. Houck (Notre Dame: University of Notre Dame Press, 1993), 8.
19. Ibid., 12.
20. See Ibid., 14–15.
21. Ibid., 22.

Faithful Citizenship: Moral Participation in the Civil Society

Catholics and most other Christians take citizenship very seriously, though some Christians believe they cannot participate in political activities because those activities are corrupt and sinful, or because the state ultimately relies on violence, which Christians must reject. Kenneth Himes helps us to explore political participation, particularly the American Catholic bishops' discussion of "faithful citizenship," in *Christianity and the Political Order: Conflict, Cooptation, and Cooperation*. The bishops published "Faithful Citizenship" in an attempt to guide Catholic voters toward an informed moral participation in the election process. Himes reminds us that moral participation requires the development and use of the virtue of prudence by which we make "wise judgments about right action, to determine how best to translate one's moral commitments into support for particular political leaders and policy choices"[22] that will benefit the common good.

In "Faithful Citizenship," the bishops observed that few if any candidates were entirely consistent with all of the principles that form CST. They asked, "How does one decide whether it is morally possible to vote for a candidate who holds a position that is not consistent with the Catholic tradition?" In fact, many candidates hold a variety of policy positions, some of which strongly support the tradition, while simultaneously holding positions that conflict with the tradition. The bishops are clear that one cannot support "intrinsically evil acts," among which are "abortion, euthanasia, human cloning, destruction of embryos in research, torture, genocide, the deliberate targeting of civilians in war or terrorist attacks, and racism."[23] This is based on the moral principle that holds that one cannot use intrinsically evil means to achieve a supposed good. The means we choose must be consistent with the good end we seek. "Formal cooperation means the cooperator [the voter] has an agreement of the will with the evil deed of the actor [the politician]." If there

22. Kenneth R. Himes, *Christianity and the Political Order: Conflict, Cooptation, and Cooperation*, 270. See United States Conference of Catholic Bishops, *Forming Consciences for Faithful Citizenship*, no. 20.

23. Ibid., 271, note 15. Reference to the USCCB, *Forming Consciences for Faithful Citizenship*, nos. 22–23.

are proportionate and sufficiently grave reasons, one may "materially cooperate" with such evil in the sense that one's "intentional will" rejects the evil willed by the actions of the politician, but that on balance the various issues the politician does support may justify voting for her or him. "In other words, the issue of *formal cooperation* always results in a negative judgment. It is wrong to so act. The question of *material cooperation* must be assessed on a case by case basis to determine if there are proportionate reasons that can be determined."[24]

Himes goes on to outline a series of "considerations in voting" relevant to living "faithful citizenship." Among them:

- The voter must assess the "intelligence, temperament, and character of a candidate."
- The voter must study the "track record of activity" of the candidate to determine what his priorities truly are and where her or his moral priorities are on the issues of importance to faithful citizenship.
- The voter must consider the political context to determine if the issues of importance are timely and have a possibility of passage in that context. Of course, one may need to be prophetic and raise the issue despite the probable lack of success in moving it forward, but one must evaluate the reasonableness of the politician's sense of timeliness for a specific issue. Part of politics is creating "timeliness" through the hard work of organizing support for important issues.[25]

Faithful citizenship requires hard work on our part. It requires the development of personal virtue, particularly prudential judgment, that forms our character and help us make the right decisions. We have to read and reflect deeply on CST as it has developed, even while we read and reflect deeply on the signs of our times that give insight into critical issues that confront us. We have to be clear in our commitments to do good and avoid evil in the political sphere and to focus on the common good. We refuse to will evil to achieve some good, but we also carefully reflect on the flawed reality in which we live that rarely provides us pure

24. Ibid., 273. Also see note 16 referring to sections 34 and 35 of *Forming Consciences for Faithful Citizenship*. Emphasis is mine.

25. See ibid., 273–74, for his full exposition.

and uncomplicated choices. Choosing to "materially cooperate" with evil because that is the only way to move forward on policies that have the likelihood of diminishing that evil is a difficult but necessary use of prudential reason in the public sphere. Such choices are always made with a commitment to achieving the common good, without formally supporting the intrinsic evil in question.

Catholic Social Doctrine, Political Community, and Civil Society

In the modern period, the church has reflected deeply on the meaning of secular civil society and the emerging democratic states. The American bishops and theologians, particularly John Courtney Murray, initially set the stage for the church's formal acceptance of the democratic state, while providing the basis for its critical reading of those concepts in light of revelation. The *Compendium* takes up the political community (the state) and civil society in its assessment of the appropriate relationship of the state to civil society. The language chosen by CST indicates the priority of the human person in community: the "human person is the foundation and purpose of political life."[26] The state fulfills its role when it is oriented to "the full growth of each of its members, called to cooperate steadfastly for the attainment of the common good."[27] This is accomplished in public policy that nurtures respect for human dignity, particularly by "promoting fundamental and inalienable human rights."[28]

Because the political community is an expression of the dignity of the human person with reason and free will, its role and responsibilities are greater than the management of the material reality of the society. The political community is called to confront "individualistic and collectivistic ideologies" through policies that nurture civil friendship in the service of the common good. This language of community results from the priority of human person who has both reason and free will, and whose fulfillment can only be realized in the context of relationships. We are social beings and we are individuals. We are "persons-in-community" where the truth

26. Ibid., para. 384.
27. Ibid.
28. Ibid., para. 388.

of our reality is found in the tension between our truth as individuals and our social identity within community. Both dimensions of our nature must be respected and appropriately supported in the political community.[29]

That respect and support are seen in the ways that political authority is enacted within the society. In the work of seventeenth-century English philosopher John Locke, whose thought influenced the founders of the United States, authority is derived from the consent of the governed, who maintain the right to hold those who exercise authority accountable according to the end that is the common good. In this sense, the political community must be "guided by the moral law . . . which in turn has God for its first source and final end."[30] Locke's thought became foundational for liberal democracy.

The Catholic Church in the nineteenth century saw both liberal democracy and economics as potential threats to the dignity of the human person, precisely because these seemed to champion the individual in ways that sacrificed the perceived good order of society and the individual's duty to promote the common good. Paul E. Sigmund writing in "Catholicism and Liberal Democracy," however, reminds us that over the church's long history, democratic notions and the right to private property are present. For example, "Gratian's *Decretum*, a twelfth century compilation of earlier church documents that was used by all medieval canon lawyers, insisted that 'Bishops are to be elected by the clergy.'"[31] Sigmund further argues that in the long history of the emergence of the constitutional democracies, particularly from the sixteenth century forward, the church hierarchy pressed for religious uniformity in society, supported absolute monarchs who cooperated with the Vatican through treaties and sharing the process of appointment of bishops with the monarchs. Some Catholic thinkers countered this support arguing "that political authority came from God through the people. . . . [They] still endorsed religious uniformity and the rule of the monarch while arguing for moral and constitutional limits on his exercise of rule."[32] The French Revolution and

29. See ibid., para. 390–92.

30. Ibid., para. 395.

31. Paul E. Sigmund, "Catholicism and Liberal Democracy," in Williams and Houck, *Catholic Social Thought and the New World Order*, 53.

32. Ibid., 54.

the seizing of the Papal States in the ultimate unification of Italy as a nation-state reinforced the papacy's distrust of democratic movements. The church's concern for social justice, however, inevitably thrust Catholic laypersons into the political debates and life of the democracies at an early stage. Catholic political parties in the European democracies emerging in the nineteenth and twentieth centuries would move from simply defending the rights of the church to engaging political authorities and the society in the dialog for social justice, particularly workers' rights and protections in the liberal economics that dominated the newly industrialized countries of Europe and the United States.

At a time when advocates of totalitarianism and advocates of democracy, however imperfect, clashed, Pius XII, in his Christmas Message of 1944, argues that with rising complexity of the modern state, the necessity of achieving the common good seems to call for democracy "as a postulate of nature imposed by reason itself."[33] Living through the consequences of a co-opted democratic state in Nazi Germany, he reminds us that "the masses" in civil society can turn from the pursuit of the common good if "the people" do not take an active responsibility to "respect the freedom and dignity of others."[34]

John XXIII and Vatican II moved the church to a full acceptance of democracy in their rejection of the necessity of the "union of church and state" and recognized the "right to worship God according to the dictates of an upright conscience, and therefore to worship God privately and publicly."[35] The acceptance of religious freedom and the principle of separation of church and state in the democratic republic were critical to the reforms proclaimed by Vatican II in the Declaration on Religious Freedom. This "meant, in effect, the abandonment of the long-standing opposition between the Vatican and liberal democracy."[36] In 1991, in his encyclical *Centesimus Annus* (On the Hundredth Anniversary), Pope John Paul II acknowledged the church's practical preference for democracy that had

33. Pius XII, "Democracy and a Lasting Peace," Christmas Message 1944, http://www.papalencyclicals.net/Pius12/P12XMAS.HTM., line 19. Accessed July 4, 2012.

34. Ibid., lines 26 and 28.

35. John XXIII, *Pacem in Terris*, quoted in "Catholicism and Liberal Democracy," 60.

36. Ibid., 61.

been cited by John XXIII and the Vatican II documents. Precisely because democracy is structured by the participation of individuals in their own governance, it holds the promise of respecting the dignity of each individual within the political community. If it is not guided by a legitimate moral vision, however, it can become unjust and unstable.

Examples of this problem abound: when political parties, civil society organizations or economic enterprises are acting only in their own interests, they are often blind to the suffering they may impose on others. Slavery, and later racial segregation, supported by businesses, civil society groups, and enforced by laws, seemed acceptable to many in society and government. Racial segregation perpetuated suffering and inequality until civil society leaders such as Martin Luther King, Jr., promoted a vision of racial equality and prompted action by the federal government to overturn the social and political structures that racists had built. The history of racism in the United States, particularly the southern states, is a stinging reminder that local civil society and government may support injustice, and that subsidiarity means action should be taken at the most appropriate level of society and political organization, which in this case meant that the federal government had to intervene to protect the rights of minorities. Study of the Nazi co-option of the German democratic state, which emerged from the widely supported Nazi movement in civil society, shows us the tragic catastrophe possible when the human person is made subservient to a totalitarian ideology and the common good of all is disregarded. The democratic German state was unable to stop the growing Nazi movement in civil society that eventually took over that state and made it a brutal totalitarian regime. More subtle ideologies of individualism, consumption-based economics, and single-issue politics can blind us to the need to protect and act for the common good of all, including a sustainable environment.

Both relativism and agnosticism threaten democracies today because without understanding the moral truths that are written into our human nature, such as the dignity, equality, and interdependence of all, and without recognition of the true transcendent end of human existence that is God, civil society and the state can move into "open or thinly disguised totalitarianism." Democratic majorities can make laws that violate social justice and moral truths such as the dignity and equality of minorities. Ultimately, the democratic system is not an end in itself, but a means to a just society.[37] It is this continuing insistence on the dignity of the human person called to unity with God and one another, participating in the love that brought us and all creation into existence, that each Christian is called to bring to the public sphere. In contemporary democratic societies each person of goodwill must speak truth to civil society and the state in order to encourage "those virtues that make it possible to *put power into practice as service.*"[38]

The relationship between the state (political community) and civil society is mediated through the moral principles of solidarity, subsidiarity, and justice. Guided by solidarity, the state enacts laws, regulations, and norms that "promote the good of every person and of the whole person."[39] Sometimes the state will have to protect people from destructive civil society organizations; not all civil society actors seek the common good. Because many individuals within civil society to a greater or lesser degree are seeking those relationships and resources that will enable them to realize their full human potential to participate in the common good, the political community strives to overcome economic, social, and cultural inequities that inhibit authentic community. The political community creates systemic structures that serve those in need, and organizes resources to meet those needs, relieve suffering, and work for the betterment of society as a whole.[40] Our communitarian vocation calls each to "cultivate a greater awareness that [all] are

37. See *Compendium of the Social Doctrine of the Church*, para. 406–7.
38. Ibid., para. 410.
39. Ibid., para. 373.
40. We are reminded of the necessary connection between charity and solidarity in the tradition. "Pope John Paul II develops his predecessors' efforts to connect charity and justice by means of solidarity. He calls charity the prototype and the very marrow of solidarity. He identifies seeds of solidarity in Leo XIII's use of 'friendship' and 'brotherly love' that will foster a cooperative and respectful relationship between capital and labor. Friendship and brotherly love give rise to Pius XI's 'social charity' and to Paul VI's 'civilization of love.' In his historical overview of the term, John Paul identifies charity expressed in human friendship as the core of solidarity (1991, par. 10). Solidarity, like charity, possesses qualities of gratuity, forgiveness and reconciliation, and communion." See Lawrence R. Cima and Thomas L. Schubeck, "Self-Interest, Love, and Economic Justice: A Dialogue Classical Economic Liberalism and Catholic Social Teaching," *Journal of Business Ethics* 30 (2001): 213–31, and chapter 9, by Pagnucco and Gichure, in this volume.

debtors of the society of which they have become part" because the "culture, scientific and technical knowledge, material and immaterial goods" which they now utilize were there before them and require an attitude of respect and gratitude.[41] Our communitarian vocation nurtures a conversion of heart founded in the experience of unity with the poor and suffering, for in solidarity the poor are not an "other." The virtue of solidarity is developed in the habit of choices that identify who I am with others, especially the poor, recognizing our mutual interdependence, for we are all brothers and sisters in service to the common good. The communitarian vocation is realized in the act of standing with the oppressed, seeking justice with them, refusing to abandon them for to do so is to abandon the truth of our vocation to the common good. The political community, the state, acts in solidarity with the poor and oppressed by protecting them from exploitation and injustice. The communitarian vocation can be fulfilled as a public servant in the government, as a member of civil society, or as a businessperson.

Guided by subsidiarity, the political community enacts laws, regulations, and norms that respect the relative capacity of each level of government and civil society to realize the common good. Subsidiarity requires that the solutions to the issues that confront us be resolved at the lowest possible level of civil and governmental organization. The solutions must be just. The small rural hamlet's local government and civil society must be allowed to work out solutions to local problems to the degree they can do so, and as long as the solutions are just. The national government needs to discern how it might shift resources to better enable the local level of government and civil society to implement their decisions, if those resources are not possessed by the local level institutions; conversely, if a higher level of government can do the job better and more justly, then it should do so. The rural hamlet's government, consisting of local citizen participation and elected public servants, and its local civil society, with its voluntary organizations and cooperative relationships, are avenues for each individual to participate in their full human development and the realization of the common good. We frequently see the collaboration of nonprofit organizations with local, county, and state governments, often with some form of federal assistance, to address community problems. This is a good example of participatory action at the local level for the common good. As those

41. *Compendium of the Social Doctrine of the Church*, para. 195.

involved in such local action will attest, however, in some cases federal or national government action will be most effective, given the nature of the problem and the local resources available. A major goal of subsidiarity is the participation of the people in solving the problems they are facing. Sometimes local government and civil society do not have the capacities to do so, or some local actors are creating the problem. Ultimately, however, preserving the autonomy of the civil society in relation to the state is critical to the realization of the common good. Without this respect for autonomy, the civil society can become subsumed into the political community, though, conversely, without the action by the political community, the strong may dominate the weak in civil society, or it may not be able to solve the problems it faces. Protecting the autonomy of civil society prevents the loss of the freedom that is necessary to realize the human vocation to love God and create a society based on love for one another.[42]

Guided by these social virtues, the political community maintains a relationship with the civil society that recognizes its role of service to it and its responsibility to encourage its development. Each of these virtues develops in mutual interdependence in public life. Catholic Social Teaching argues that even this is a reductionist view of the cooperative relationships that form the civil society and its ability to mediate the power of the state in ways consistent with the common good. In the fullest sense, the virtues arise from love, which is "the highest and universal criterion of the whole of social ethics."[43]

Common Good

How might we understand the nature of the common good to which the civil society strives? The dialogue on the common good is one of the great themes of Western philosophy and politics, with its equivalents in the great civilizations of the East. In practical life experience, we first learn (or not) about our relationship as individuals to a common good within the family, with its ties and natural demands of provisioning and nurturing children and one another. Maturing into adulthood is the process of a child coming to know that the greater good of the whole family

42. See ibid., para. 419–20.
43. Ibid., para. 204.

takes precedence over his or her self-centered views—to see, in fact, that the good of the family is their good as well.

Pluralistic cultural environments, such as the United States, inevitably increase social tensions as competing visions of acceptable patterns and norms come into conflict within the society. In addition, the corrosive nature of a philosophy and culture focused on liberal individualism is felt not only at the level of society but within the family sphere. One of the recurring themes in the religions of the world, however, is some equivalent form of overcoming the ego-self in service to one's community, particularly with those who are poor, suffering, and without a voice in the public sphere. For example, Buddhists assert that realizing freedom from the attachments, aversions, and confusions that define the ego-self allows one to understand the origin of all suffering, stand with those who are suffering, and act compassionately for the betterment of each person and society as a whole. To paraphrase St. Paul, we can live in the world but not be of the world.

Herman Daly and John Cobb, Jr., remind us that economic theory and practice are central to the dialogue on the common good. Most liberal theorists from Adam Smith forward have argued that rational self-interest is the basis for economic exchange and the invisible hand of the market. "Economists typically identify intelligent pursuit of private gain with rationality, thus implying that other modes of behavior are not rational. Those modes include other-regarding behavior and actions directed to the public good."[44] Although later denied by some liberal economists, the moral context of Adam Smith's assessment of the wealth of nations and the free market in his earlier book, *The Theory of Moral Sentiments*, recognizes the contingent nature of the market and economic exchange. Both are instrumental means to the ends perceived by the participants in the exchange. Consumerism and its foundation, materialism, are the derailments resulting from the imposition of lust for power, fear of death, and revolt against the truth of our relationship with God who calls us into existence.[45] In the end, the market can be a vehicle for satisfaction

---

44. Herman Daly and John Cobb, Jr., *For the Common Good* (Boston: Beacon Press, 1989), 5.

45. See John Paul II, "*Sollicitudo Rei Socialis*: On Social Concern (1987)," in *Catholic Social Thought: The Documentary Heritage*, ed. David J. O'Brien and Thomas A. Shannon (Maryknoll, NY: Orbis Books, 1992), 411–19.

of needs and a relatively comfortable life in a community of mutually interdependent persons and nature. Alternatively it can be understood as an individualistic end-in-itself, a vehicle for self-isolation, greed, social and ecological destruction.

> However much driven by self-interest, the market still depends absolutely on a community that shares such values as honesty, freedom, initiative, thrift, and other virtues whose authority will not long withstand the reduction to the level of personal tastes that is explicit in the positivistic, individualistic philosophy of value on which modern economic theory is based.[46]

Catholic Social Teaching and the Common Good

The common good, the central responsibility of our vocation as social beings, is defined by the *Compendium* as "the sum total of social conditions which allow people, either as groups or as individuals, to reach their fulfillment more fully and more easily."[47] Achieving perfection in one's life is the process of accepting responsibility for one's actions and intentions, particularly in regard to the building up of the human community through love and justice. For John XXIII, the practical implications of such a life are an engagement with people and institutions to work toward: universal employment for all who desire work and greater access to goods and services necessary for a better life through productive work; more equitable relationships across the society; equality between sectors of the economy; balance between new production and services for citizens; a more humane way of existence that is sustainable and which respects the needs of future generations.[48] Put simply, "The common good would be achieved when through the fulfillment of rights and obligations, duties, and responsibilities, all members of the global human family had the means of subsistence and dignity."[49]

46. Daly and Cobb, *For the Common Good*, 51.

47. Ibid., 72, para. 164.

48. See ibid., 97.

49. Brenda Appleby and Nuala P. Kenny, "Relational Personhood, Social Justice and the Common Good: Catholic Contributions toward a Public Health Ethics," *Christian Bioethics* 16, no. 3 (2010): 302. Advance Access publication on December 24, 2010, doi:10.1093/cb/cbq022304.

As related in some detail by my colleagues in chapter 7 on human rights, liberal individualism assumes the autonomy of the individual in the family and society. The rights of the individual are primary, and reason serves self-interest. Self-interest tends to lead one to create transactional relationships through which one can achieve personal inclinations. In its best sense, the human person uses reason to understand the human situation and seeks to achieve happiness by living a virtuous life. Contemporary culture, however, tends to nurture patterns of instrumental relationships, seeing the other as the means to attain our interests. It reduces meaning to what we can possess, fostering the excitement of the hunt for things that, when finally possessed, can be easily thrown away in favor of the hunt for the next thing that will surely bring me happiness.

Catholic Social Teaching argues that the dignity of the individual is grounded in God's love that brings us into existence. This dignity is manifest in the social character of the human person. We truly become who we are by entering into relationships that seek the good of the other person, or in the broadest sense, the common good. These transformational relationships nurture virtue in our lives, what Robert Bellah called, "the habits of the heart." Such habits focus our desires and commitments toward solidarity with all, especially the least among us. Our lives participate in the Love that calls us into community with God, self, others, and creation itself, enabling us to choose for others and work for the sustainable common good.

Detractors, like Michael Novak, argue that this notion of the "common good" is a feel-good concept that is subjective, defined according to class perspective, difficult to apply to public policy, and policies created to further the "common good" may in fact have consequences that harm the welfare of most people. He finds the term "common good" vacuous because he does not accept the communitarian assumptions that underlie its usage in the Catholic tradition. While Novak is interested in democratization and increased individual participation, not to mention justice, he simply does not think that the realization of any of these goals results from anything other than autonomous individuals contracting for their realization through political institutions. In Novak's view, economic justice is best realized through the self-interested activity of individuals.[50]

---

50. See Michael Novak, "Liberty and Social Justice: Rescuing a Virtue," in Williams and Houck, *Catholic Social Thought and the New World Order*, 269–84.

Thomas R. Rourke sums up the problems with Novak's approach as an uncritical belief that self-interested actions taken together suffice for the common good and that his notion of freedom amounts to license. The communitarian social ethic underlying CST argues that true freedom is consistent with the social ends of the human person in community seeking the common good. "It is precisely this transcendent commitment to the good beyond any particular goods which sets us free from being mastered by circumstances and a variety of inclinations."[51]

Catholic Universities and the Common Good

One example from my home university, Chaminade University of Honolulu, may be helpful in understanding how Catholic universities can effectively work toward the common good, mobilizing their resources in service to the common good. Chaminade University of Honolulu created a new associate of arts program in the Micronesian state of Chuuk. Working with our partner, the Very Reverend Amando Samo, bishop of the Diocese of the Caroline Islands, we created new opportunities for the students of Chuuk to access higher education through the new Caroline College and Pastoral Institute (CCPI) created by the diocese. We have come to see this effort as a profound expression of our mission and identity as a Catholic and Marianist university.

Recruiting students from Micronesia to our main campus almost inevitably means that they will not be able to return to their homeland because of the level of debt they will likely incur while attending the university. For the target students of this project, all of whom qualify for Pell Grants, the chance of coming to our main campus was indeed remote. The new program promised a real opportunity to use their education for the betterment of their own society.

One of the key problems for the students is that English is their second language, and their academic preparation leaves them at risk in English language-based education. Using standardized placement exams that give us a relative sense of their abilities in reading, writing, and mathematics, along with their high school or College of Micronesia transcripts, we build

51. Thomas R. Rourke, "Michael Novak and Yves R. Simon on the Common Good and Capitalism," *Review of Politics* 58 (Spring 1996): 246–47.

the cohort for entry in the fall semester. The first semester focuses on these three areas, allowing students the opportunity to improve their English and math skills so that they can succeed in the rest of their college classes.

We created a new hybrid model that utilizes adult tutors at CCPI working with the online professors during scheduled lab times. This allows us to structure the study time of the students, help them focus appropriate time on each of their courses, and enable faculty members to interact with the students through some synchronous activities if they desire. At the least, faculty, through their professional tutors, are able to better sequence learning activities at specific times in the students' day.

As students progress in the program, we offer the most proficient students opportunities to work as peer tutors, emphasizing their responsibility to use their accomplishments for the good of the whole learning community. Within the culture, the peer-to-peer tutoring allows for more open questioning by the students who will not readily ask questions directly of the instructor. Through the peer tutors assigned to each of the online courses, small group discussions and exercise sessions are held and nagging questions can be answered. The tutors are able to give the instructor a different perspective on the learning process for the students. It is clear that the peer tutors also benefit from their leadership roles in the cohort and generally accelerate their own learning.

We continue to adapt the program to meet specific needs identified by the students, the church, and their future employers in Chuuk. Our faculty create opportunities for the students to express their identity within their own culture while helping them to understand both the religious and secular cultures out of which their education model is drawn. We are focusing on environmental sustainability and health issues through the science courses.

The program continues to improve because of the efforts of the many full-time faculty members who work in it. It is one of those rare times when the service we offer is so close to our mission and identity and the values and priorities we hold as a Marianist and Catholic institution in the Pacific: developing partners in the Pacific, working with local Chuukese immigrant communities in Hawaii, providing access to higher education, and giving students opportunities to make a difference for the better in their own society. In other words, it is preparing them for life, service, and careers that will contribute to the common good of their own societies and creating new opportunities for us to grow in the social virtues of solidarity, subsidiarity, and justice. An uncommon joy and a profound challenge! We are grateful!

Discussion Questions

1. Why does Catholic Social Teaching contend that seeking the common good is integral to our dignity as human beings?

2. Why is the "communitarian vocation" central to the church's understanding of human well-being?

3. How do the bishops approach "Faithful Citizenship," and why do they argue that living faithful citizenship requires the development of the virtue of prudential judgment?

4. As you live your commitments to justice and a sustainable future, how do you resolve the conflicts between men and women of goodwill as to what specific policies and solutions we will adopt to meet the needs of the common good?

5. Why are the social virtues of solidarity, subsidiarity, and justice central to the realization of a just political community that is working for the common good?

6. Should a Catholic university have Catholic Social Teaching at the core of its mission? How might Chaminade University of Honolulu improve its outreach in justice to the people of Chuuk in Micronesia?

Chapter 4

Linda Plitt Donaldson and
Susan Crawford Sullivan

Catholic Social Teaching, Poverty, and the Economy

In responding to the question "Who is my neighbor?" Jesus told the parable of the Good Samaritan. In this story, we learn that our neighbor is one who is vulnerable, left for dead, and even our enemy. In the last judgment, Jesus makes clear that our neighbor is the one who is hungry, thirsty, marginalized, naked, sick, and in prison (Matt 25:41-43). Jesus clearly aligns himself primarily with those who are poor, vulnerable, and marginalized in both his teachings and his life example. Guided by Jesus' example, Catholic Social Teaching (CST) calls for a preferential option for the poor and solidarity with the poor, where we put the needs of those who are poor and vulnerable first. To that end, CST calls for an economy that functions "as an instrument for the overall growth of . . . the human quality of life"[1] and should be measured "not by what it produces but . . . whether it protects or undermines the dignity of the human person."[2] It is the moral dimension of the economy that addresses some of the underlying causes of poverty and human suffering.

In selecting the name Pope Francis, Cardinal Jorge Mario Bergoglio offered new relevance to the life and example of St. Francis of Assisi, who rejected a family context of wealth, prestige, and status to radically emulate Jesus' life and teachings by embracing poverty, simplicity, service, and true solidarity with people living in poverty. In explaining why he chose the name Francis, the Pope stated:

1. *Compendium of the Social Doctrine of the Church*, 326.
2. *Economic Justice for All*, para. 2.

During the election, I was seated next to . . . Cardinal Claudio
Hummes . . . a good friend! When things were looking dangerous, he encouraged me. And when the votes reached two thirds,
there was the usual applause. . . . And he gave me a hug and a
kiss, and said "Don't forget the poor!" And those words came to
me: the poor, the poor. Then, right away, thinking of the poor, I
thought of Francis of Assisi. . . . That is how the name came
into my heart: Francis of Assisi. For me, he is the man of poverty,
the man of peace, the man who loves and protects creation. . . .
How I would like a Church which is poor and for the poor![3]

In the early months of his papacy, Pope Francis made clear that his ministry
will be characterized by an effort to rebuild God's church in a way that
service to and solidarity with the poor will be given primacy. Onlookers
have taken notice of his humble actions in the first days of his papacy:
forgoing the ermine-rimmed cape to dress in simple garments at the public
announcement of his election; asking for the people's blessing as he undertook his position, rather than blessing the people; selecting simple quarters
rather than the palatial papal apartment; washing the feet of young men
and women in a juvenile detention center on Holy Thursday, and visiting
an impoverished *favela* in Brazil, to name just a few examples.

In the first homily of his papacy, Pope Francis called attention to everyone's responsibility to "embrace with tender affection the whole of
humanity, especially the poorest, the weakest, the least important, those
whom Matthew lists in the final judgment on love."[4] Furthermore, he also
addressed the notion of power and its expression in the person of the pope
when stating, "Let us never forget that authentic power is service, and that
the Pope too, when exercising power, must enter ever more fully into that
service which has its radiant culmination on the Cross."[5] In a later homily,

---

3. Pope Francis, Address of the Holy Father to Representatives of the Communications Media, Saturday, March 16, 2013, http://www.vatican.va/holy_father/francesco
/speeches/2013/march/documents/papa-francesco_20130316_rappresentanti-media
_en.html.

4. Pope Francis, Homily of the Holy Father at the Inauguration of his Papal Ministry, March 19, 2013, http://www.vatican.va/holy_father/francesco/homilies/2013
/documents/papa-francesco_20130319_omelia-inizio-pontificato_en.html.

5. Ibid.

Pope Francis added, "Real power is service. . . . And there is no other way in the Church to move forward. For the Christian, getting ahead, progress, means humbling oneself. If we do not learn this Christian rule, we will never, ever, be able to understand Jesus' true message on power."[6]

Similarly, the pope has also called attention to the role of the economy in exacerbating wealth inequalities, poverty, human suffering, and the subjugation of people, echoing Pope Benedict's warning about "the scandal of glaring inequalities."[7] He has called for a "return to person-centered ethics in the world of finance and economics" and a "balanced social order that is more humane."[8] In a powerful speech in a poor Brazilian *favela,* Francis spoke directly to and about the poor:

> And the Brazilian people, particularly the humblest among you, can offer the world a valuable lesson in solidarity, a word that is too often forgotten or silenced, because it is uncomfortable. I would like to make an appeal to those in possession of greater resources, to public authorities and to all people of good will who are working for social justice: never tire of working for a more just world, marked by greater solidarity! No one can remain insensitive to the inequalities that persist in the world! Everybody, according to his or her particular opportunities and responsibilities, should be able to make a personal contribution to putting an end to so many social injustices. The culture of selfishness and individualism that often prevails in our society is not what builds up and leads to a more habitable world: it is the culture of solidarity that does so, seeing others not as rivals or statistics, but brothers and sisters. . . . The measure of the greatness of a society is found in the way it treats those most in need, those who have nothing apart from their poverty![9]

6. Pope Francis, Homily, May 21, 2013, http://en.radiovaticana.va/news/2013/05/21/pope_at_mass:_true_power,_even_in_the_church,_is_in_serving_others/en1-694087.

7. *Caritas in Veritate*, 22.

8. Pope Francis, Address to the New Non-Resident Ambassadors to the Holy See: Kyrgyzstan, Antigua and Barbuda, Luxembourg and Botswana, May 16, 2013.

9. "Full Text: Pope Francis Visits Rio Shanty Town," Catherine Harmon, *The Catholic World News Report*, July 25, 2013, http://www.catholicworldreport.com/Blog/2446/full_text_pope_francis_visits_rio_shanty_town.aspx#.UgJ9CdKsg6Y; accessed August 7, 2013.

Pope Francis' early papacy continues a long history of CST in emphasizing our responsibility for creating a society where all people can flourish, giving special attention to those who are poor and marginalized and to an economy that promotes human development. CST assumes that participation in societal life, local and global, public and economic, is an inherently moral undertaking. To that end, CST can be a powerful tool in guiding ethical and moral dimensions of professional practice and good citizenship where the preferential option for the poor can be used as a primary principle through which to assess one's action in the world.

This chapter will discuss issues of poverty in light of CST. We will provide an overview of the prevalence of poverty in the United States and globally, briefly review CST on poverty and the economy, and then offer some examples of how Catholic colleges and universities are teaching about issues of poverty and the economy through the lens of CST. This chapter comes with several disclaimers. First, it is written by two social scientists who study poverty, not by moral theologians. We are not scholarly experts in CST, but out of interest, we have pursued courses and independent reading in order to bring CST to light in our own disciplines. Second, theologians have written extensively about CST, poverty and the economy, and we do not intend this chapter to be an exhaustive analysis of all the relevant encyclicals and other documents. Our intent in this chapter is to present a basic overview of both poverty and CST as it relates to poverty and the economy.

Poverty

Poverty is a global experience that violates human dignity, undermines the common good, and requires us to respond to the call of the prophets to "do justice, love goodness, and walk humbly with God" (Mic 6:8). In 2011, 15 percent of Americans lived in poverty. This represents 46.2 million people, including 16.1 million children[10] and is the largest number of Americans living in poverty since the government started tracking this statistic in 1952. In addition, 6.6 percent of Americans, or 20.4 million people, live in "deep poverty" where their incomes are only one-half of the poverty threshold (see table 1). In other words, there are families of

10. Census, 2011.

four in America who are trying to live on less than $11,525 per year, and 1 in 50 Americans report no other source of income other than food stamps.[11]

Families who rely on food stamps as their sole source of income are either homeless, living with friends and family members, drawing on meager savings, staying in subsidized apartments, bartering services, searching for under-the-table jobs, or engaging in some other survival strategy. As the most recent recession was taking its toll, food-stamp enrollment exploded from 26.3 million recipients in 2007 to 46 million recipients in 2011.[12] Around this same time (2007 to 2010), family homelessness increased by 20 percent, and families using emergency or transitional housing increased from 30 to 35 percent. Homelessness is the most severe expression of poverty in the United States.

Table 1. 2012 Poverty guidelines for the forty-eight contiguous states and the District of Columbia[13]

Persons in Household	Annual Income
1	$11,170
2	$15,130
3	$19,090
4	$23,050
5	$27,010
6	$30,970
7	$34,930
8	$38,890

11. J. DeParle, "Living on Nothing but Food Stamps," *The New York Times*, January 3, 2010. Retrieved from http://query.nytimes.com/gst/fullpage.html?res=940D E4DD173EF930A35752C0A9669D8B63&ref=thesafetynet&pagewanted=print

12. P. Edelman, *So Rich, So Poor: Why It's So Hard to End Poverty in America.* (New York: The New Press, 2012).

13. U.S. Department of Health and Human Services (2012). "Poverty guidelines." Retrieved from http://aspe.hhs.gov/poverty/12poverty.shtml.

Poverty has been creeping up from its 2000 level at 11.3 percent to its current rate of 15.1 percent where it has held steady for the past two years.[14] We also know that poverty can have devastating consequences for children. Children growing up in poverty have worse health outcomes compared with children growing up in financially stable households. They have higher rates of asthma, diabetes, and other chronic illness versus their non-impoverished counterparts.[15] Due to stressful family contexts, children in poverty start to lag behind in school at an early age and generally attend lower-quality schools, causing them to be less prepared for high school. Consequently, they have higher high school dropout rates, are less likely to attend college, and have less education overall and fewer contacts in the labor market to compete for better paying jobs.[16] So children growing up in poverty often stay in poverty or enter the ranks of the "near poor."

The number of low-income or "near-poor" working families continues to rise and is projected to reach 50 million people in the next few years.[17] Figure 1 shows the percentage of working families by poverty status. Over 30 percent of working families meet the threshold of being low-income or poor, and like their nonworking counterparts, they struggle to cover basic expenses such as housing, utilities, day care, transportation, and food. They tend to work low-paying jobs such as food service, retail, housekeeping, and health care (e.g., medical assistants). Cashiering is the most common occupation for low-income families.[18]

14. Ibid.

15. K. Magnuson and E. Votruba-Dryzal, "Enduring Influences of Childhood Poverty," in *Changing Poverty, Changing Policies*, ed. Maria Concian and Sheldon Danziger (New York: Russell Sage Foundation, 2009).

16. Ibid., and H. Holzer, "Penny Wise, Pound Foolish: Why Tackling Child Poverty during the Great Recession Makes Economic Sense" (2010). Retrieved from http://www.americanprogress.org/issues/2010/09/pdf/hit_childpoverty.pdf.

17. Working Poor Families Project (2012–2013). "Low-Income Working Families: The Growing Economic Gap." Retrieved from http://www.workingpoorfamilies.org/wp-content/uploads/2013/01/Winter-2012_2013-WPFP-Data-Brief.pdf.

18. Ibid.

Figure 1. Working families by poverty status

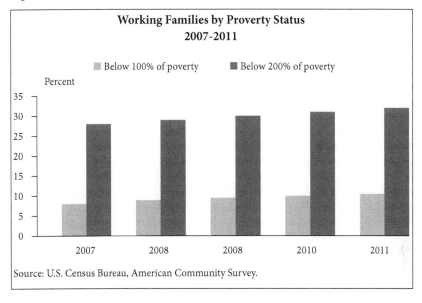

Source: U.S. Census Bureau, American Community Survey.

Labor analysts predict that occupations such as retail sales, home health aides, and personal care aides will be among the fastest growing occupations,[19] yet these jobs represent some of the lowest paying jobs in the economy. Because low-wage, low-income members of working families often hold more than one job to make ends meet, they have little time to spend with their families, participate in their communities, or attend to spiritual or leisure activities, among other things. CST stresses that participation in such spheres of life gives meaning to our lives and helps us realize our human dignity.

While poverty, low-wage jobs, and homelessness in America are growing, the gap in wealth among Americans is widening, i.e., the rich are getting richer and the poor are getting poorer (see figure 2.) Wealth refers to one's total assets, including real estate, stocks, bank accounts (savings, checking), minus total liabilities (credit card debt, mortgages, etc.). Wealth, more than income, speaks to a family's security and ability to

---

19. M. Lockard and M. Wolf, "Occupational Employment Projections to 2020," *Monthly Labor Review* 135, no. 1 (2012): 84–108. Retrieved from http://www.bls.gov/opub/mlr/2012/01/art5full.pdf.

pursue opportunities (e.g., borrowing on home equity for college) or withstanding economic setbacks (e.g., liquidating assets to cover expenses in the event of job loss). One's wealth can explain differences in how families manage during an economic recovery. For example, stock markets tend to recover faster than labor markets, so families with wealth will recover from economic setbacks faster than those whose assets are primarily tied to family income versus physical or investment assets. Wealthy households are more insulated from the effects of stagnating wages, increasing health costs, high rates of unemployment, and the impact of foreclosures experienced by the majority of Americans.

Figure 2. Share of total household wealth growth accruing to various wealth groups

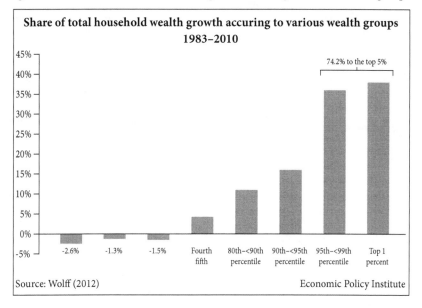

While numerically more white people experience poverty than other groups, blacks and Hispanics, whose poverty rates are 27.6 percent and 25.3 percent respectively, disproportionately experience poverty.[20] People of color disproportionately work in low-wage jobs, have less-than-

20. U.S. Census Bureau, "Income, Poverty, and Health Insurance Coverage in the United States" (2011). Retrieved from http://www.census.gov/prod/2012pubs /p60-243.pdf.

desirable educational opportunities, have greater exposure to violence, and are subject to racism and discrimination, all of which impede their economic opportunity. Poverty also has a disproportionate effect on women. About 34 percent (34.2 percent) of families headed by single women are poor with 16.9 percent of such families living in "deep poverty."[21] This feminization of poverty is largely related to employment in low-wage occupations wage disparity between men and women,[22] lack of affordable housing and child care, experience of violence and abuse, and an inadequate safety net.[23] The poverty rate for children has risen from 16.2 percent in 2000 to 21.9 percent in 2011, and 9.7 percent of children under 18 live in deep poverty.[24]

The feminization of poverty is a global phenomenon. Of the 1.4 billion people in the world living in extreme poverty,[25] 70 percent of them are women.[26] Throughout the world, discrimination against girls and women undermines their access to education, employment, and participation in government.[27] All over the world, violence (physical, sexual, psychological) is a universal experience for women and girls that cuts across class and culture. The percentage of women reported to have experienced physical violence at least once in their lifetime ranges from 12 percent to 59 percent, depending on the country, and between 6 percent and 35

21. Ibid.

22. According to the Institute for Women's Policy Research, women earn 77 cents on every dollar earned by their male counterparts ("The Gender Wage Gap: 2011," September 2012).

23. While food stamp enrollment skyrocketed from 2007 to 2010 (46 million), households receiving Temporary Assistance for Needy Families (TANF) have remained surprisingly low at 4.5 million households in 2011 (Edelman, 2012), giving evidence of the challenges to getting cash assistance since the 1996 welfare reform bill was passed.

24. U.S. Department of Health and Human Services, "Information on Poverty and Income Statistics: A Summary of 2012 Current Population Survey Data" (2012). Retrieved from http://aspe.hhs.gov/hsp/12/povertyandincomeest/ib.shtml.

25. United Nations defines "extreme poverty" as living on less than $1.25 per day.

26. UN Entity for Gender Equality and the Empowerment of Women, http://www.unifem.org/gender_issues/women_poverty_economics/.

27. United Nations, "The Millennium Development Goals Report," 2012.

percent report having experienced sexual violence.[28] Violence against women is both a cause and consequence of poverty. Furthermore, violent conflicts throughout the world have uprooted many people. The United Nations reports that by the end of 2011, approximately 42.5 million people were "living in a place to which they had been forcibly displaced due to conflict or persecution."[29]

With poverty comes hunger. Approximately 850 million people in the world suffer from hunger and malnutrition, contributing to disease, illness, and death. The World Health Organization estimates that malnutrition is the root cause of more than one-third of childhood deaths.[30] Due to malnutrition and unsanitary and environmental conditions, children are susceptible to serious diseases like cholera, malaria, yellow fever, dengue fever, and tuberculosis. Every year, a million people die of malaria, and 90 percent of those are children who live in sub-Saharan Africa.[31] Lack of access to healthy, nutritious food is a problem even in wealthy countries like the United States, as 20 percent of all U.S. households with children under age 18 suffered from food insecurity in 2011.[32]

Catholic Social Teaching on Poverty and the Economy

Catholic Social Teaching on poverty begins with the Hebrew prophets crying out for justice for the most vulnerable in their societies and continues in the example of Jesus and the formation of the earliest Christian communities, who demonstrated love of God and love of neighbor in their everyday interactions. While concern for and charity toward the poor existed for many centuries, the first "official" document of CST appeared in 1891, with Pope Leo XIII's *Rerum Novarum* (On the Condition of Labor). Coming against the backdrop of the Industrial Revolution, this encyclical aligned the church with social justice concerns such as the

28. UN Entity for Gender Equality and the Empowerment of Women.

29. United Nations, "The Millennium Development Goals Report," 2012.

30. World Health Organization, "World Health Statistics," 2009.

31. World Health Organization.

32. United States Department of Agriculture Economic Research Service, http://www.ers.usda.gov/topics/food-nutrition-assistance/food-security-in-the-us/key-statistics-graphics.aspx#.UeMLVtKsiSo, accessed July 12, 2013.

right to a living wage, just working conditions, and the right of workers to form labor unions.[33] Through this encyclical, Pope Leo XIII was reading and responding to "signs of the times," specifically, the condition and exploitation of workers during the industrial revolution.

Catholic Social Teaching speaks to the responsibility of the church to scrutinize the signs of the times and interpret them in light of the gospel.[34] Developing a thoughtful method of social analysis enables the church's teaching to deepen, evolve, and respond to contemporary questions that effect human existence and social relationships. As noted in the introduction, in addition to official documents that comprise CST, the broader Catholic social tradition also encompasses the work of organizations such as Catholic Charities, the Catholic Campaign for Human Development, and Catholic Relief Services, as well as the example of leaders such as Dorothy Day and Mother Teresa.

Catholic Social Teaching is often discussed in terms of "key themes," and commentators have used various schemas to present these key themes. Several common themes are of particular importance when considering issues of poverty and the economy. The first two are the dignity of the human person and the concept of the common good.[35] These themes undergird CST and are critically important for considering the moral implications of poverty and inequality.

The dignity of the human person, simply put, states that every person is valued and loved in the eyes of God. Too often our society marginalizes people who are poor, homeless, or hungry, but CST asserts that they have inherent dignity and equal value as human beings. Thomas Massaro, SJ, explains that CST calls for a more equal sharing of economic resources and power and extends the theological doctrine of human dignity into

---

33. See Thomas Massaro, *Living Justice: Catholic Social Teaching in Action*, 2nd ed. (Lanham, MD: Rowman & Littlefield, 2012), 33–76, for an excellent discussion of the historical development of Catholic Social Teaching.

34. *Gaudium et Spes.*

35. Lists of key themes of Catholic Social Teaching generally begin with the dignity of the human person, but Todd David Whitmore argues that starting with the concept of the common good is actually a better starting ground. See Todd David Whitmore, "Catholic Social Teaching: Starting with the Concept of the Common Good," in *Living the Catholic Social Tradition: Cases and Commentaries*, ed. Kathleen Maas Weigert and Alexia K. Kelley (Lanham, MD: Sheed & Ward), 59–81.

the social and political realm.[36] The concept of the common good runs counter to the prevailing cultural ethos of individualism and calls us to see that we are *interdependent* members of one human family. In this light, the fact that people in our midst are living in deep, despairing poverty and lacking basic needs (food, shelter, education, health care, and so on) is not a problem only for the poor. It is a problem for all of us, since we are interdependent. Catholic Social Teaching views human nature as fundamentally social in that people live together in a community, not as self-maximizing individualists. If we are fundamentally social, then the notion of the *common* good prevails, not a notion of "what's in it for me?"

Catholic Social Teaching defines the common good as "the sum of all social conditions which allow people, either as groups or as individuals, to reach their fulfillment more fully and more easily."[37] Included among the social conditions that promote human development are "a commitment to peace; the organization of State powers; a sound juridical system, the protection of the environment, and the provision of essential services to all, some of which are at the same time human rights: food, housing, work, education and access to culture, transportation, basic health care, the freedom of communication and expression, and the protection of religious freedom."[38]

Theologian David Todd Whitmore believes that the notion of the common good is the fundamental starting point of CST, as human dignity arises from the relationships people have with each other,[39] including economic relationships. David Hollenbach, also a theologian, reflects that our economic choices can promote relationships that support or undermine human dignity and the common good:

> [Some choices may result in greater] inequality or exclusion from resources necessary for the realization of human dignity. . . . Such negative interdependence is evident between groups whose interactions are marred by domination or oppression, by conflict

36. Massaro, *Living Justice*, 82.
37. *Compendium*, 164.
38. *Compendium*, 166.
39. Whitmore, "Catholic Social Teaching," 60.

or war, or who are living under economic institutions that exclude some people from relationships that are prerequisite for decent lives. Morally positive [choices are] . . . marked by equality and reciprocity. Those who are interacting show respect for each other's equal human dignity and relate to each other in ways that reciprocally support each other's dignity and freedom.[40]

Pope Benedict's 2009 encyclical letter *Caritas in Veritate* (Charity in Truth) highlights the importance of interdependent relationships: "As a spiritual being, the human creature is defined through interpersonal relations. The more authentically he or she lives these relations, the more his or her own personal identity matures. It is not by isolation that man establishes his worth, but by placing himself in relation with others and with God."[41] David Coleman offers a fuller philosophical reflection on CST and the common good in chapter 3 of this volume.

Flowing from the ideas of the common good and dignity of the human person is the notion of solidarity, as it emphasizes interdependence and common humanity as opposed to individualism. Solidarity is an especially important theme when learning about poverty and the economy as it is considered both a "social principle" and "moral virtue" that calls for the transformation of "structures of sin" into "structures of solidarity."[42] When Pope Francis called us to "embrace the whole of humanity, especially the poorest,"[43] he was referring to the universal quality of solidarity (i.e., solidarity with everyone, especially people who are poor) in order to restore them to fully participating members of the community. College students who have come from privileged backgrounds may have had little interaction with people who are poor. If they have done social service in high school, they have likely perceived and experienced it as doing charity

40. D. Hollenbach, "Economic Justice and the New Challenges of Globalization," in *The Almighty and the Dollar*, ed. Mark Allman (Winona, MN: Christian Brothers Publications, 2012), 102.

41. Pope Benedict XVI, *Caritas in Veritate* (2009), 53, http://www.vatican.va/holy_father/benedict_xvi/encyclicals/documents/hf_ben-xvi_enc_20090629_caritas-in-veritate_en.html.

42. *Compendium*, 193.

43. Pope Frances, Homily of the Holy Father at the Inauguration of his Papal Ministry, March 19, 2013.

for those who are other. In college, public service programs and immersion trips to poor areas domestically and abroad can reinforce a charity model. Students taking social science classes may read books and articles that inadvertently contribute to the notion of the poor as "other."

Considering poverty through a lens of solidarity can confront a charity model which treats the poor as unfortunate "others" lower in the social hierarchy. Solidarity, by contrast, emphasizes that the poor are equal members of the human family. Further, solidarity implies interdependence—something which people who might be volunteering in or doing service learning in poor communities need to keep in mind. In this way of thinking, privileged volunteers are not "rescuing" people, but rather are learning from people and working together with them in partnership. Both solidarity and interdependence lead to a model of community engagement which highlights both charity and justice, seeking to understand the social structural reasons underlying many problems and working with neighborhood residents to develop solutions together rather than imposing solutions as outsiders.

Pope John Paul II's 1987 encyclical *Sollicitudo Rei Socialis* (On Social Concern) states the following:

> [Solidarity] is not a feeling of vague compassion or shallow distress at the misfortune of so many people, both near and far. On the contrary, it is a firm and persevering determination to commit oneself to the common good; that is to say to the good of all and of each individual, because really we are responsible for all. . . . Solidarity . . . helps us to see the other . . . as our neighbor . . . on a par with ourselves, in the banquet of life to which all are equally invited by God. . . . The motivating concern for the poor must be translated at all levels into concrete actions, until it decisively attains a series of reforms.

In chapter 9, the essay by Ron Pagnucco and Peter Gichure explores a variety of ways in which solidarity has been theorized and practiced and relates these broader understandings to the Catholic notion of solidarity.

Participation is another important theme of CST linked to notions of solidarity and the common good. In summary this theme says that a test of a good society is one in which everyone has the opportunity to participate. Injustices that block participation in educational, economic, and social spheres, for example, deny people who are poor their right to play a full role in society. The church has a long-standing concern with worker rights and underscores the belief that people have a fundamental right to participate fairly in economic life.

Pope Leo XIII outlined a number of labor-related rights in the 1891 Papal encyclical *Rerum Novarum*. Subsequent encyclicals have also addressed the dignity of work, safe working conditions, and a living wage where one could support a family. In his 1981 encyclical *Laborem Exercens* (On Human Work), Pope John Paul II identified work as the "key to the social question," where work is the way in which human beings participate in the creative activity of God, realize their dignity, and contribute to the common good. Furthermore, he made clear that human beings are the subject of work versus instruments or objects of work. If one views workers merely as instruments of work, one might ignore the ultimate purpose of labor (i.e., promoting human development and participation). In connecting the dignity of work with poverty, Pope Benedict XVI wrote that "poverty results from a violation of the dignity of human work, either because work opportunities are limited (through unemployment or underemployment), or because a low value is put on work and the rights that flow from it, especially the right to a just wage and to the personal security of the worker and his or her family."[44]

Catholic Social Teaching particularly concerns itself with people who are poor. The "preferential option for the poor" in CST states that the measure by which any society should be judged as a moral society depends upon how it treats its poorest members.[45] The preferential option for the poor was forcefully stated in the U.S. context in the U.S. bishops 1986 letter, *Economic Justice for All: Pastoral Letter on Catholic Social Teaching and the U.S. Economy*. "The obligation to evaluate social and economic activity from the viewpoint of the poor and the powerless arises from the radical command to love one's neighbor as one's self. Those who

44. *Caritas in Veritate*, para. 63.

45. The term "preferential option for the poor" derives from liberation theology in Latin America in the 1970s. While some aspects of liberation theology were criticized by the Vatican as Marxist in their notions of class struggle and polarization, the theme of the preferential option for the poor has become an important part of Catholic Social Teaching.

are marginalized and whose rights are denied have privileged claims if society is to provide justice for all."[46]

The letter goes on to explicitly address a variety of public policies, stating, "The way society responds to the needs of the poor through its public policies is the litmus test of its justice or injustice."[47] Catholic poverty policy analyst and Harvard public policy professor Mary Jo Bane, who resigned her post as the assistant secretary at the U.S. Department of Health and Human Services in protest of the 1996 welfare reform law, has written on the impact of Catholic social thought in viewing poverty and poverty policy. Bane, an accomplished social scientist and experienced high-level social services administrator, assesses poverty policy initiatives in some detail in her essay "A Catholic Poverty Analyst Looks at Poverty."[48] For Bane, the challenge of poverty in the United States "lies in the fact that some Americans lack one or more of the most important capabilities necessary for human flourishing in this society" in that they "lack income, or opportunities to work, or opportunities to participate fully in society."[49]

Catholic Social Teaching tells us that people with resources have responsibilities to others who do not. As Thomas Massaro, SJ, puts it, "To recognize our property as coming under a social mortgage means that we cannot disregard the needs of the less fortunate, use our property in ways that harm them, or exclude them from full participation in society."[50] The notion of social mortgage relates to the CST concept "universal destination of goods" where one's right to private property and ownership is not for self-enrichment, but for facilitating the "development of the whole person and all of humanity."[51]

---

46. *Economic Justice for All*, 87.

47. *Economic Justice for All*, 123.

48. Mary Jo Bane and Lawrence M. Mead, "A Catholic Policy Analyst Looks at Poverty," in *Lifting up the Poor: A Dialogue on Religion, Poverty, and Welfare Reform* (Washington, DC: Brookings Institution Press, 2003), 12–51.

49. Ibid, 21.

50. Massaro, *Living Justice*, 95.

51. *Compendium*, 177.

Catholic Social Teaching describes a business enterprise as a "community of solidarity"[52] where interdependent and mutually beneficial relationships are present. Catholic Social Teaching speaks out forcefully against consumerism. Pope John Paul II warned against the "civilization of consumerism" that involves the over-accumulation of material goods, making us "slaves of possession and of immediate gratification"[53] where the focus is on *having* rather than on *being*. He even drew similarities between consumerism and other "ideological evils" such as Marxism, Nazism, and Fascism, stating that all tend to elevate the individual to the exclusion of the common good and the dignity of all human beings.[54]

Recently, Pope Francis has condemned the excesses of unbridled capitalism. "While the income of a minority is increasing exponentially, that of the majority is crumbling. This imbalance results from ideologies which uphold the absolute autonomy of markets and financial speculation, and thus deny the right of control to States, which are themselves charged with providing for the common good." Francis has condemned "a savage capitalism [that] has taught the logic of profit at all cost, of giving to get, of exploitation without looking at the persons . . . and we see the results in the crisis we are living."[55] Again and again, we see CST on the economy connecting with the key CST principles of solidarity, dignity of the human person, the importance of worker rights, and the preferential option for the poor. Scholar Rebecca Todd Peters comments, "If the principle of solidarity was central to the development of . . . economic

52. *Compendium*, 340.

53. *Sollicitudo Rei Socialis*, 28.

54. Message of His Holiness Pope John Paul II for the celebration of the World Day of Peace, January 1, 1999. Retrieved from http://www.vatican.va/holy_father /john_paul_ii/messages/peace/documents/hf_jp-ii_mes_14121998_xxxii-world-day -for-peace_en.html.

55. M. S. Winters, "Pope Francis Spotlights Social Teaching with Blunt Calls for Ethical Economy," *National Catholic Reporter* (June 1, 2013). Retrieved from http:// ncronline.org/news/vatican/pope-francis-spotlights-social-teaching-blunt-calls -ethical-economy.

policy, it could contribute to the development of an alternative vision of economic life rooted in the common good."[56]

While a thorough historical discussion of the complexities of CST on the economy is beyond the scope of this essay, CST calls for an economy that serves the common good and integral human development.[57] According to the *Compendium of the Social Doctrine of the Church* compiled by the Vatican Pontifical Council for Justice and Peace in 2004, modern CST affirms free markets but underscores their limitations and condemns their excesses.[58] Individual profit can never be the sole objective of the economy, and the market alone cannot supply all important human needs.[59] The market must be socially useful and in service to the common good, otherwise it becomes "an inhuman and alienating institution."[60] Markets must be regulated so as to serve the common good. "Freedom in the economic sector, however, must be regulated by appropriate legal norms so that it will be placed at the service of integral human freedom."[61]

In his encyclical *Caritas en Veritate* (Charity in Truth), Pope Benedict XVI highlights the importance of distributive justice and social justice for the market economy. He notes, "It must be remembered that the market does not exist in the pure state. It is shaped by the cultural configurations which define it and give it direction. Economy and finance, as instruments, can be used badly when those at the helm are motivated by purely selfish ends. . . . The economic sphere . . . must be structured and governed in an ethical manner"[62] Benedict continues, "The economy

---

56. R. T. Peters, "Considering a Solidarity Economy as a Framework for Justice," in *The Almighty and the Dollar*, ed. Mark Allman (Winona, MN: Christian Brothers Publications,2012), 137.

57. *Compendium*, 348.

58. Some critics contend that competitive economic systems such as markets are not compatible with Catholic Social Teaching. See, for example, Joe Torma's "The Cooperatist: Catholic Social Principles and Economics." While not rejecting markets, Rebecca Todd Peters calls for solidarity economies as alternatives to global free markets, such as barter economies, worker cooperatives; see R. T. Peters, "Considering a Solidarity Economy," 137.

59. *Compendium*, 349.

60. *Compendium*, 348.

61. *Compendium*, 350.

62. *Caritas in Veritate*, 36.

needs just laws and forms of redistribution governed by politics, and what is more, it needs works redolent of the spirit of gift."[63]

Catholic Social Teaching and Catholic Campuses in Solidarity with the Poor

Catholic Social Teaching demands that we stand in solidarity with people who are poor, engage in service to ameliorate their immediate needs, and work for justice to address the structural dimensions that violate their dignity and undermine the common good. Catholic campuses are using a variety of strategies to give students an opportunity to stand in solidarity with the poor at home and abroad. This section of the chapter highlights a few of many examples.

At the University of St. Thomas in Miami, the Center for Justice and Peace has engaged its students in global and local initiatives that seek social and economic justice. Their Global Solidarity Partnership (GSP) combines faculty research, curriculum development, student engagement, and community outreach to build the economic infrastructure of local communities in Haiti's Northwest region. The three long-term initiatives are a fair-trade coffee partnership, a women's artisan initiative, and sustainable solar energy initiatives. All three are designed to connect students and faculty with the people of Haiti in a collaborative partnership that enables relationships built on mutuality.

Closer to home, the Center for Justice and Peace helped students participate in a local faith-based organizing effort called People Acting for Community Together (PACT). Students intern with PACT, joining with the local community on issues residents care about, such as the drug problem and school safety, while taking courses on ethics and theology. Through the Center, students have also joined with the Coalition of Immokalee Workers while taking full 3-credit immersion courses that focus on the integration of CST, immigration, and farm labor.

In a graduate social work class on homelessness at the Catholic University of America, National Catholic School on Social Service students are invited to practice the principle of human dignity by engaging in a *regular* conversation with someone who is homeless that they meet on

---

63. *Caritas in Veritate*, 37.

the street. For these regular conversations, students are directed to talk about everyday things such as the weather, local sports, politics, etc., and not to explore the personal story of the individual, which may underscore difference and is often disrespectful. Students are invited to meet with this person at least three times over the course of the class to allow a relationship to emerge that is based on mutuality and respect for human dignity, not a relationship based on power, have-have not, or doing-for dynamics. Students then write a paper that reflects on this experience and course content and then identify whether or not it is possible to end homelessness.

At the College of the Holy Cross, a sociology seminar called Catholic Thought and Social Action challenges students to engage in a leadership project for social change while reading social science theories of leadership and democratic citizenship. The course is heavily steeped in Catholic social thought with students reading parts of social encyclicals, learning about the work of Catholic social agencies, and reading autobiographies of lay leaders such as Dorothy Day. Coordinating with community organizations, students in the seminar have worked to mobilize support for legislative issues with regard to affordable housing, education, the environment, and school nutrition and have been involved in community efforts to help low-income youth get summer jobs and expand college access.[64] Guided by Catholic social thought, students learn to work together with others toward a greater common good and learning to see the poor and marginalized people with whom they may be working not as charity recipients, but as people sharing a common dignity and humanity—people who are equals and partners in a struggle for greater justice.

At the University of Notre Dame, undergraduates can minor in the Catholic Social Tradition. This minor was established in 1997 in order to provide graduates entering a wide variety of professions a solid grounding in the social justice teachings of the Catholic Church. As opposed to a primary emphasis on volunteer work, the program's emphasis is on preparing students for service through their professional vocations. To obtain the minor, students must complete fifteen credit hours, including the Catholic Social Tradition core course, two three-credit electives, a

---

64. Sullivan and Post, "Combining Community-Based Learning and Catholic Social Teaching," 126.

senior capstone, and three one-credit seminars or colloquia on social concerns. Electives can include service learning and internship courses in the United States and abroad, as well as topical courses on issues relevant to CST, such as poverty or immigration. After completing the minor, graduates are well-prepared to take the rich social justice teaching of the Catholic Church into their future careers.

A number of Catholic colleges and universities partner with Catholic Relief Services (CRS) to integrate Catholic social thought and action on issues of international poverty. Cabrini College hosted the first campus CRS ambassadors' program where students who are committed to global humanitarian concerns raise awareness about global conditions on their campuses, hold regular meetings for students to learn more about and discuss issues of global poverty, and even engage in legislative initiatives to advance human rights and social and economic justice. One outcome of the Cabrini College-CRS partnership was student involvement in lobbying for comprehensive immigration reform. This lobbying effort was the culmination of a semester-long study of immigration issues and CST. Cabrini College was able to link this effort to their institutional identity, as St. Francis Cabrini is the patron saint of immigrants.

William Vos, Agnes Kithikii, and Ron Pagnucco[65] describe how the principle of mutuality (a core element of solidarity) informed the growth and development of a partnership between the Dioceses of St. Cloud and Homa Bay, Kenya. This CRS Global Solidarity Initiative includes faculty, students, and staff of the College of Saint Benedict/Saint John's University in the partnership. The partnership began in 1999 with an intention to create a collaboration based on a recognition that each partner has gifts to be shared, responsibility for creating a shared vision, along with mutually developed roles and responsibilities in the partnership. It was designed with an intention toward avoiding the traditional "sister diocese" or "sending church/receiving church" relationship. The essay identifies factors that lead to developing strong partnerships that truly reflect global solidarity. Catholic Relief Services has extensive resources for classroom use, which can be accessed online at www.crscollege.org.

---

65. W. Vos, A. Kithikii, and R. Pagnucco, "A Case Study in Global Solidarity: The St. Cloud-Homa Bay Partnership," *Journal for Peace & Justice Studies* 17, no. 1 (2008): 45–60.

Conclusion

Jesus conveyed the essence of his ministry when he stated, "He has sent me to bring good news to the poor, to proclaim liberty to the captives, and to set the oppressed free" (Luke 4:18). Catholic Social Teaching is a rich resource for students to use as the lens through which they see, judge, and act in the world. Catholic colleges and universities are in a unique position to help students carry on that ministry on their campuses and beyond in concrete ways that show a preferential option for and solidarity with the poor. Several Catholic campuses offer powerful examples of how to use CST to deepen students' understanding of the structural dimensions of poverty and to give them opportunities to act on that analysis. A variety of tools exist to help students promote CST as a lens for understanding. The signs of the times call on us to put these tools into action.

Discussion Questions:

1. Discuss an immersion or community-based learning experience that deepened your understanding or experience of being in solidarity with people who are poor. What aspect of that experience helped move you from a place of being in service to others to a place of solidarity with others?

2. What principles of CST resonate most with you in terms of one's responsibility to people who are poor and vulnerable? Explain.

3. What might be some of the barriers to building solidarity relationships with people who are poor? What can we do to overcome these barriers?

4. Discuss whether or not CST (particularly principles of human dignity, the common good, solidarity, and the preferential option for the poor) adds anything to the secular discourse on the condition of poverty, the state of the economy, and societal responses to it.

5. Using a CST lens, how would you address the tension between profit-making and human development in a business enterprise?

Chapter 5

Daniel Groody, CSC, and
Colleen Cross

From Neighbor to Brother and Sister: Immigration in Catholic Social Teaching[1]

The migration of peoples is one of the most defining moral issues of our time. Although people have been migrating since the dawn of human history, the scope and scale of migration today is unprecedented. According to the International Organization of Migration, more than 214 million people are migrating around the world today, which means that approximately one of every 33 people around the world is living away from their

---

1. Portions of this article are drawn from Daniel G. Groody, *Globalization, Spirituality, and Justice: Navigating a Path to Peace*, Theology in Global Perspective Series (Maryknoll, NY: Orbis Books, 2007), 91–121; and Daniel G. Groody, "Homeward Bound: A Theology of Migration," *Journal for Catholic Social Thought* 9, no. 2 (2012): 409–24. For further reading, see Daniel G. Groody, "A Mission of Reconciliation: Theological Perspectives of Pilgrim People," in *On "Strangers No Longer": Perspectives on the Historic U.S.-Mexican Catholic Bishops' Pastoral Letter on Migration* (Mahwah, NJ: Paulist Press, 2013), 63–86; and Daniel G. Groody, "Crossing the Divide: Foundations of a Theology of Migration and Refugees," *Theological Studies* 70 (September 2009): 638–67.

homelands.[2] Nearly 42 million of these are forcibly uprooted,[3] including 16 million refugees and 26 million who are internally displaced.[4] This movement of peoples is so extensive that it touches essentially every aspect of human life. Studied by virtually every academic discipline, migration is transforming not only the social, cultural, and economic landscape of our communities but the theological, ecclesial, and spiritual territory as well. With good reason, some scholars today refer to our own times as the "age of migration."[5]

This chapter seeks to examine the reality of migration and the mission of the church through the lens of Catholic Social Teaching (CST) and the context of Catholic higher education. Here we will investigate not simply the economic or political costs related to this debate but also human and social costs related to the search for the international common good and the God-given dignity of each and every person.

2. See http://www.iom.int/jahia/Jahia/about-migration/facts-and-figures/lang /en (accessed November 29, 2011). An immigrant is defined as a person who moves to another country to take up permanent residence. See United States Conference of Catholic Bishops and Conferencia del Episcopado Mexicano, *Strangers No Longer Together on the Journey of Hope*, issued by the USCCB on January 22, 2003, glossary.

3. The United Nations defines a long-term migrant as one who has lived away from his or her homeland for a duration of at least twelve months (see United Nations, *Recommendations on Statistics of International Migration, Revision 1*, 1998). A refugee is defined as "any person, who, owing to a well-founded fear of being persecuted for reasons of race, religion, nationality, membership in a particular social group, or political opinion, is outside the country of his or her nationality and is unable or, owing to such fear, is unwilling, to avail himself or herself of the protection of that country; or who, not having a nationality and being outside the country of his or her habitual residence as a result of such events, is unable or, owing to such fear, is unwilling to return to it." For the definition of *asylee*, see the definition of refugee above. "The definition conforms to that of a refugee except regarding the location of the person upon application for asylum: The asylee applies for protection in the country of asylum, whereas the refugee applies for status in either his or her home country (under certain circumstances) or in a country of temporary asylum." For all definitions, please see *Strangers No Longer*, glossary.

4. See http://www.unhcr.org/4a3b98706.html, accessed November 29, 2011.

5. Stephen Castles and Mark J. Miller, *The Age of Migration: International Population Movements in the Modern World*, 4th ed. (New York: Guilford Press, 2009).

In the first part of this essay we will explore the issue of migration in light of central themes of CST. Second, we will examine this teaching with respect to the church's mission of reconciliation. And third, we will look at this mission in the context of Catholic colleges and universities, particularly as it deals with migration to the United States and the plight of undocumented immigrants. In many ways this perspective will offer a theological exploration of migration, through which we hope to offer not only more information about this complex issue but also a new imagination about it. Our aim is to help educate and animate students on college campuses to contribute to the important task of immigration reform and the building of a more just and humane society.

Catholic Social Teaching and Migration

As it looks at the world today and its social issues, CST seeks to challenge those dimensions of society that diminish people's relationships with God, others, the environment, and themselves, and promote those factors that enhance these relationships. Because its universal message is directed to all nations and all peoples, CST is concerned with all aspects of the human being and the full human development of every person.[6] It is addressed not only to Roman Catholics but also to other ecclesial communities, other religions, and all people of goodwill.[7]

As Pope Benedict XVI and previous popes have noted, the purpose of CST is not to replace the state nor to organize society but to challenge, guide, and form the conscience of the human community as it seeks a new social order.[8] The church is concerned that this process leads to the

6. Pope Paul VI, *Populorum Progressio* (On the Development of Peoples), March 26, 1967, 42.

7. Pope John XXIII first began speaking of CST in terms of addressing all people of goodwill and not simply Catholics in *Pacem in Terris* (On Establishing Universal Peace in Truth, Justice, Charity, and Liberty), April 11, 1963. See United States Conference of Catholic Bishops, *Sharing Catholic Social Teaching: Challenges and Directions* (Washington, DC: United States Conference of Catholic Bishops, 1998), for further discussion on the role of Catholic Social Teaching in Catholic education.

8. Pope Benedict XVI, *Deus Caritas Est* (God Is Love), December 25, 2005, 28; Pontifical Council for Justice and Peace, *Compendium of the Social Doctrine of the Church*, May 26, 2006, 81.

integral development of the human person in society. Catholic Social Teaching sees the process of transformation as central to its mission of evangelization,[9] which it understands not as proselytism but as a way of helping people, under the light of the gospel, to relate to each other in life-giving ways. It not only seeks to denounce injustices and inequities of the current global order but also actively announce, in Pope John Paul II's words, "a culture of life." Alongside many social issues such as homelessness, racism, genocide, capital punishment, abortion, and many other issues, the church takes up the issue of immigration because it touches upon the areas that are at the heart of the reign of God.

As Vatican II noted, the reign of God is about a kingdom of truth and life, holiness and grace, love, peace and justice.[10] In Christian theology there are two principal notions of justice: internal justice and external justice. Internal justice deals with one's experience of justification or being put in right relationship with God through the saving work of Jesus Christ. External justice deals with the promotion of good works. Internal justice refers to God's activity within a person; external justice refers to one's response to God's grace. Internal justice relates to the first and the greatest command: to love the Lord God with all one's heart, soul, and mind (Matt 22:37-38). External justice relates to the second command: to love one's neighbor as oneself (Matt 22:39). It seeks humanizing activity leading to right relationships with one's self, the community, its social structures, and finally to the environment itself.[11] God's justice, in other words, is not principally about vengeance or retribution but about restoring people to right relationship with God, themselves, others, and the environment.[12]

When the church comments on issues related to injustices, like immigration, it does so principally because it directly affects the quality of

9. Pope John Paul II, *Sollicitudo Rei Socialis* (On Social Concern), December 30, 1987, 41.

10. *Lumen Gentium* (Dogmatic Constitution on the Church), promulgated by Pope Paul VI, November 21, 1964, 36.

11. This definition is drawn in part from an excellent article by Michael Crosby, "Justice," in *The New Dictionary of Catholic Spirituality*, ed. Michael Downey (Collegeville, MN: Liturgical Press, 1993), 597.

12. For more on this topic, see Daniel G. Groody, *Globalization, Spirituality, and Justice: Navigating the Path to Peace* (Maryknoll, NY: Orbis Books, 2007).

our relationships. Our current economic system, which greatly influences the movement of peoples, is one such example. The current, asymmetric distribution of the goods of the earth leaves much to ponder in view of the designs of a loving Creator and the human choices that have constituted the current world (dis)order. At present 19 percent of the world's population lives on less than a dollar per day; 48 percent lives on less than two dollars per day; 75 percent lives on less than ten dollars per day; and 95 percent lives on less than fifty dollars per day. The top 1 percent have as much as the poorest 57 percent taken together, and the three richest *people* have as much as the poorest 48 *nations* combined.[13] These disorders are rooted in unjust structures, but as Vatican II says, they are also rooted in the disorders of the human heart.[14] They stem from complex interplay of original, personal, and social sin that fragment and alienate various levels of our relationships.

When addressing immigration, the church's social teaching highlights important themes such as: (a) the right to stay in one's homeland, (b) the right to move when conditions require it, (c) the unity of the nuclear family, (d) the international common good and our responsibility to and solidarity with the larger human family, especially the most vulnerable, (e) the national common good and the right of nations to protect borders, and (f) the dignity of the human person. We will touch briefly on some of these themes, but since space does not allow us to examine these themes in detail, our primary focus will be on one of the most foundational themes in CST: the promulgation of human dignity.

Although people on the move are labeled in various ways, the vast majority of them are simply human beings in search of better lives. Most are not seeking to get rich but more often survive and live above the level of mere subsistence. Their arduous trials and dangerous border crossings are well documented, but surprisingly, when asked about the most difficult

---

13. For more on these statistics and their sources, see Daniel G. Groody, *Globalization, Spirituality, and Justice: Navigating the Path to Peace* (Maryknoll, NY: Orbis Books, 2007), 3-10.

14. *Gaudium et Spes* (Pastoral Constitution on the Church in the Modern World), 10, promulgated by Pope Paul VI, December 7, 1965); http://www.vatican.va/archive /hist_councils/ii_vatican_council/documents/vat-ii_const_19651207_gaudium-et -spes_en.html (accessed November 27, 2012).

part of migration, they often point to challenges that go beyond the physical hardships. Despite swimming across canals and oceans, hiding in cargo ships and train cars, and enduring extreme temperatures in deserts and mountains, the migrants often point to difficulties that go to the heart. One migrant from Mexico said, "I have stowed away on baggage compartments of buses and almost suffocated in a box car; I almost froze to death in the mountains and baked to death in the deserts; I have gone without food and water for days, and nearly died on various occasions. As difficult as these are, these are not the hardest parts of being a migrant. The worst is when people treat you like you are a dog, like you are the lowest form of life on earth."[15] Such stories reveal that no wound cuts more deeply than the feeling that others do not even regard you as a human being, that you are no one to anyone. Many migrants today struggle simply to reclaim their status as human beings, especially in the context of a world that demeans, diminishes, and dehumanizes them. At the heart of the church's mission is the affirmation of the human person in the depth of who they are as a child of God.

In its efforts to safeguard the dignity of all people, CST has consistently argued that the moral health of an economy is measured not in terms of financial metrics like the gross national product or stock prices but in terms of how the economy affects the quality of life in the community as a whole.[16] Catholic Social Teaching states that an ordered economy must be shaped by three questions: What does the economy do *for* people? What does it do *to* people? How do people participate in it?[17] It puts strongest emphasis on what impact the economy has on the poor. It stresses that the economy is made for human beings, not human beings for the economy. In the immigration debate this means that the primary focus has to do first with human and relational costs; CST asks to what extent the economy of a country enhances the dignity of every human being, especially those who are vulnerable and deemed insignificant.

15. Groody, "Homeward Bound," 411.

16. United States Conference of Catholic Bishops, "Economic Justice for All," no. 14, available at: http://www.osjspm.org/economic_justice_for_all.aspx (accessed May 3, 2009).

17. Ibid., 1.

Although it sees the first ideal as people's right to stay in their home-lands, the church also acknowledges that people have a right to migrate when conditions are insufficient in their homelands to live a dignified life.[18] What is underneath this vision is the notion that God alone is the ultimate owner of all that the earth contains, and consequently, all the goods of the earth are given in trust as a patrimony to the whole of the human community, not just a privileged few.

The bishops of the United States have added that "any limitation on international migration must be undertaken only after careful consider-ation of the demands of international solidarity. These considerations include development, trade and investment programs, education and training, and even distribution policies designed to narrow the wide gaps between the rich and the poor."[19] In other words, controlling borders must be addressed only after the issues of distributive justice have been met, otherwise we end up looking at immigration as a problem in itself rather than a symptom of deeper social imbalances which precipitate the movement of people.

In 2003 the bishops of Mexico and the United States jointly issued the pastoral letter *Strangers No Longer: Together on the Journey of Hope* in response to the ongoing migration phenomenon between their two coun-tries. Pointing to migration as a "sign of the times" that makes a claim on the human conscience, they identified five principles based on Scripture and CST to guide the church in its discussions of migration.[20] The first highlights the individuals' right to economic, political, and social oppor-tunities in their homelands. Such rights not only safeguard human dignity but also are essential to human flourishing. Second, when individuals cannot find employment necessary to support themselves and their fami-lies in their home countries, they have the right to migrate and find work. Third, the church recognizes the right of nations to control their borders, but this right is not absolute. Rather, it must be exercised in light of the

18. *Pacem in Terris*, 25.

19. United States Conference of Catholic Bishops, *One Family under God: A Statement of the U.S. Bishops' Committee on Migration*, rev. ed. (Washington, DC: United States Conference of Catholic Bishops, 1998), 6. For a further discussion of solidarity, see chapter 9 by Pagnucco and Gichure in this volume.

20. *Strangers No Longer*, 34–38.

principle of the global common good and exigencies of distributive justice. The bishops explicitly state that nations possessing an abundance of resources "have a stronger obligation to accommodate migration flows."[21] Fourth, because of the extreme vulnerability that refugees and asylum seekers face, the bishops argue that their cases require special attention and protection.[22] They consistently affirm that the moral health of an economy is gauged by how it treats its most vulnerable members.[23] Finally, the bishops emphasize that the dignity and rights, inherent to each person irrespective of citizenship status, must be protected. Giving expression to the injustices present in the current migration reality and the search for a more just and humane social order, *Strangers No Longer* calls us to understand this justice first and foremost in light of right relationship with God and with one another.

The heart of the bishops' vision of justice is rooted in the scriptural vision of the reign of God. When Jesus proclaimed the reign of God, he did most of his ministry around tables. This "table fellowship" offered a vision of God's invitation to all to accept the message of salvation and consequently to create through a community of sharing through the gift of hospitality. In *Welcoming the Stranger Among Us*, the U.S. bishops affirmed, "Immigrants, new to our shores, call us out of our unawareness to a conversion of mind and heart through which we are able to offer a genuine and suitable welcome, to share together as brothers and sisters at the same table, and to work side by side to improve the quality of life for society's marginalized members."[24] In its care for all, especially those

---

21. Ibid., 36.

22. Although not as explicitly relevant to the discussion on undocumented migration, a number of individuals enter the United States seeking this status. Rather than welcome such individuals and hear their case in an efficient manner to determine an adjustment in legal status, many seeking protection are sent to detention facilities, sometimes for durations upwards of a year before the appropriate legal authorities evaluate their cases. The church in the United States sees this as a grave injustice that needs to be addressed.

23. United States Conference of Catholic Bishops, "Economic Justice for All," 123, available at http://www.osjspm.org/economic_justice_for_all.aspx (accessed October 7, 2013).

24. U.S. Catholic Bishops, "Welcoming the Stranger among Us: Unity in Diversity" (2000).

most in need, the church not only goes beyond borders but unites itself with those on the other side of them, giving expression to its interconnectedness as the body of Christ.

In this spirit, CST is enacted each year along the U.S./Mexico border, when the bishops gather people from both countries to celebrate a binational Mass, in the open air. What is unusual about this Eucharist is not only that people from different countries come together but also that the altar is joined on either side of the border divide. With the bishops concelebrating the Eucharist on both sides, the Christian community gives testimony to what it means to be united in Christ in table fellowship, even amidst the fractured sociopolitical and economic reality of migration today. In the end the church examines the issue of migration under the light of the Gospel message and the centrality of the Eucharist, which at its core deals with getting our relationships right, or, in other words, the mission of reconciliation.

Migration and the Church's Mission of Reconciliation

In many ways, at the heart of CST on migration is a vision of the church's mission of reconciliation, which gives primacy to the human and relational costs associated with migration over, and sometimes against, the political and economic costs. Here we would like to look at this theological foundation in more depth. Our argument here is that CST seeks to foster justice-as-right-relationships by overcoming (1) the inhuman-human divide; (2) the divine-human divide; (3) the human-human divide; and (4) the country-kingdom divide. Healing these relationships through the church's ministry of reconciliation addresses the issue of immigration reform at the most fundamental levels of human experience.

Imago Dei: *Reconciling the Inhuman-Human Divide*

The Scriptures give us important insight into who we are before God and ways we can find a more liberating approach to some of the dehumanizing undercurrents in the process of migration. In the book of Genesis we are introduced to *imago Dei* ("image of God"), a central truth, which emerges throughout the Scriptures, that human beings are created in the image and likeness of God (Gen 1:26-27; 5:1-3; 9:6; 1 Cor 11:7; Jas

3:9). Defining all human beings in terms of *imago Dei* provides a very different starting point for the discourse on migration and creates a very different trajectory for the discussion than commonly used labels from a sociopolitical sphere (that is, alien, migrant, refugee, internally displaced person), or worse, the degrading stereotypes used by nativist groups. *Imago Dei* names the personal and relational nature of human existence and the mystery that human life cannot be understood apart from of the mystery of God.

For many forced migrants, moving across borders is connected to finding a job. Pope John Paul II addressed the connection between human dignity, social justice, and work when he noted, "the person working away from his native land, whether as a permanent emigrant or a seasonal worker, should not be placed at a disadvantage in comparison with the other workers in that society in the matter of working rights. Emigration in search of work should in no way become an opportunity for financial or social exploitation."[25]

Most migrants leave their homes not only to realize a greater dignity for themselves but also for their families. Statistics on global remittances offer one indicator of the connection between migration and relationships. In a recent study, migrants sent home to their families more than $325 billion, often in small amounts of $100 to $300 at a time.[26] Meanwhile, the total Overseas Development Aid from donor nations to poorer countries was $128 billion.[27] This means that migrants living on meager wages spent two and a half times as much money helping alleviate global poverty as did the wealthiest countries of the world. Contrary to dehumanizing stereotypes, *imago Dei* is a two-edged sword that positively functions as an affirmation of the value and worth of every person and evaluates and challenges any tendencies to dominate or oppress the poor and needy, or degrade them through various manifestations of racism, nativism, and xenophobia.

25. Ibid., 23.

26. *Migration and Remittances Fact Book 2011*, 2nd ed. (Washington, DC: The World Bank, 2011), vii. Available online at http://siteresources.worldbank.org/INTLAC /Resources/Factbook2011-Ebook.pdf.

27. See http://www.oecd.org/document/35/0,3746,en_2649_34447_47515235 _1_1_1_1,00.html (accessed December 1, 2011).

Verbum Dei: *Reconciling the Divine-Human Divide*

Christ is the perfect embodiment of *imago Dei* and the one who helps people migrate back to God by restoring in them what was lost because of sin. A theology of migration is fundamentally about God's migration into our sinful, broken existence, and our return migration to our ancestral, spiritual homeland, where at last we find our lives and our relationships made whole again. Through Jesus, God enters into the broken and sinful territory of the human condition in order to help men and women, lost in their earthly sojourn, find their way back home to God. From this perspective the incarnation is the great migration of human history: God's movement in love to humanity makes possible humanity's movement to God.

The *verbum Dei* ("word of God") manifests that, even as human beings erect barriers of every sort, God walls off no one from divine fellowship. In the journey into otherness and vulnerability, Jesus enters into total identification with those who are abandoned and alienated. The incarnation moves people beyond a narrow, self-serving identity into a greater identification with those considered "other" in society, particularly those like migrants and refugees who are poor and regarded as insignificant. In becoming neighbor to all in the incarnation, that is, all who live in the sinful territory of a fallen humanity, God redefines the borders between neighbors and opens up the possibility for new relationships. Migration becomes a descriptive metaphor for the movement of God toward others in the human response of discipleship.

Missio Dei: *Reconciling the Human-Human Divide*

A central dimension of the *missio Dei* ("mission of God") is Jesus' ministry of reconciliation which deals largely with overcoming human constructions that divide the insider from the outsider, particularly those generated by law in its various forms. The *missio Dei* challenges a tendency that very often human beings have to idolize the state, religion, or a particular ideology and use it as a force that excludes and alienates, even when it does so under the guise of obedience to a greater cause.

When thousands of immigrants and refugees die each year trying to cross areas like the deserts of the American Southwest or the waters dividing North Africa from Europe, the structures of a society must be seriously examined under the entirety of legal reasoning. Here many different kinds of law are at work: laws of nations that control borders; laws of human nature that lead people to seek opportunities for more dignified lives; natural law that deals with ethical dimensions of responding to those in need; and divine law that expresses the Creator's will for all people. The fact that so many migrants are dying in their efforts to meet basic human needs raises serious questions about current civil laws and policies and their dissonance with other forms of law.

Catholic Social Teaching, drawing on the thought of Thomas Aquinas and others, brings out that when people cross borders without proper documentation, most are not simply breaking civil laws but obeying the laws of human nature, such as the need to find work in order to feed their families and attain more dignified lives. Moreover, crossing international borders without papers in most countries is an administrative infraction, not a felony; it is not a violation of divine law or natural law, and in such cases undocumented immigration should in no way be confused with serious criminal activity or threats to national security. Much misunderstanding and injustice occur when immigrants and immigration are perceived primarily as problems in themselves rather than as symptoms of more systemic social ills and inequities, as matters of national security rather than as responses to human insecurity, as social threats rather than as foreign neighbors.

Visio Dei: *Reconciling the Country-Kingdom Divide*

The way we perceive those considered as "other" in the phenomenon of migration is rooted not only in how we see those who are different from ourselves but also in the way we see God. Meister Eckhart says that the goal of Christian life is not so much to seek the *visio Dei* ("vision of God") in heaven as to see things in this life as God sees them.[28] While our journey through life is situated within the citizenship in this world, ultimately it is grounded in citizenship of, and movement toward, our citizenship in the next. In addition to pledging allegiance to a particular country, the *visio Dei* brings out that one's ultimate obedience is to God alone, which leads one beyond any national and political boundaries to ultimate fidelity to the kingdom of God. Our focus here is how this vision

---

28. Bernard McGinn, "*Visio Dei*: Seeing God in Medieval Theology and Mysticism," in *Envisaging Heaven in the Middle Ages*, ed. Carolyn Muessig and Ad Putter with Garth Griffith and Judith Jefferson (New York: Routledge, 2007), 24–27.

takes root in human history, how it influences social transformation, and how it transfigures the way we understand migrants and refugees. In its care for all, especially those most in need, the church not only goes beyond borders but unites itself with those on the other side of them, giving expression to its interconnectedness as the body of Christ. In imitation of its founder, the church serves all people regardless of their religious beliefs, their political status, or their national origins.

The *visio Dei* comes into focus in the person of Jesus Christ and the kingdom he proclaimed. It is based not on geography or politics but on divine initiative and openness of heart, leading to a different kind of vision of the current world order, where many of the first are last and the last first (Matt 19:30; 20:16; Mark 10:31; Luke 13:29-30). Jesus clearly taught that many of the values and metrics people employ to measure others will be inverted and that the excluded will be given priority in the kingdom. The kingdom calls people into movement, making the church exiles on earth, strangers in this world, and sojourners en route to another place.[29] The *visio Dei* also challenges people to move beyond an identity based on a narrow sense of national, racial, or psychological territoriality. It holds out instead the possibility of defining life on much more expansive spiritual terrain consistent with the kingdom of God. In the end, CST reminds us that the work of Christian mission as reconciliation and the pursuit of justice as right relationships must be understood not only in light of religious conversion but moral, intellectual, affective, and social conversion as well.[30]

Journeying with the Migrant: The Work of Catholic Colleges and Universities

Guided by CST and the mission of the church, Catholic colleges and universities work against the forces of injustice in society in order to stand

29. Christine D. Pohl, "Biblical Issues in Mission and Migration," *Missiology* 31 (2003): 3–15.

30. For more on these notions of conversion, see Bernard Lonergan, *Method in Theology.* (Minneapolis: Winston/Seabury, 1972); and Donald L Gelpi, *Committed Worship: A Sacramental Theology for Converting Christians*, vols. 1 and 2 (Collegeville, MN: Liturgical Press, 1993).

in solidarity with migrants, regardless of their immigration status. Through education, advocacy, and direct service, and through providing scholarships and educational opportunities that open doors to the marginalized and excluded, they seek to foster right relationships that promote human dignity among those who are excluded and rejected in our society. To cite one example, the University of Notre Dame explicitly articulates in its mission statement, "The aim is to create a sense of human solidarity and concern for the common good that will bear fruit as learning becomes service to justice."[31] In similar ways, other Catholic colleges and universities stand in solidarity with the migrant through a multidimensional commitment that is grounded in a vision of justice and the key principles of human dignity, evangelization, and integral human development. Although intellectual formation is a primary goal of these institutions, their curricula and dedication to advocacy and outreach fundamentally serve to witness the gospel call, promoting human flourishing not only in their students but also in the world at large.

Through the three pillars of education, advocacy, and direct service, Catholic colleges and universities seek to promote this understanding of justice and illuminate the *imago Dei* that has been dimmed, and even defiled.[32] A faithful and authentic expression of this aim is one that creates an environment where transformation of mind *and* heart is not only possible but encouraged, where learning truly does become "service to justice."[33] In this manner, the first pillar of education is the most important aspect of the mission of Catholic institutions of higher education. In pursuit of this transformation, environments nurturing and fostering the development of the whole person are constitutive to classes offered in such institutions. By creating a space where education, faith, spirituality, and reflection can mutually inform one another, Catholic colleges and universities provide a unique opportunity for students to foster right

31. University of Notre Dame Mission Statement, http://www.nd.edu/about/mission-statement/ (accessed February 2, 2013).

32. Latin American Episcopal Conference (CELAM) at Puebla. Translated by Gustavo Gutiérrez in *On Job: God-Talk and the Suffering of the Innocent* (Maryknoll, NY: Orbis, 1987), xiii.

33. University of Notre Dame Mission Statement, http://www.nd.edu/about/mission-statement/ (accessed February 2, 2013).

relationships and work toward the common good. And while migration, particularly in an increasingly globalized world, is a complex and often divisive subject, CST teaches that it must be fundamentally concerned with the promulgation of human dignity. In this manner, educational opportunities are designed to encourage personal and communal growth and to look toward an authentic and faithful expression of solidarity within the community and ultimately within the entire human family.

Promoting the formation of the whole person, many Catholic colleges and universities provide classes and immersion opportunities that are cognizant of this reality, seeking the development of right relationships between students, migrants, and the world. One such program is "Justice Matters" run by Cabrini College in Pennsylvania. This core curriculum, required during the first, second, and third years, and finished with a capstone project in the fourth year, seeks to combine academics with social justice to encourage transformation and personal development. Fostering academic theory that will be brought into conversation with the community and the world, students are exposed to a variety of disciplines and social issues.

Another program is the Migrant Experience Seminar at the University of Notre Dame. This one-unit course, combined with an alternative break, immerses students in the reality of migrant farm workers. Classes before the trip examine CST and the social and economic factors associated with migration while the trip itself allows students to work in the fields alongside the migrants. Classroom learning, combined with hands-on experience, provides a space for theory and practice to mutually inform and strengthen one another, leading to transformation of both mind and heart.

Of particular importance to the educational community is the situation of undocumented immigrant youth living in the United States. Often forced to hide in the shadows, lacking the opportunity to develop their God-given gifts, and often denied the fullness of their human dignity, these young people are unable to attain true human development and face the risk of becoming a permanent underclass in society. Although they possess significant potential, the door remains closed to them.[34]

34. Content drawn from Colleen Cross, "Achieving a DREAM: Catholic Support for Immigrant Youth," in *On "Strangers No Longer,"* 231–50.

Recognizing this injustice, and attempting to change the status quo, a number of Catholic colleges and universities have stepped forward to provide these youth educational opportunities, regardless of financial means or the promise of future employment.

Santa Clara University, Dominican University, Holy Cross College, and the University of Notre Dame, among others, have instituted programs that provide scholarships for undocumented students seeking higher education. One of the leaders in such programs, Santa Clara University in California provides over twenty need-based scholarships to undocumented students.[35] Covering full tuition and room and board, this program is sponsored by the Jesuit community of Santa Clara, and funded in part by the Jesuits' personal salaries. With over fifteen undocumented students, Dominican University in Illinois is also a national model. Known as a "welcoming, hospitable place" for these students, Dominican fosters academic growth and leadership, recognizing their potential.[36] Holy Cross College in Indiana has a similar, though significantly smaller, program. Through the "Juan Diego" fund, Holy Cross provides a select number of full scholarships to undocumented students. Sponsored through contributions from the community and outside donors, these Juan Diego scholarships open a door to these students that would otherwise remain closed. And while the question of legal employment after graduation is present, and the reality not ensured, economic efficiencies and pragmatic reasoning are not the ultimate ends of these programs; rather, they are committed to realizing our greatest potential as human beings in the kingdom of God.

Advocating for the future of these students, the second pillar, many colleges and universities are working toward comprehensive immigration reform. The Development, Relief, and Education for Alien Minors (DREAM) Act is one aspect of this reform, seeking to provide educational opportunities

---

35. Kurt Wagner, "25 Undocumented Immigrants Find a Home—and Free College Education—at Santa Clara University," *USA Today* (September 24, 2011); http://www.usatodayeducate.com/staging/index.php/ccp/25-undocumented-immigrants-find-a-home-at-santa-clara-university (accessed January 11, 2013).

36. Libby Nelson, "DREAMing at Catholic Colleges," *Inside Higher Ed* (January 31, 2012) http://www.insidehighered.com/news/2012/01/31/catholic-colleges-urged-support-undocumented-students (accessed March 1, 2013).

and create an earned path to citizenship for qualified immigrant youth. Embodying many key principles of CST, the DREAM Act allows undocumented students the chance to develop their God-given potential and capabilities, promoting the fullness of human dignity and human flourishing. If undocumented students are denied this opportunity through postsecondary education, this serves to unravel the fabric of our society, undermine the common good, and weaken our nation in the long run.[37]

The third pillar of involvement by Catholic institutions of higher education is that of direct service. Seeking the kingdom of love and life that Jesus Christ proclaimed, direct service helps to bring to life a vision of a new world order where the last become first (Matt 19:30; 20:16; Mark 10:31; Luke 13:29-30). La Salle University, St. Joseph University, and DePaul University all have such programs that encourage faculty, students, and staff to assist immigrants throughout their communities. Sending students of varying disciplines across Philadelphia to organizations aiding immigrants, La Salle University connects its students with the needs of the community. Students are able to provide valuable services such as education, social work, and medical services, among others, while entering into deeper communion with the migrant community. St. Joseph University in Philadelphia has designed service-learning classes focused on current migration realities that require a weekly commitment from students at social agencies across Philadelphia. Such classes not only provide a space for service, education, and reflection, but foster a commitment to community involvement among students. Several outreach efforts are also present at DePaul University in Chicago. The law school is actively involved in assisting DREAM-eligible and deferred-action

37. It is important to note that DREAM can change. As of August 2013, DREAM legislation has not been passed. In August 2012, U.S. President Barack Obama announced deferred action for undocumented students. While deferred action contains many provisions similar to DREAM legislation, it is not considered a substitute for such legislation and larger comprehensive immigration reform. United States Conference of Catholic Bishops, *The Announcement of Deferred Action for DREAM Eligible Youth*, Statement of Most Reverend José H. Gomez, Archbishop of Los Angeles, chairman, USCCB Committee on Migration (Washington, DC: United States Conference of Catholic Bishops, June 15, 2012). Content on DREAM in this chapter drawn from Colleen Cross, "Achieving a DREAM: Catholic Support for Immigrant Youth" in *On "Strangers No Longer,"* 231–50.

students while the campus promotes involvement not only at the local level but in public policy initiatives as well. Programs such as these challenge us to see the crucified and risen face of Christ in the stranger and confront attitudes that serve to defile the *imago Dei*. In this manner, Catholic colleges and universities seek to live out a vision of our faith, a faith that acts on behalf of justice for the good of all.

Conclusion

Migration is one of the most defining moral issues of our times, and Catholic colleges and universities *can* make a difference. Catholic Social Teaching reminds us that responses to social problems such as migration must be rooted not in models of political pragmatism, economic efficiency, nor cultural imperialism, but most fundamentally in the gospel message and Christ's proclamation of the kingdom of God. In part this involves denouncing the structures and systems of society that divide and dehumanize people in order to foster human dignity in the vulnerable and disenfranchised, opening a space for all to grow and develop. Through education, advocacy, and direct service, we see in the vulnerable stranger a mirror of ourselves, a reflection of Christ, and a challenge to human solidarity. Though the result is not always immediate, the ability to inspire minds and hearts, creating an environment where faith seeks understanding, understanding seeks contemplation, and contemplation leads individuals into deeper conversion, and conversion leads not only to future changes but also fuller lives.

Discussion Questions

1. To what extent do colleges and universities with financial resources have moral obligations to help migrants and immigrants? In what ways?

2. What is the contribution of CST to migration? In what ways is it similar to or different from other groups responding to the humanitarian crisis?

3. What is the contribution of migration to colleges and universities?

4. What understanding of justice do you bring to these readings? How would you define it?

5. If social and economic distinctions mean nothing to God, why do they mean so much to human beings?

6. How does the statement "Action on behalf of justice is a constitutive dimension of preaching the gospel"[38] relate to the role of Catholic colleges and universities in the area of migration?

38. *Justice in the World*, Synod of Bishops (1971), 6.

Chapter **6**

Bernard F. Evans

Care for Creation

"We cannot stay here. The sea is rising up. This is the end of the island."

"Most of our culture will have to live in memory. That part of our life will be washed away."[1]

On a small island in the South Pacific, the people know that their life in this paradise will soon end. The sea is rising, already spreading salt water over their fertile farmland and destroying their ability to grow the food upon which their survival depends. The story of the Cateret Islanders, as told in the documentary film *Sun Come Up*,[2] is one of people traveling to Bouganville—a province of Papua, New Guinea—in search of land to resettle their families. It is a narrative of climate change's first refugees.

Global Climate Change

The story of the Cateret islanders is a story of hope. Certainly there is tragedy in this account of a people losing their ancestral homeland and way of life. But there is also hope in this community's determination to face a monumental challenge and in other peoples' willingness to help.

---

1. *Sun Come Up* (New York: New Day Films, 2010).
2. Ibid.

95

This story is a piece of the growing evidence that something both remarkable and ominous is happening to the earth's climate. For decades scientists around the world have been warning that our planet is warming, and this phenomenon likely will lead to devastating consequences. While some people doubt the accuracy of this claim, none of them live on the Cateret Islands. The extent of global warming as well as its causes may be open to debate, but few scientists deny that a major shift is occurring in weather patterns, one that points to measurable and lasting climate change.

Faced with this news it becomes ever more difficult to ignore the likelihood that our style of living may be contributing to these unwanted changes. If that is the case, then we of this generation have some obligation to make adjustments in how we live. The way we live today must reflect an awareness of what is happening to the world around us, and the price these happenings will inflict on people in other parts of the world, and on our own children through multiple generations. It seems evident we face a number of moral choices, and we need to be clear about the values that inform such decisions.

In more practical terms, if we recognize that climate change is occurring and that one of its expressions is global warming, then we must examine some of the most predictable and habitual acts we carry out. This will involve more than recycling cans or observing an annual earth day. It will mean radical changes in the many ordinary activities we so take for granted every day.

Among these is the simple task of getting us from one place to another. Our unchallenged reliance upon driving ourselves to the grocery store, to school, or to work deserves a critical reassessment. Our individualistic tendency toward independence and self-reliance may need to be recognized for what it is—an unaffordable luxury. We would do well to educate ourselves about the benefits—to the environment and to our social and psychological well-being—that come with reliance upon others. The exam accompanying this learning is to test our willingness to use car-pooling, buses, trains, bicycles, and our feet.

Of course, our chances of passing this exam will increase with greater societal commitment to public transportation and new models of residential living. In too many of our nation's suburbs residents are miles from basic services and have only their own automobiles to rely on, for example, when they need to go grocery shopping. Our individual commitment to use alternative forms of transportation obviously depends upon the larger community's willingness to provide such opportunities.

Our eating habits also may need to change. Paying more attention to what we eat and where it comes from can lead to a decline in greenhouse-gas emissions. Consuming foods that are out of season and that must travel fifteen hundred miles to reach our dining room tables feeds the gluttony of unnecessary emissions. Learning to eat more foods grown locally and within the current season is a relatively painless contribution most of us can make to addressing climate change. It is as simple as it is radical because it moves us to transformation in one of the most fundamental human acts—eating.

There are many other areas of daily living, besides eating and driving, where we can and must embrace far-reaching changes. Some of these are adjustments and adaptations we long ago recognized needed to be made. Now, like our sisters and brothers in the South Pacific, we know that procrastination in favor of convenience is neither a practical nor moral option.

In fact it is more than a matter of lifestyle changes. To continue living as we do now brings into question our continued existence as a species. Granted, it is easy to overstate the problem, and crying "wolf" too frequently is a sure way to disengage people from the seriousness of the issue. This is especially the case when many people remain doubtful that climate change is a grave threat or that their individual efforts will make any difference. And yet, if the scientists' data seem distant and unreal, the flooding of a peoples' homeland is not difficult to grasp.

Beyond the practical matters of survival and willingness to alter lifestyles, global climate change offers a religious and theological challenge as well. This involves our understanding of humankind's place within the rest of creation and how that location speaks of our relationship with God. That connection with our Creator defines our roles and responsibilities within the created order and points to the actions and behavior consistent with what it means to be fully human. That vision of the human person in right relationship with God holds the potential to guide our choices in responding to any environmental challenge.

The sacred texts of the Hebrew Scriptures present two complimentary but distinct emphases for that vision. The first creation story (Gen 1:1–2:3) speaks of humans—and humans alone—being made in the image and likeness of God. Humans are told to "be fruitful and multiply, and fill the earth and subdue it" and have dominion over every other creature that flies, swims or walks upon this earth.

This is one biblical emphasis that shapes our sense of who we humans are among all God's creatures. It is an accent that too often leads to an arrogant, overconfident appraisal of our place and responsibility. In the most positive light this emphasis leads us to employ our God-given talents to work with God in bringing creation to fulfillment. It leads us to discover and even create, to work with the elements of nature to improve life for all humans. Scientific developments in such areas as medicine and food production reflect this vision of humankind's place within God's creation.

This stress on the uniqueness and power of humans over the rest of creation has a darker side as well. Throughout human history we have demonstrated a tendency to overdo it—that is, to read the biblical command "to have dominion over" as a divine directive to do whatever we wish to the natural world. It spawns a confidence that in turn breeds a tragic belief that we can fix anything we break. It finds little cause for considering the needs of future generations, because down the road some intelligent human will discover the solutions to any problems created by the excesses of our current lifestyles. This may be the thinking that so readily embraces fracking as this generation's answer to oil independence, with minimal concern for the environmental dangers that accompany the blasting of sand, water, and chemicals deep into the earth to release petroleum and natural gas. This also may be the unarticulated rationale behind the rapid production and marketing of genetic-engineered human foods even before testing for long-term costs to human health or to environmental safety.

The book of Genesis provides a second creation story (Gen 2:4-25) and with it an alternative emphasis or understanding of humankind's place within the rest of creation. This story says nothing about humans being made in the image and likeness of God, nor is there any mention of us having dominion over the other creatures. The emphasis here is upon all of us being like the rest of creation, being part of creation. Humans are formed "from the dust of the ground" as are the trees and animals and birds.

People, in this account, are far more creaturely than they are godly, less the creators and more the created. This is a perspective that offers a more modest sense of our place and role within the rest of creation. It challenges us to "regain humility and recognize the limits of our powers, and most importantly, the limits of our knowledge and judgment."[3]

Ongoing Scientific Research

While recognizing those human limitations, we nonetheless can acknowledge a benefit deriving from the way God chose to shape human beings: our ability to study, analyze, and draw conclusions about the world in which we live. That capacity for research and reflection on the natural world engenders hope that we may adequately comprehend and respond to all forms of environmental degradation.

Already there is much research and data gathering on such critical matters, including that of climate change. The international scientific community has warned repeatedly that areas of this planet are warming at alarming rates and that humans are contributing significantly to this development. A very small percentage of scientists counter that this problem is not as great as is often reported. Some believe that the current warming trends are part of a long-established cyclical pattern of the earth warming and cooling. Still others acknowledge that serious warming is taking place, but natural happenings are a greater cause than human behavior.[4]

Climatologists present their data and argue their various perspectives with numbers and language that is not always intelligible to those of us

3. "Common Declaration of Pope John Paul II and the Ecumenical Patriarch His Holiness Bartholomew I," June 10, 2002.

4. There are many publications and resources related to debates on climate change. A good place to begin is with the Intergovernmental Panel on Climate Change (IPCC). This is an international panel of scientists who review current research and issue periodic reports on the status of climate change (www.ipcc.ch/). Another source, especially helpful to Catholics, is the Environmental Justice program sponsored by the United States Conference of Catholic Bishops (www.environmentaljusticeusccb). One publication on this topic from the U.S. Catholic Bishops is *Global Change: A Plea for Dialogue, Prudence and the Common Good* (http://www.usccb.org/issues-and-action/human-life-and-dignity/environment/global-climate-change-a-plea-for-dialogue-prudence-and-the-common-good.cfm).

who are not scientists. For the average layperson to make sense of this information and to be moved to new actions requires that this data be presented or taught by way of recognizable phenomena. Media reports on the findings of scientists can facilitate that process as can the teaching efforts of environmental organizations.

Examples of this include accounts of polar ice cap melting or the stories about the temperatures of West Antarctica rising much more rapidly the past fifty years than previously thought. Warnings about polar bears becoming an endangered species bring home the point, as do accounts of various types of birds changing their migratory patterns in response to changing temperatures.

Perhaps no consequence of global warming captures our attention as strikingly as the concern about rising sea levels. It takes little imagination to see what this might portend for human existence, especially with two-thirds of the world's largest cities located in areas vulnerable to rising sea levels. That fear may gradually but steadily change into the sober realization that for a small number of people living on a South Pacific island, it has already begun.

Scientific discoveries about environmental harm and especially about climate change must lead to education of the public, an education that goes beyond describing what is happening and why. This education will help people to recognize the specific human behaviors that contribute most to climate change. Scientific research in any area may not have the goal of changing human behavior but that always is an anticipated benefit that may follow the work of such focused studies. It is difficult to imagine an activity within the realm of science where this connection between the gathering of data and human living patterns is more critical than this research related to climate change.

Recognizing the facts of climate change is but one step on the road to corrective human behavior. The scientific community can tell us that the earth is warming. Equally important is clarity about those daily activities that result in the emission of greenhouse gases and that contribute so significantly to this warming. This may be the task of educators in various settings—to make the connection between scientific findings and peoples' activities in daily living.

There is a second educational need that follows the findings of scientists on this issue: that is to help us see global warming within the broader context of environmental stress and degradation. How, for example, do we understand resource consumption and depletion? The United States for some time has worried about the depletion of fossil fuel energy resources as well as our heavy dependence upon other nations for meeting these needs. Those concerns may have spurred remarkable technological developments that now allow us to recover natural gas and oil through the fracking process. What are the negative side effects of this process, and do these developments contribute to global warming?

Likewise, pollution (land, water, air) is a reality we commonly understand: putting something into the ecosystem that the ecosystem cannot assimilate. This may be introducing something into our water in such large amounts that the rivers, lakes, and aquifers cannot handle. The same can be said about our food-producing land as well as the air we take into our respiratory systems. Are we able to see the emission of excessive amounts of greenhouse gasses as another form of pollution—something we so commonly understand and connect with various activities in daily living?

A third example of the kind of education needed for addressing climate change relates to human population growth. Should we look at the expanding global population as a contributor to climate change as well as to other forms of environmental stress? This is a much-debated question. Some environmentalists argue that the growing human population is the number one threat to the environment. Every environmental problem, they claim, is exacerbated by an expanding population of humans, and the earth can sustain only so many of us. Others counter that the greatest threat comes not from numbers but from lifestyles of the current human community, especially those of us living in North America and Western Europe.

In their 1991 pastoral statement, *Renewing the Earth*, the U.S. Catholic bishops stress that point when they state: "Consumption in developed nations remains the single greatest source of global environmental destruction. A child born in the United States, for example, puts a far heavier burden on the world's resources than one born in a poor developing country."[5] The bishops note, "Regrettably, advantaged groups often seem more intent on curbing Third-World births than on restraining the even

5. *Renewing the Earth: An Invitation to Reflection and Action on the Environment in Light of Catholic Social Teaching* (A Pastoral Statement of the United States Catholic Conference, 1991), 9.

more voracious consumerism of the developed world."[6] In this document, however, the bishops acknowledge that rapid population growth presents environmental challenges, stating, "Even though it is possible to feed a growing population, the ecological costs of doing so ought to be taken into account."[7] This document calls for prenatal care, education, good nutrition, and health care for poor families in order to encourage hope for the future and responsible parenthood. *Renewing the Earth* states that the Catholic Church addresses population issues within the context of CST concepts such as just development, dignity of the human person, care for the environment, and justice for the poor. According to the document, "Respect for nature ought to encourage polices that promote natural family planning and true responsible parenthood rather than coercive population control programs or incentives for birth control that violate cultural and religious norms and Catholic teaching."[8]

The point here is simply to ask if there is a connection between what most people recognize as environmental problems—resource depletion, pollution, human population growth, climate change. As we explain each of these phenomena on the theoretical level are we able to see any connections among them? More importantly, can we see the connections between these various threats to the environment and our living habits?

An example of making such connections appears in a recent report from the global justice organization Coopération Internationale pour le Développement et la Solidarité (CIDSE)[9] which explores the connections between global food security, agricultural systems, and climate change. The report begins with the acknowledgment that every person on this planet has a right to adequate food—to the means for producing it or the means of procuring it. It then explores what might be the best

6. Ibid.

7. Ibid.

8. Ibid.

9. CIDSE is an international alliance of seventeen Catholic development agencies working together for global justice. Priority issues for the alliance are development finance, food and climate justice, and business and human rights. The acronym stands for the organization's French full name, "Coopération Internationale pour le Développement et la Solidarité" (International Cooperation for Development and Solidarity).

agricultural systems to help satisfy this human right. The report further argues that agriculture is not just about producing large quantities of food to satisfy a growing human population. Rather, agriculture needs to be multi-functional—producing food, reducing poverty, and regenerating the environment.[10]

Drawing on studies from various global organizations, the CIDSE report delineates why the international community needs to give more support to agricultural systems that feature small-scale, local production units. These are systems that allow the majority of the world's poor people to continue working as small-scale food producers[11] using farming methods that contribute far less greenhouse gases to climate change than do the large industrial-style farms so prevalent throughout North America. Additionally, these locally-adapted, smaller units of food production are likely to prove more resilient to the demands of climate change. In short, they enjoy the greatest likelihood of being sustainable long into the future.

Ongoing scientific research related to climate change is essential. The fruit of that research, however, must be translated into language and images comprehensible to the ordinary person. This educational effort also must help us to see how the growing knowledge on climate change relates to other, more familiar environmental issues, and how our daily lives connect with all of the above. That information provides the starting point for moral discernment about what, if anything, needs to change in our lives.

Needed Ethical Reflection

So how do we respond to the new realities before us? What changes in living should accompany our growing realization that there are serious problems within the environment? If we accept what scientists are telling

10. "Agriculture: From Problem to Solution" (Achieving the Right to Food in a Climate-Constrained World). Available at http://www.cidse.org/.

11. "In Africa and Latin America, small-scale farming represents approximately 80 percent of all farms. In Latin America small-scale farms produce up to 67 percent of total output and create up to 77 percent of employment in the agricultural sector (FAO, 2001)" ("Agriculture: from Problem to Solution," 20, 4).

us about climate change, what actions are we morally compelled to pursue? And, most fundamentally, what values inform our decisions? Three sources of moral guidance immediately present themselves: the Sacred Scriptures, Catholic Social Teaching, and the ethical teachings of our ecumenical and interfaith colleagues.

The Christian's starting point for moral reflection on how we might respond to climate change must be the biblical wisdom regarding creation. What the Scriptures tell us about the Creator is central to how we see our activity within this world. How we envision our own relationship with God determines how we utilize but also protect the garden we are charged to till and care for.

The Scriptures say nothing about climate change, but they have everything to tell us about the loving God who created and who walks with us. Likewise they teach us how we are to care for one another, and that our respect for and treatment of our sisters and brothers directly impacts our standing with this God whom we worship as the Creator of the universe. These same Scriptures remind us that our relationship with God and with our neighbor is shaped by how we treat the rest of creation. The prophet Hosea warns that we cannot possibly be in right relationship with God if we are not in right relationship with all of God's children and with the rest of creation (Hos 4:1-3).

From the biblical wisdom we learn that the Creator, humans, and the earth exist in a three-way relationship. Moral reflection might lead us to consider deeply the practical, day-to-day expectations that issue from this web of life-giving relationships. And so we return to the fundamental question about our place within creation and the kind of behavior that honors this location.

Another source of wisdom for moral reflection on the environment is CST. These encyclicals and other documents present a number of universal principles regarding the human person and organized social life. Three of them have particular relevance to this discussion. One is the claim that every human being enjoys a sacred dignity by the fact that each of us has been created by God, redeemed through the cross of Jesus Christ, and called to communion with God. The dignity of the human person is the foundation for all Catholic social thought, and the starting point for exploring what it means to protect human beings and at the same time to give adequate consideration to the rest of creation.

A second principle of CST important to this discussion is that every person must contribute to the common good—that is, all those basic conditions of living that make it possible for each of us to do reasonably well (food, clothing, education, housing, safe communities). Surely one of these conditions is a secure and healthy natural environment. Catholic Social Teaching reminds all of us that every one of us is required to work for these conditions.

The third principle deserving consideration here is the preferential option for the poor. Pope Paul VI first used this terminology in his 1971 apostolic letter, *A Call to Action*.[12] This teaching suggests that we do more than perform charitable actions on behalf of persons or groups with great needs. It also means that we work to change programs and public policies to benefit persons with the greatest needs. How we address environmental issues should reflect an awareness that the poor and the marginalized suffer most from human behavior that harms the natural world—in the Cateret Islands and everywhere.

Within CST we find a few documents with a more direct focus upon caring for God's creation. One of these is Pope John Paul II's 1990 World Day of Peace message, *The Environmental Crisis: A Common Responsibility* (originally titled, *Peace with God the Creator, Peace with All of Creation*). In this short statement the Holy Father presents a number of challenging observations about humankind's failure to carry out God's command to care for the garden. One of the most striking points comes at the very end of the document: "At the conclusion of this Message, I should like to address directly my brothers and sisters in the Catholic Church. . . . Respect for life and for the dignity of the human person extends also to the rest of creation, which is called to join man in praising God."[13] We Catholics who place such an emphasis on respect for life, on the right to life, and on the dignity of the human person, we must regard the rest of creation as worthy of similar consideration.

12. "In teaching us charity, the Gospel instructs us in the preferential respect due to the poor and the special situation they have in society: the more fortunate should renounce some of their rights so as to place their goods more generously at the service of the poor" (Pope Paul VI, *A Call to Action* [1971], 23).

13. Pope John Paul II, *The Ecological Crisis: A Common Responsibility*, World Day of Peace Message (1990), 16.

In 1991 the U.S. Catholic bishops quoted that same statement from Pope John Paul II in their pastoral letter *Renewing the Earth*.[14] Among the points they offer is the assertion that consumption in developed nations—more than population growth—represents "the single greatest source of global environmental destruction."[15] Their statement also provides a brief and beautiful reflection on the sacramentality of creation. The natural world is a privileged place for encountering God. The whole universe is sacramental. We care for the garden not just because it is the source of our food and other basic necessities. We do so because it is a place where we find God.

Pope Benedict XVI has written abundantly on caring for creation. An example is his 2007 World Day of Peace message, *The Human Person, The Heart of Peace*. Reflecting on the thought of his immediate predecessor, Pope John Paul II, Benedict wrote that "disregard for the environment always harms human existence."[16] There is, he continues, an inseparable link between peace with creation and peace among peoples, both of which are founded on peace with God. Pope Benedict's message further acknowledges the "increasingly serious problem of energy supplies," a topic he addressed earlier in his encyclical, *Charity in Truth*.[17]

In his 2010 World Day of Peace message, this pope names some of the most serious environmental challenges the world now faces, and then he reflects on the tragic consequences of these developments. "Can we disregard the growing phenomenon of 'environmental refugees,' people who are forced by the degradation of their natural habitat to forsake it—and often their possessions as well—in order to face the dangers and uncertainties of forced displacement?"[18]

Our moral reflection on environmental issues, including that of climate change, can draw upon the wisdom of our biblical texts as well as the guidance we find in CST. A third source for this effort is the teachings

14. *Renewing the Earth*, 7.

15. Ibid., 9.

16. Pope Benedict XVI, *The Human Person, the Heart of Peace*, World Day of Peace Message (2007), 8.

17. Pope Benedict XVI, *Charity in Truth* (2005), 49–50.

18. Pope Benedict XVI, *If You Want to Cultivate Peace, Protect Creation*, World Day of Peace Message (2010), 4.

we find among our ecumenical and interfaith colleagues. Most Protestant denominations have social statements on the environment, and they are easily accessible through the internet. Some of these are quite similar to Catholic statements, but there are differences worth noting.

The 1993 Lutheran statement, *Caring for Creation: Vision, Hope and Justice*, grants considerable attention to practical aspects of caring for creation. Included in its statement are several recommendations for actions local congregations can pursue. An American Baptist statement from 1989, *Creation and the Covenant of Caring*, offers a position on the threat of population growth that differs from the Catholic document, *Renewing the Earth*. Beyond Christian sources, we might consider the Jewish teaching on *bal-tashchit*—do not destroy, do not waste. Staying with the People of the Book, we note that the Islamic emphasis on moderation offers a much-needed corrective to our present-day indulgence in excessive consumption.

A more serious engagement of all these sources of moral wisdom—Catholic, Protestant, Jewish, Muslim—can lead us to a richer vision of humankind's place within the rest of creation. That vision provides the starting place for initiating a religious response to the science on climate change.

Catholic Colleges and Universities

Colleges and universities that bear a Catholic identity have an important place in this discussion. They are in a strong position to help all of us comprehend the challenges we face in responding to any threat to our environment, however large or small. These Catholic institutions of higher education need not be in the forefront of scientific research on a topic like global warming, but they certainly can translate those findings into meaningful concepts and images for the larger public, particularly their current students.

They also have a role to play in the needed moral reflection around these issues. Part of that is to make meaningful connections between CST and environmental issues of the day. Another dimension of this is to further the development of CST, not simply to hand on what the larger church has been given to date by the Vatican and episcopal leaders.

One area ready for development in Catholic colleges and universities is that of relating the church's social teachings to specific environmental problems, like climate change. Herein lies a twofold task for students, professors, and researchers in Catholic educational settings. First is to make clearer the significance of the church's teaching on a particular topic in terms of moral choices, prudential judgments, and daily living. For example, when the U.S. Catholic bishops state in *Global Climate Change* that we should "take steps now to mitigate possible negative effects in the future,"[19] what does this mean for the daily lives of persons sitting in a college classroom? How do we go from the bishops' declaration of moral principle to living the principle in choices we make on a day-to-day basis?

The second part of this task entails raising questions about the teachings we have at this point, by recognizing their incompleteness, or by engaging in discussion on the adequacy or usefulness of a particular teaching related to an issue of the day. We need to actively engage CST on the environment so as to know these teachings and to assess them with a critical mind.

This might include a critique of the language used in church documents related to the environment. For example, is the use of "dominion language" from the first creation story in Genesis 1 the most effective way of presenting or understanding humankind's place within the rest of creation? It may be one thing to assert that all the Abrahamic faiths use this language, but quite another to presume this is the most effective vocabulary or terminology to inspire fresh appreciation of the beauty and grandeur of all that the Creator has placed upon this earth and throughout the universe.

Examples of Campus Engagement

Saint John's University (SJU) in Collegeville, Minnesota, and the College of Saint Benedict (CSB) in nearby St. Joseph offer several examples of how Catholic colleges and universities can help promote greater community awareness of our call to care for creation. Both institutions are committed to embracing the goals of sustainability, defined as "meeting the needs of the present generation without compromising the ability of

---

19. *Global Climate Change: A Plea for Dialogue, Prudence and the Common Good*, A Statement of the U.S. Catholic Bishops (2001), 2.

future generations to meet their needs."[20] Along with numerous other colleges, CSB and SJU are committed to carbon neutrality by 2035. Among the many steps taken to reach that goal is the printing policy adopted on both campuses which limits every student, club, and organization to twenty-five dollars a semester for printing and duplicating.

In its Sustainability Master Plan CSB includes a sustainability building policy for all new buildings and renovations over five thousand square feet. More directly related to students, faculty, and staff, CSB now bans the sale of plain, plastic bottled water on campus as well as the purchase of such bottles elsewhere using institutional funds.

The Monastery of St. Benedict sponsors the Common Ground Garden, a CSA (Community Supported Agriculture) farm.[21] Community members from the St. Joseph area purchase a share of vegetables and each week during the summer growing season receive a box of fresh produce. The Garden provides an opportunity during the fall and spring for students from CSB and SJU to learn about sustainable farming practices as well as local food systems.

The Arboretum at SJU offers another model for how Catholic colleges and universities in rural areas can educate around creation care, and do so outside the classroom. Saint John's Arboretum encompasses more than twenty-eight hundred acres of land including prairie, wetland, lake, oak savanna, and forest habitats. The educational programs of the Arboretum annually serve over sixty-five hundred students from prekindergarten to senior year of high school through on-site field experiences and in-class curricula. "The Saint John's Arboretum celebrates the unique beauty and richness of God's creation in central Minnesota and fosters the Benedictine tradition of land stewardship, education, and environmental respect."[22] The Arboretum provides opportunities for research by students

20. www.csbsju.edu/SJU-sustainability. Another resource and action for sustainability is the St. Francis Pledge to Care for Creation and the Poor. This is a promise and a commitment to live our faith by protecting God's creation and advocating on behalf of people in poverty who face the harshest impacts of global climate change (www.catholicclimatecovenant.org).

21. See the Saint Benedict's Monastery website, www.sbm.osb.org, and then search for "Common Ground Garden."

22. www.csbsju.edu/Arboretum/AboutUs.

and faculty as it works to preserve native plant and wildlife communities. To the central Minnesota community beyond campus, the Arboretum models practices of sustainable land use and offers a natural environment for spiritual renewal.

Catholic Foundations

Our biblical texts, CST, and the varied works of Catholic academicians offer a foundation for moral deliberation on climate change and other environmental issues. That foundation includes the principles and observations we explored earlier in the essay, which are part of at least four points summarized here that Catholics—and others—recognize relative to humankind's place and responsibility within the rest of creation.

1. *Creation is God's.* The absolute starting point for a discussion about caring for the environment in general, or responding to climate change more specifically, is this simple acknowledgment that all of creation belongs to God. Psalm 24:1 makes this point with stunning clarity: "The earth is the LORD's and all that is in it, the world, and those who live in it." The world in which we live, the land and water upon which we depend for food, recreation, and commerce—all of it belongs to God. This is the recognition needed to form a religiously sound vision of who we humans are and how we are to conduct ourselves on this planet.

2. *Creation is good.* Our activity on this earth, our sense of obligation to care for God's creation is guided also by the recognition that creation is good. It is good not because of its usefulness to humans but because it was formed by a good and loving God. The first creation story in the Book of Genesis repeatedly testifies to this truth in the words: "And God saw that it was good" (Gen 1:3-25). An important corollary to this recognition is to see that we humans are part of this good creation. The second creation story says that we are made from the dust of the ground—the same stuff from which God made the trees and the animals and the birds. We are connected to the rest of creation. We are part of the same creation over which God proclaimed: "It is good."

3. *Humans are called to be stewards.* Of all the creatures that God placed upon this earth, none were given the responsibility to care for creation as were humans. In Genesis 1 we read that humans are to "have dominion over" the rest of creation (1:28). The biblical language here suggests the responsibility of "ruling over" in the place of God and to do so as God would, with love and compassion and with a particular concern for the most marginalized and vulnerable aspects of this beautiful creation. Genesis 2 speaks of God placing the human in the Garden of Eden to till and keep it (2:15). The garden image is an easy metaphor for our duty to care for the earthly "garden" that is now home to more than seven billion people.

4. *Environmental degradation is most harmful to the poor.* All humankind is threatened by climate change and other forms of environmental abuse. Yet no one suffers more from these developments then individuals and groups who live on the margins of society. People anywhere who live in involuntary economic poverty and relative political powerlessness have extremely limited resources for shielding themselves from the harsh effects of environmental decline. They also are least able to deal with the aftereffects of such happenings and therefore are compelled to live in compromised environmental conditions long after their more affluent brothers and sisters have put such experiences behind them. Today the story of the Cateret people—the world's first climate change refugees—makes clear that the poor and the marginalized are often the first to experience the effects of humankind's failure to care properly for God's good creation.

Conclusion

These are a few of the foundational points in Catholic teaching and scholarship regarding humankind's place and responsibilities on this earth. They can provide a starting point for thinking and acting on the most pressing environmental challenges of our time. Surely one of those is climate change. Catholic colleges and universities are not without resources and opportunities for engaging this most critical challenge of our lifetime.

As Christians, we live in hope. However serious the challenge we face, we always know that within the human community we will find the needed gifts, wisdom, and compassion to move forward. We know also that through our communal efforts the Spirit is at work renewing the face of the earth. As one of the Cateret Islanders stated after they had been given new land to settle their families, "We have plenty of friends now. It's begun."

Discussion Questions

1. If scientists determine that polar ice caps are melting at a dangerous level, what moral obligation do we have to respond to this news—and what should our response look like?
2. What obligations do we have to ensure a relatively comfortable life for the children of this generation without endangering the same expectations for future generations?
3. What duties do we have toward other species?
4. How morally significant are scientific conclusions that are less than one hundred percent certain?
5. Choose an environmental issue and use the four points noted above as a framework to think about it. How might this framework differ from another framework for thinking about an environmental issue?

Chapter 7

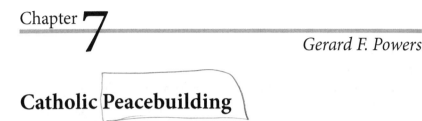

Gerard F. Powers

Catholic Peacebuilding

If Catholic Social Teaching (CST) is the church's best-kept secret, peacebuilding is CST's best-kept secret. But, one might object, isn't the church's teaching on just war and pacifism among the oldest and best known parts of CST? Although this is true, peacebuilding is much broader than the ethics of war. The United Nations (UN), governments, and many scholars define peacebuilding as efforts to promote economic, social, and political reconstruction and reconciliation after internal conflicts with a primary focus on governments and public policies. In this chapter peacebuilding is defined more broadly to cover the church's teaching and practice related to the entire conflict cycle (before, during, and after war), as well as both interstate and intrastate conflicts. This involves not only government actors and public policies and institutions, but also a range of other actors, factors, and practices at all levels that are integral to healing broken societies and building and sustaining a just peace. The church's peacebuilding involves a broad spectrum of activities, from advocacy and mass mobilization to facilitation of peace negotiations and participation in truth and reconciliation processes. This broad approach to peace is evident in the following anecdotes.

Iraq. On Ash Wednesday 2003, Cardinal Pio Laghi, Pope John Paul II's special envoy, met with President George Bush at the White House to deliver a message from the pope urging the president not to go to war in Iraq. The pope's letter repeated what had become his common refrain—and that of church leaders in the United States and around the world—in

113

the months leading up to the war: "War is not the answer!" The answer, according to the pope, was negotiation and dialogue. In his press statement after the meeting, Cardinal Laghi explained that Iraq should be handled within the framework of the UN and international law. He concluded that military intervention, especially intervention justified by a doctrine of preventive war, would be illegal and immoral. He decried "the grave consequences" of going to war in Iraq, "the suffering of the people of Iraq" and "further instability in the region and a new gulf between Islam and Christianity."[1]

President Bush repeated what he said many times before and after: in effect, that war *was* the answer. He dismissed the cardinal's dire warnings and instead insisted that war would not only eliminate the gathering danger posed by a "rogue" regime with ties to global terrorist networks and weapons of mass destruction, but war would also bring freedom for the people of Iraq, new stability to the region, and would be a catalyst for the spread of democracy throughout the Middle East. In what observers considered an unprecedented snub and an indication of the White House's desire to mute the pope's moral critique, Cardinal Laghi was not permitted the usual privilege of talking with the media on White House grounds.

The LRA in Northern Uganda. The video *Kony 2012* was incredibly successful in bringing attention to the Lord's Resistance Army (LRA), an extremist group that has terrorized populations in Northern Uganda and neighboring countries for many years. Fifteen years before that video went viral, Roman Catholic Archbishop John Baptist Odama joined with his Anglican, Muslim, and Orthodox counterparts to form the Acholi Religious Leaders' Peace Initiative. Archbishop Odama had the courage to risk his life and go four times into the bush, alone and with the other religious leaders, to meet Joseph Kony, the brutal LRA leader (and former altar boy) who has been indicted for war crimes by the International Criminal Court (ICC). Their appeals to stop the violence and pursue a negotiated peace are widely credited with helping to convince Kony to enter formal peace negotiations. Given their role and the credibility they have with the Acholi people, the religious leaders were invited to be official facilitators of the peace process. As facilitators, they were outspoken in opposing the ICC indictments, arguing that they were obstacles to

---

1. See "On File," *Origins* 32, no. 39 (March 13, 2003): 642.

finalizing a peace agreement and an unnecessary imposition given that traditional Acholi methods of accountability and reconciliation would be more appropriate.

Sudan. On July 9, 2011, South Sudan became an independent state that January after a referendum on independence that many feared would ignite a new genocidal conflict in a country that had seen little else in the past half century. The independence referendum was part of the 2005 Comprehensive Peace Agreement, which brought a cease-fire in a conflict that had raged in southern Sudan from 1955 to 1972 and again from 1983 to 2005. The path to a cease-fire and full independence would not have been laid without a multipronged peacebuilding effort by the Catholic and Anglican Churches. These churches were, for all intents and purposes, the only functioning institutions in southern Sudan. They were responsible for most education, health care, humanitarian aid, development programs, and human rights monitoring. Moreover, their "People-to-People" peace process in the 1990s helped reconcile warring tribes in southern Sudan, their parallel civil society peace process helped cement the 2005 peace agreement, and their civic education campaign and logistical support were instrumental in ensuring a peaceful and credible referendum on independence.

The fact that these anecdotes would be news to even otherwise well-informed Catholics illustrate why it is appropriate to say that peacebuilding is CST's best-kept secret. The church is able to play a significant role in peacebuilding in these and other cases because it brings three sets of assets—what political scientists call "soft power"—to the peace puzzle: (1) ritual, spirituality, theology, and social teaching; (2) the people power of the people of God; and (3) enormous institutional capacity.

Places like Sudan and Northern Uganda are laboratories of Catholic peacebuilding—not fluff courses like Rocks for Jocks, but something more like Organic Chemistry. It is not enough to understand the church's official teachings on war and peace, as foundational as those are. A full understanding of the church's approach to peace requires considering how this teaching finds institutional expression through the work of countless Catholic educational institutions, lay organizations, and church agencies from the Vatican to the local parish. It is through these institutions that individuals are formed in their faith and (hopefully) come to embrace peacebuilding as part of their Christian vocation. It is this combination of the church's teaching on peace, its faith-filled artisans of peace, and its institutional work for peace that makes the Catholic peace tradition a living tradition. It is also a living tradition insofar as the church's peace-building practices are informed by its teaching and, in turn, inform new developments in official teaching. Robert Schreiter calls this interplay between practice and teaching a practical theology of peacebuilding.[2]

This chapter begins with a brief overview of the "signs of the times" related to contemporary issues of war and peace. The bulk of the chapter then considers the church's peacebuilding assets in more detail. It concludes with a successful student-led initiative for peacebuilding.

Signs of the Times: The Reality of War and Peace

The Pastoral Constitution on the Church in the Modern World begins by saying that in order to serve the world as Christ did, the church has "the duty of scrutinizing the signs of the times and of interpreting them in the light of the Gospel."[3] While the theological implications of this passage are much disputed, it is clear that the church cannot be a peacebuilder absent a cogent analysis of today's conflicts and ways of resolving them.

The Iraq war, the LRA, and the break-up of Sudan highlight several features of today's conflicts.[4] First, since the end of the Cold War, most violent conflicts are intrastate, not interstate. These internal conflicts are often less about ideology and more about identity—religious, ethnic, tribal, or national. The problem of conflict, therefore, is often inseparable from the problem of failed and failing states riveted by identity conflicts.

Second, since 9/11, the threat posed by global terrorist networks and other nongovernmental actors has dominated international affairs, as terrorists networks often thrive in failed and failing states.

---

2. Robert Schreiter, "A Practical Theology of Healing, Forgiveness, and Reconciliation," in *Peacebuilding: Catholic Theology, Ethics and Praxis*, ed. R. Schreiter, S. Appleby, and G. Powers (Maryknoll, NY: Orbis Books, 2010), 366 [hereinafter *Peacebuilding*].

3. *Gaudium et Spes*, 4. Translations of Vatican II documents in this chapter are from *The Documents of Vatican II*, ed. Walter M. Abbott (New York: The America Press, 1966).

4. See *Human Security Report 2012* (Vancouver: Human Security Press, 2012).

Third, since World War II, civilians, not soldiers, have become the main victims of war, and many of these victims are not directly targeted by armed actors but are indirect casualties of war.

Fourth, the world no longer faces the threat of global nuclear war, a defining characteristic of international affairs during the Cold War. But the threat of nuclear proliferation and nuclear use remains a central concern while nuclear disarmament, dismissed as a utopian dream just a few decades ago, is now the rallying cry of "hawks" like Henry Kissinger and the stated policy goal of the United States and Russia.

Fifth, like the splitting of the atom, rapidly evolving technology continues to pose new ethical challenges, from the proliferating use of drones to cyber warfare.

Finally, since the end of the Cold War, peacebuilding has become a cottage industry among secular actors at all levels, from the establishment of the UN Peacebuilding Commission in 2005 to countless grassroots' peacebuilding initiatives by nongovernmental organizations (NGOs). Similarly, the Catholic Church has seen a proliferation of programs that consciously seek to nurture the peacebuilding capacity of the church. Most well-known is Sant'Egidio, a lay community based in Rome that was instrumental in facilitating a peace agreement in Mozambique in 1992.[5] Less well-known is the peacebuilding of Catholic Relief Services and other Caritas agencies.[6]

These (and other) "signs of the times" pose challenges to CST and Catholic action. The first set of challenges relate to the ethics of war. The principal challenge during the Cold War was the morality of nuclear deterrence amid a superpower arms race that threatened global annihilation. The principal challenge in the 1990s was the morality of humanitarian intervention in the face of genocide in Bosnia-Herzegovina, Rwanda, Kosovo, and East Timor. The principal challenges of the 2000s have been the ethics of counterterrorism, the preventive war doctrine used to justify

---

5. See, for example, Andrea Bartoli, "Mediating Peace in Mozambique: The Role of the Community of Sant'Egidio," in *Herding Cats*, ed. P. Aall, C. Crocker, and F. Hampson (Washington, DC: U.S. Institute of Peace, 1999), 245–73.

6. See *Pursuing Just Peace*, ed. M. Rogers, T. Bamat, and J. Ideh (Baltimore: CRS, 2008) [hereinafter *Pursuing Just Peace*]; *Peacebuilding: A Caritas Training Manual* (The Vatican: Caritas Internationalis, 2002, 2006).

the Iraq intervention, and the ethics of occupation (or *just post bellum*) in Iraq and Afghanistan.

The second set of challenges relates to the need for further development of a broader peacebuilding ethic. In addressing the roots of terrorism, stopping nuclear proliferation, preventing and ameliorating identity conflicts, and promoting the nation-building and reconciliation needed in places like South Sudan, Iraq, and Afghanistan, the common challenge is peacebuilding. Just as just-war norms are often racing to keep pace with new technology and strategies of warfare, a peacebuilding ethic needs to catch up to the practice of peacebuilding.

The Church's Peacebuilding Assets: Ritual, Spirituality, Theology, and Ethics

The Catholic Church is a large, complex, and incredibly diverse global religious institution that brings a rather unique mix of ideals, people, and institutions to the challenges of peacebuilding. Most articles on Catholic approaches to war and peace focus on the first, most fundamental, set of assets: beliefs, spirituality, and social teachings. Two distinct but complementary and interrelated methods are used to address two distinct but overlapping audiences. Teaching addressed to Catholics emphasizes the biblical conception of peace, the centrality of peace in the church's sacraments and mission, and a distinctively Christian theological and ethical approach to war and peace. Teaching addressed to the wider community uses the natural law tradition, which presumes that the demands of justice and peace are knowable and binding on all persons, regardless of their religious convictions. A short article cannot begin to do justice to the breadth and complexity of Catholic teaching on peace, but the following elements of the church's approach will serve as a starting point: peacebuilding as vocation, the role of spirituality and sacraments, a cosmopolitan ethic, a positive conception of peace, solidarity, the centrality of international law and institutions, just war and nonviolence, and a theology and ethics of peacebuilding.[7]

---

7. For a more detailed overview of the elements of peacebuilding, see Gerard Powers, "Catholic Approaches to Security and Peace," in *The Routledge Handbook of Religion and Security*, ed. C. Seiple, D. Hoover, and P. Otis (Routledge, 2012), 33–44;

The foundation for individual Catholics and the church as a whole is an understanding of peacebuilding not as an optional commitment but as integral to our *Christian vocation* and, therefore, central to the mission of the church. This sense of vocation and mission give peacebuilding a depth and texture that is distinct from most secular approaches. Understanding the dynamics of conflict, training in conflict resolution skills, education to change attitudes, and developing strategies of social change are essential. But, frankly, some of this work sometimes looks and feels a bit like "drive-by" peacebuilding. What motivates and sustains Cardinal Laghi, Archbishop Odama, members of Sant'Egidio's Mozambique mediation team, and countless other peacebuilders around the world is a deeper sense of vocation or mission. For bishops and priests, peacebuilding is an integral part of their roles as teachers and pastors; for the laity, peacebuilding is an integral part of assuming their principal responsibility for transforming the social order in light of the gospel through their work, family, and civic activities.

Cultivating peaceable virtues is a *sine qua non* of the peacebuilding vocation. As the U.S. bishops said in *The Harvest of Justice Is Sown in Peace*:

> True peacemaking can be a matter of policy only if it is first a matter of the heart. . . . Amid the violence of contemporary culture and in response to the growing contempt for human life, the Church must seek to foster communities where peaceable virtues can take root and be nourished. We need to nurture among ourselves *faith and hope* to strengthen our spirits by placing our trust in God, rather than in ourselves; *courage and compassion* that move us to action; *humility and kindness* so that we can put the needs and interests of others ahead of our own; *patience and perseverance* to endure the long struggle for justice; and *civility and charity* so that we can treat others with respect and love.[8]

---

and Gerard Powers, "From an Ethics of War to an Ethics of Peacebuilding," in *From Just War to Modern Peace Ethics*, ed. Heinz-Gerhard Justenhoven and William Barbieri (Boston: De Gruyter, 2012), 275–312.

8. National Conference of Catholic Bishops, *The Harvest of Justice Is Sown in Peace* (Washington, DC: USCC Office of Publishing, 1993), 6.

In other words, the peacebuilding vocation entails being individuals and a church that personify a certain kind of character—individuals and a community who are "habitually disposed to love and seek justice for their neighbors as if such a disposition were a second nature."[9]

Since peacebuilding is part of our Christian vocation, peace is integral to the church's *sacramental life and a healthy spirituality*. In fact, John Paul Lederach, a prominent Mennonite peace studies scholar who has worked with the Catholic Church in Uganda, Colombia, the Philippines, and elsewhere, points out that in situations of protracted conflict like these, the church's sacramental tradition, particularly the Eucharist, "stands as an important, perhaps unique, contribution of the Catholic tradition" because it has the power to mobilize "both the sacramental and the moral imagination in reference to reconciliation, restoring the broken community, and taking personal and corporate responsibility for the suffering of others."[10] The sacrament of reconciliation can be part of a process of trauma healing on a personal level and also can serve as a metaphor for post-war communal reconciliation. Spiritualities of non-violence and reconciliation offer ways to integrate peacebuilding into the faith life of Christian communities in ways that sustain them during the often long, arduous struggle against violence and injustice.[11]

The central role of ritual, sacrament, and spirituality in the church's peacebuilding work was evident in Sudan. Veteran missionary John Ashworth argues that the "value added" by the church amid the well-funded secular NGOs, powerful foreign governments, the UN, warring factions, and other actors was its ability to bring about "transformation, metanoia."[12] It was not surprising that the centerpiece of the church's program of civic education, logistical support, and monitoring for the

---

9. Daniel M. Bell, *Just War as Christian Discipleship: Recentering the Tradition in the Church Rather Than the State* (Grand Rapids, MI: Brazos Press, 2009), 83.

10. John Paul Lederach, "The Long Journey Back to Humanity: Catholic Peace-building with Armed Actors," in *Peacebuilding*, 51.

11. See Robert Schreiter, "The Catholic Social Imaginary and Peacebuilding: Ritual, Sacrament, and Spirituality," in *Peacebuilding*, 221–39.

12. Interview with John Ashworth, long-time advisor to Catholic Relief Services and other church agencies in Sudan, University of Notre Dame, South Bend, Indiana, April 1, 2013.

2011 independence referendum was "101 Days of Prayer for Peace." When religious leaders were selected to play a leading role in the government's reconciliation commission in 2013, they made it clear that they considered the process to be ultimately about religious, not just political, reconciliation.

A third element of Catholic peacebuilding is its grounding in a *cosmopolitan or communitarian ethic*. This ethic is more compatible with notions of "human security" than "national security," the preoccupation of the varieties of political realism that tend to dominate U.S. foreign policy debates.[13] It is a human-centric, not state-centric, ethic. The duty to protect national security and state-centric principles of sovereignty, the equality of states, and nonintervention are critically important. But they are not absolutes. These principles are instrumental norms that serve the more fundamental principles of the dignity of the human person and the common good. While the United States has, at times, been a leader on human rights, its emphasis is on civil and political rights, and even this limited human rights agenda rarely trumps military, political, or economic interests. As Mark Ensalaco and Ron Pagnucco explain in more detail in chapter 8, a Catholic approach includes not only civil and political rights but also economic, social, and cultural rights.[14] U.S. policy, like that of all countries, is focused primarily on the national common good, defined primarily in terms of political, economic, and military security. In Catholic teaching, a state's first obligation is to protect the national common good, but states—especially the most powerful—also have a heavy obligation to protect and promote the global common good. Unlike realist approaches that exclude or marginalize religion and

13. The United Nations Development Programme used the concept of human security in its 1994 *Human Development Report*. The concept focuses on the security of individuals rather than states, the focus of traditional notions of national security. A narrow definition focuses on violent threats whereas the broader definition used in the 1994 Report defines security in terms of freedom from hunger, disease, pollution, affronts to human dignity, threats to livelihoods, and other harms as well as violence. See Human Security Report Project: http://www.hsrgroup.org/ (accessed July 2, 2013).

14. See in this volume chapter 8 on human rights, by Ron Pagnucco and Mark Ensalaco and chapter 9 on solidarity by Ron Pagnucco and Peter Gichure; *Gaudium et Spes*, 74.

morality, this cosmopolitan ethic insists that religion and morality must be factors in policymaking.

A fourth element of Catholic peacebuilding is a *positive conception of peace*. Like much of U.S. foreign policy and international relations theory, a major function of Catholic teaching, particularly the just-war tradition, is to maintain a negative peace (that is, avoiding war and helping to prevent and manage violent conflicts around the world). But Catholic teaching is not satisfied with preventing, limiting, and stopping violence and war. Catholic teaching also insists on the much more ambitious goal of building a positive peace.

Kenneth Himes describes three ways of talking of positive peace in CST, each of which reinforces and complements the others. The Shalom of Isaiah, where the wolf and lamb lie down together (Isa 11:6), is the *eschatological meaning* of peace. The *spiritual meaning* of peace is the interior peace that comes through communion with, and by being part of, the Body of Christ. *Tranquilitas ordinis* is the *political meaning* of peace—the peace of a rightly ordered political community—with people living in truth, charity, freedom, and justice directed toward the common good.[15] This political peace is not merely a utopian ideal but something that is achievable in human history. As Pope Paul VI noted, moving beyond a state of affairs where war is a sad necessity is a moral obligation akin to abolishing slavery and eradicating diseases.[16]

Solidarity is a fifth element of Catholic teaching.[17] As Ron Pagnucco and Peter Gichure explain in chapter 9, solidarity reminds us that one's own good is intimately bound up with that of the wider community. Solidarity challenges the idea that international relations is a zero-sum game in which the pursuit of U.S. interests invariably puts the United States in competition and conflict with other countries. It calls for collaboration, not competition, among individuals, groups, and nations to

15. Kenneth Himes, "Peacebuilding and Catholic Social Teaching," in *Peacebuilding*, 268–69.

16. Pope Paul VI, "Homily on the World Day of Peace" (January 1, 1970), cited in Himes, "Peacebuilding and Catholic Social Teaching," 280.

17. See chapter 9 in this volume by Ron Pagnucco and Peter Gichure, "The Challenge of Solidarity: A Catholic Perspective."

build structures of cooperative security that can promote authentic human development and the common good.[18]

In considering the ethics of war, solidarity reinforces the duty of care owed civilians (that is, in targeting decisions, civilians should be treated as if they were our own parents, siblings, and children). Solidarity suggests a special option for the victims of war akin to the option for the poor. Solidarity also impels the church to overcome, through its own peacebuilding and accompaniment efforts, the chasm that divides the world's zones of peace and prosperity from the zones of war and deprivation. Lederach finds that church actors in places like Colombia and Uganda consistently emphasize the church's role of accompaniment, "the quality of being present with, being alongside people as they make a journey." According to Lederach, "[s]ociologically, the church is, literally, present in and with the communities most affected by violence. Theologically, Church leaders consider their active presence, their engagement with both victims and perpetrators, as an expression of their pastoral vocation." Consequently, they rarely use secular terms, such as mediation or negotiation, to describe their engagement with armed actors but prefer terms such as "pastoral dialogue."[19]

Strengthening *international law and international institutions* is a concrete manifestation of the virtue of solidarity and a necessary means to achieve both a negative and positive peace. For many realists, the terms "international community" and "world order" are oxymorons. Given a quasi-anarchic collection of mostly competing states, they argue that the shared values and common institutions needed for a genuine international community do not exist. Catholic teaching is realistic about the weaknesses of the current international system but insists that there are universally shared values—natural law—that can and must find expression in international law and institutions.[20] While realists focus on collective security

18. See Himes, "Peacebuilding and Catholic Social Teaching," in *Peacebuilding*, 273–75.

19. Lederach, "The Long Journey Back to Humanity," in *Peacebuilding*, 43, 48–50.

20. Pontifical Council for Justice and Peace, *Compendium of the Social Doctrine of the Church* (Washington, DC: United States Conference of Catholic Bishops, 2005), 433–34 [hereinafter *Compendium*].

alliances like NATO to defend the shared interests of groups of allied states, Catholic teaching envisions a cooperative security regime based on the shared values of all states and the people they do, or at least should, represent.

The UN and other international institutions are central to this vision of cooperative security.[21] The church does not support a "global super-state" that would limit or replace the role of individual nations and local communities in addressing conflict. That would violate an element of the principle of subsidiarity: authority should be exercised at the *lowest level possible*.[22] But the UN and other international institutions are intended to fulfill a second element of subsidiarity: authority should be exercised at the *highest level necessary*. These institutions contribute to global solidarity by developing norms to govern armed conflict, such as the Geneva Conventions, and helping to resolve complex conflicts, such as those borne of failed and failing states, that individual nations are unwilling or unable to address.[23] In response to the obvious inadequacies of international norms and institutions, the church has supported major reforms, as well as more serious measures to counter the indifference, lack of political will, and lack of resources that impede international peacebuilding.

A seventh element is the church's rich tradition of reflection on *just war and nonviolence*. Of the four main approaches to the ethics of war—holy war, amoral realism, just or limited war, and pacifism or principled nonviolence—only the latter two are now considered options for Christians. Contemporary holy war is exemplified by Al Qaeda's so-called jihad against the West and extreme forms of religious nationalism. Amoral realism claims that national security interests trump moral and legal norms in war and that "war is hell" and therefore somehow beyond morality. Both holy war and amoral realism violate Catholic teaching because they assume, for different reasons, that war can be unlimited or at least not subject to moral constraints. Catholic teaching is realistic insofar as

21. The Second Vatican Council urged "the establishment of some universal public authority acknowledged as such by all, and endowed with effective power to safeguard, on the behalf of all, security, regard for justice, and respect for rights" (*Gaudium et Spes*, 82).

22. *Compendium*, 441.

23. Pope John XXIII, *Pacem in Terris*, 140.

it accepts that in a sinful world without an international authority to control and resolve conflict, military force is sometimes a tragic necessity to establish or maintain order. But Catholic teaching rejects total war and the notion that national security, vital interests, and the "necessities" of war trump norms.

The just war tradition and pacifism, or principled nonviolence, are the two morally legitimate approaches to the ethics of war. In their 1983 peace pastoral, the U.S. Catholic bishops suggested that the two traditions share a common starting point: a strong presumption "in favor of peace and against war," a starting point which makes them "distinct but interdependent methods of evaluating warfare."[24] Some Catholics have always embraced the principled nonviolence of those like Dorothy Day and the Catholic Worker Movement who believe nonviolence is central to the gospel. But since Vatican II and especially since the end of the Cold War, nonviolence has received greater emphasis and legitimacy in official church teaching. Papal and other statements are replete with condemnations of the "savagery" and "scourge" of war, descriptions of war as "an adventure without return" and a "defeat for humanity," and hortatory appeals, such as "war never again" and "war is not the answer."[25] The experience of total war in the twentieth century, the threat of a nuclear holocaust, and the fact that civilians have increasingly been the main victims of war have led the church to be deeply skeptical of the ability of modern war to meet just-war criteria. At the same time, successful nonviolent change, from the demise of Marcos in the Philippines to the mostly peaceful dissolution of the Soviet bloc, has demonstrated the efficacy of nonviolence.[26]

Nevertheless, principled nonviolence is considered an option for individuals, not governments. In the words of the Second Vatican Council,

24. National Conference of Catholic Bishops, *The Challenge of Peace: God's Promise and Our Response* (Washington, DC: USCCB Publishing Office, 1983), 51.

25. *Compendium*, 497.

26. Pope John Paul II, *Centesimus Annus* (1991), 23. For John Paul's teaching on war, see Drew Christiansen, "Catholic Peacemaking, 1991–2005: The Legacy of Pope John Paul II," *The Review of Faith and International Affairs* 4, no. 2 (Fall 2006). A growing body of literature analyzes the efficacy of nonviolent resistance. See, for example, Erica Chenoweth and Maria J. Stephan, *Why Civil Resistance Works: The Strategic Logic of Nonviolent Conflict* (New York: Columbia University Press, 2011).

faced with aggression, "governments cannot be denied the right to legitimate defense once every means of peaceful settlement has been exhausted."[27] The just-war criteria limit when, why, and how force may be used. The *jus ad bellum* criteria restrict resort to war: just cause, comparative justice, legitimate authority, right intention, probability of success, proportionality, and last resort. *Jus in bello* criteria restrict the conduct of war: noncombatant immunity, proportionality, and right intention.[28]

In public policy debates on U.S. military interventions, the just war versus pacifism debate is of marginal relevance. The more relevant debate is between two different interpretations of the just war tradition. The more permissive approach of the traditionalists begins with a presumption in favor of justice and considers war a tool of statecraft, making it easier to justify resort to military force.[29] President Bush's moral justification for preventive war in Iraq represents the most permissive of this interpretation. Cardinal Laghi's arguments against war in 2003 reflected the increasingly strict, or restrictive, approach of official teaching. This approach begins with a strong presumption against war and considers war a failure of statecraft. This latter approach creates a hermeneutic

---

27. *Gaudium et Spes*, 79. The just-war tradition has been deeply skeptical of revolutionary violence because revolutionaries lack clear legitimate authority, and revolutionary violence often blurs the distinction between combatants and noncombatants. See James Turner Johnson, *Can Modern War Be Just?* (New Haven, CT: Yale University Press, 1984), 54–55. According to the *Catechism of the Catholic Church* (New York: Image Books, 1995), 2243, "Armed resistance to oppression by political authority is not legitimate, unless all the following conditions are met: (1) there is certain, grave, and prolonged violation of fundamental rights; (2) all other means of redress have been exhausted; (3) such resistance will not provoke worse disorders; (4) there is well-founded hope of success; and (5) it is impossible reasonably to foresee any better solution."

28. U.S. Conference of Catholic Bishops, *The Harvest of Justice Is Sown in Peace* (Washington, DC: United States Conference of Catholic Bishops, 1993), 12–14.

29. See George Weigel, "The Development of Just War Thinking in the Post-Cold War World: An American Perspective," in *The Price of Peace: Just War in the Twenty-First Century*, ed. C. Reed and D. Ryall (Cambridge: Cambridge University Press, 2007). See also George Weigel, *Faith, Reason, and the War against Jihadism: A Call to Action* (New York: Doubleday, 2007).

which interprets the just-war criteria narrowly, making it very difficult to justify military force.[30]

The challenge for adherents of either interpretation of just war and proponents of principled nonviolence is to enlarge the (rather tired) debate over the ethics of war. All sides must reflect much more seriously and systematically on a wider *theology and ethic of just peace or peacebuilding*, an area where they should be able to find common ground. The just-war tradition and an ethic of peacebuilding are inherently complementary approaches. Properly used, the just-war tradition is an element of peacebuilding. The U.S. bishops, for example, have used just-war criteria as a form of conflict prevention, opposing military intervention in Iraq in 1991 and 2003. Adherence to *jus in bello* norms of civilian immunity and proportionality not only limit violence during war but also enhance prospects for a peace agreement and postwar reconciliation.

As helpful as it can be as a form of peacebuilding, however, the just-war approach risks becoming a sort of procedural checklist unmoored from its deeper foundations in social ethics unless it is linked to a broader peacebuilding ethic. Cardinal Laghi was not relying solely on just-war arguments to prevent the Iraq War; his arguments reflected a much wider ethic of peacebuilding. His appeal to the power of dialogue (even when dealing with one of the world's worst dictators), the importance of upholding and strengthening international law, and the need to defer to the UN on Iraq reflect a broader cosmopolitan ethic of a just peace without which his just-war arguments are incomprehensible.

The Responsibility to Protect (R2P), adopted at the 2005 World Summit, is another example of the interrelationship between an ethics of war and an ethics of peacebuilding. R2P is based on the principle that in cases of serious human rights violations, such as genocide, war crimes, crimes against humanity, and ethnic cleansing, principles of order (state-centric norms of

---

30. J. Bryan Hehir, a principal author of the U.S. bishops' peace pastoral, is a leading proponent of this strict interpretation. See Hehir, "From the Pastoral Constitution of Vatican II to *The Challenge of Peace*," in *Catholics and Nuclear War*, ed. Philip J. Murnion (New York: Crossroad, 1983), 71–87. For an overview of the U.S. bishops' application of this strict approach to U.S. military interventions since the 1980s, see Gerard Powers, "The U.S. Bishops and War since the Peace Pastoral," *U.S. Catholic Historian* 27, no. 2 (Winter 2009): 73–96.

sovereignty and nonintervention) must give way to principles of justice (human-centric norms of human rights). It was developed as an alternative to the "humanitarian" military interventions in Kosovo and Bosnia. R2P's first two pillars are about conflict prevention: the state's responsibility to protect its own citizens and the international community's obligation to assist states in doing so. If a state is unwilling or unable to protect its own citizens, even with international support, then the third pillar envisions collective action through the Security Council to protect citizens.

In his 2008 address at the United Nations, Pope Benedict endorsed R2P in the name of protecting basic human dignity and human rights.[31] On the controversial issue of intervention under pillar three, church statements contend that the international community has not only a right but a duty of humanitarian intervention in the face of threats to the survival of whole groups or serious violations of basic human rights. While strong priority is given nonmilitary forms of intervention, it can be legitimate as a last resort for the international community to "take concrete measures to disarm the aggressor" and protect innocent victims.[32] While there might be exceptional cases, intervention should be through the UN Security Council in accord with the UN Charter so as to help ensure, as the U.S. bishops have said, that "humanitarian intervention is an authentic act of international solidarity and not a cloak for great power dominance."[33]

The genius of R2P is that it combines a peacebuilding ethic (pillars 1 and 2) with an intervention ethic (pillar 3). But R2P's intervention ethic needs to be supplemented by a post-intervention ethic. The Iraq intervention, while very different from that envisioned by R2P, is a case in point. Once the United States invaded Iraq, the moral debate changed from an ethics of intervention to an ethics of exit and faced a host of issues not addressed by the just-war tradition or pacifism. If it was immoral to intervene, was it immoral to stay? What did the United States, as a *de jure* and then *de facto* occupying power, owe Iraqis? Was it the responsibility of the United States to help bring about reconciliation among Iraqis, and, if so, what did that entail?[34] Some of these are issues related to an emerging

---

31. Benedict XVI, Address to UN General Assembly, April 18, 2008.

32. *Compendium*, 220, quoting John Paul II, 2000 World Day of Peace Message, 11.

33. *Harvest of Justice Is Sown in Peace*, 16.

34. Bishop William Skylstad, president, USCCB, "Call for Dialogue and Action on Responsible Transition in Iraq," November 13, 2006; Gerard Powers, "Our Moral

theory of a *jus post bellum*, but some of them involve a wider set of issues that have not been addressed in depth in official CST.[35]

In some ways, the practice of peacebuilding is ahead of the theology and ethics of peacebuilding. Reading the peacebuilding "signs of the times" today requires a much better mapping and analysis of the mostly unheralded peacebuilding work of the Catholic community around the world. It also requires identifying ways in which existing teaching can be enriched by insights from practice and practice can be enriched by developments in teaching. For example, the field of conflict resolution could inform CST.[36] From civil war in Syria to dealing with the Lord's Resistance Army, the church has called for dialogue and negotiation as an alternative to military force. But as Himes points out, the church's communitarian ethic can present an overly optimistic sense of the ability to resolve deep-seated conflicts like these through negotiation.[37]

Catholic teaching also provides little guidance on how to deal with the ethical dilemmas and tradeoffs usually present in such cases. Bishops

---

Duty in Iraq," *America* (February 18, 2008): 13–16; George Lopez, "Ethics Outflanked," *America* (March 6, 2006): 14–18.

35. Several chapters in *Peacebuilding* address post-intervention issues: Daniel Philpott, "Reconciliation: A Catholic Ethic for Peacebuilding in the Political Order"; Maryann Cusimano Love, "What Kind of Peace Do We Seek? Emerging Norms of Peacebuilding in Key Political Institutions"; Peter-John Pearson, "Pursuing Truth, Reconciliation, and Human Dignity in South Africa: Lessons for Catholic Peacebuilding"; and Robert Schreiter, "A Practical Theology of Healing, Forgiveness, and Reconciliation." See also Brian Orend, "Justice after War," *Ethics and International Affairs* 16, no. 1 (April 2002): 43–56; Gary Bass, "*Jus Post Bellum*," in *Philosophy & Public Affairs*, 384–412; William Bole, Drew Christiansen, and Robert Hennemeyer, *Forgiveness in International Politics* (Washington, DC: United States Conference of Catholic Bishops, 2004).

36. The literature on conflict resolution and peace studies is vast. See, for example, *Strategies of Peace: Transforming Conflict in a Violent World*, ed. D. Philpott and G. Powers (Oxford: Oxford University Press, 2010); *Leashing the Dogs of War: Conflict Management in a Divided World*, ed. C. Crocker, F. Hampson, and P. Aall (Washington, DC: U.S. Institute of Peace Press, 2007); *Human Rights and Conflict: Exploring the Links between Rights, Law, and Peacebuilding*, ed. J. Mertus and J. W. Helsing (Washington, DC: U.S. Institute of Peace, 2006).

37. See Himes, "Peacebuilding and Catholic Social Teaching," in *Peacebuilding*, 282.

from war-torn places like Northern Uganda, Rwanda, and Colombia wake up in the morning worrying, not about the next round of confirmations or parish openings, but about how they can prevent full-scale war from breaking out in their dioceses between different tribes or rebel groups. What does it mean to celebrate the Eucharist in parishes where these violent groups and their victims share a pew at Sunday Mass?

The Vatican supported the establishment of the International Criminal Court (ICC) as a critical means to strengthen international norms and international institutions. Yet the Acholi Religious Leaders in Uganda strongly opposed the first indictments handed down by the ICC because they undermined prospects for achieving a peace agreement with the LRA's indicted leaders. How should one weigh the tradeoffs between achieving a negative peace and holding war criminals accountable? From Sudan to Northern Ireland, the church has taken a variety of positions on the issue of secession, a key concern in about half the world's conflicts, but these positions are based almost entirely on pragmatism because there is little in CST on the question. In short, there are a variety of areas in need of further development of a theology and ethics of peacebuilding.

To review, the first set of Catholic peacebuilding assets includes a variety of elements: a commitment to peacebuilding as vocation, a spiritual and sacramental imagination, a cosmopolitan ethic centered on human dignity and the common good, a positive conception of peace, an embrace of solidarity, support for international law and institutions, a highly restrictive approach to just war with a priority given nonviolent methods, and a broader theology and ethics of peacebuilding to address issues beyond the ethics of war.

The Church's Peacebuilding Assets: People Power and Institutional Presence

The church's teachings and rituals are of little more than academic importance if they are not lived; if they do not shape people's lives and the life of the institutional church. That the church's teaching on peace is, indeed, a living tradition is most evident in the stories and writings of a rather small pantheon of past and present Catholic peacebuilding saints. Some are well known: St. Francis of Assisi, Archbishop Oscar Romero, Dorothy Day. The risk in focusing on these figures is that we can end up with the impression that peacebuilding is an exceptional thing, a counsel of perfection, not something all of us are called to and capable of. In fact, countless ordinary Catholics reside in every conflict zone in the world and are performing courageous but mostly unheralded acts of peacebuilding. They are bishops like Paride Taban, a kind of "religious elder statesman" who has been selected to be vice chairman of the official reconciliation commission in South Sudan. But most are priests, women religious, and laypeople who are working for Catholic Relief Services or Solidarity with Sudan, or a local parish trying desperately to keep competing tribes from turning the village into a free-fire zone.

But it is not just about individuals; it is also about the people power of the people of God. The Catholic Church in the Philippines invented the term with its mass mobilization to overthrow the long-standing dictator Ferdinand Marcos in 1986.[38] Also in the 1980s, the Catholic Church was a prime mover behind the Solidarity trade union movement in Poland, which negotiated an end to five decades of communist rule in 1989, the first domino to fall in the demise of the Soviet bloc. In the United States, following their widely acclaimed pastorals on peace (1983) and the economy (1986), the bishops undertook a much more focused effort, beginning in the late 1980s, to develop diocesan and parish education and advocacy networks around issues of justice and peace. In the 1990s and early 2000s, the Catholic Campaign to Ban Landmines and the campaign for debt relief for poor countries were two of the most sustained and successful efforts to mobilize large numbers of Catholics around complex policy issues.

An often overlooked dimension of Catholic peacebuilding is its institutional context. The church's moral and religious power and its people power are mediated through an extensive set of institutions, from local parishes and grassroots peace organizations to Vatican offices and global development agencies. An increasing number of people, mostly youth, are skeptical of or indifferent to institutions, especially religious institutions. But the fact is that the Catholic peace tradition would not be a

---

38. Peter Ackerman and Jack Duvall, *A Force More Powerful: A Century of Nonviolent Conflict* (New York: St. Martin's Press, 2000), 369–95; Christina A. Astorga, "Culture, Religion, and Moral Vision: A Theological Discourse on the Filipino People Power Revolution of 1986," *Theological Studies* 67 (2006): 567–601.

living tradition without Catholic institutions, and Catholic institutions are part of what makes Catholic peacebuilding distinctive.

In South Sudan, for example, the dearth of political and civil society institutions of the kind taken for granted in developed countries like the United States left the church to fill the void. As mentioned earlier, the church there played a substitute political role, providing most of the education, health care, humanitarian aid, development programs, and human rights monitoring, sponsoring civil society peace processes that contributed to the 2005 peace agreement, and undertaking a civic education campaign and logistical support for the referendum on independence. The church can play these kinds of roles because, unlike many international NGOs, development agencies, and governmental institutions, it is an indigenous institution deeply rooted in the fabric of society that does not withdraw when violence erupts.

According to Lederach, in war-torn areas like South Sudan, Uganda, Congo, the southern Philippines, and Colombia, the church's "ubiquitous presence" gives the church a "unique if not unprecedented presence in the landscape of. . . conflict." In these areas, the church has relationships with every level and nearly every area of conflict, creating a depth and breadth of access that few religious or secular institutions enjoy. He concludes, "There are few places where the infrastructure and ecclesiology of church structure so neatly aligns with the multilevel and multifaceted demands of peacebuilding."[39]

A distinctive element of Catholic peacebuilding is that the church is not only an indigenous local actor, but it is also one of the world's largest and most complex transnational institutions. Its global reach is greater than the U.S. government, the UN, and the world's largest corporations. The 1.2 billion Catholics are served by more than 200,000 parishes, 400,000 priests, 700,000 religious sisters, and hundreds of thousands of lay staff in Catholic schools, health care agencies, charities, and other institutions. In comparison, Walmart, one of the world's largest corporations, has 10,800 stores in 27 countries with 2.2 million employees.[40]

---

39. Lederach, "The Long Journey Back to Humanity," in *Peacebuilding*, 50–51.

40. *Annuario Pontificio* (Vatican City: Libreria Editrice Vaticana, 2013); Walmart website accessed June 15, 2013: http://corporate.walmart.com/our-story/?povid =P1171-C1093.2766-L5.

The church's peacebuilding work is done through a variety of entities. The widely respected Vatican foreign service, with representatives serving 179 states, the UN, and other international organizations and regional organizations, such as the European Union, are deeply involved in promoting peace and justice. There are also staffed peace and justice offices at the Vatican, at over 100 regional and national bishops' conferences, and at thousands of dioceses and some parishes. Many of the 164 national Catholic caritas agencies have programs devoted specifically to peacebuilding. In South Sudan alone, Catholic Relief Services spent four million dollars on peacebuilding in 2010-2011. The church's peacebuilding work is also done by a multiplicity of lay movements, such as Focolare, and independent organizations, such as the Sant'Egidio Community and Pax Christi International, which have affiliates in dozens of countries. Catholic institutions and individuals also play a prominent role in many interfaith organizations, such as Religions for Peace. The 135,000 Catholic elementary and high schools worldwide provide education and formation in CST, and 1,358 Catholic universities teach, research, and provide expertise to the church and the wider public on matters of peace and justice.[41]

Through this extensive institutional infrastructure, the church has an enormous capacity for peacebuilding. It is the most vertically integrated religious institution, with a hierarchical structure with clearly defined leaders. The church has institutions at all levels and clear lines of teaching and organizational authority (though it is quite decentralized in its operations). Its vertical integration is complemented by a capacity for what sociologists call "horizontal integration," the ecclesial bonds of solidarity that unite the Catholic community across geographical, cultural, national, and economic divides.

The Acholi Religious Leaders Peace Initiative in northern Uganda, for example, operated at many levels. They formed local and later district-level peace committees within northern Uganda to educate their own people about peacebuilding, to address land issues, to organize peace rallies and prayers, to mediate local conflicts, and to develop programs

---

41. *Annuario Pontificio* 2013. One example of collaboration for peace among universities and various Catholic institutions is the Catholic Peacebuilding Network at http://cpn.nd.edu/.

of trauma healing. They advocated on national legislation on amnesty and were official observers at the peace negotiations. They worked closely with their religious counterparts in the United States as well as other key countries and the UN to bring greater attention to an often-ignored conflict. They also urged these governmental bodies to play a constructive role in the peace process by, among other things, supporting indigenous alternatives to the indictments handed down by the International Criminal Court.[42]

Another example of how the church's vertical and horizontal integration can contribute to peacebuilding is the Catholic Peacebuilding Network (CPN). The CPN is a network of university institutes, bishops' conferences, development agencies, and independent peace organizations. It enhances the study and practice of Catholic peacebuilding by: (1) deepening engagement among scholars and practitioners, (2) improving understanding of best practices in peacebuilding, (3) further developing a theology and ethics of peace, and (4) enhancing the peacebuilding capacity of the church in conflict areas. Starting with seven partner institutions in 2004, the CPN numbered twenty-two in 2013. Through a series of international conferences around the world, CPN has enabled scholars to engage directly with Catholic peacebuilders in several dozen countries suffering from conflict and has facilitated sharing of best practices among these peacebuilders, who often have little contact with their counterparts in other conflict zones. Because it can bring together a diverse array of Catholic institutions engaged in peacebuilding to assist with strategic planning, training, and other needs of the church, CPN has been able to contribute to the development of the peacebuilding capacity of the church in the Great Lakes Region of Africa, Colombia, and the Philippines.

These and other examples illustrate how the Catholic peace tradition is a living tradition because it shapes the minds, hearts, and souls of people. But the way the church reaches people and mobilizes them to act in effective, sustained ways that can engage the multiple factors, actors, and levels of conflict is through its remarkable presence as a global institution that is deeply rooted in the local.

---

42. Kelsie Thompson, "Uganda: Alliances for Peace: The Acholi Religious Leaders Peace Initiative," in *Pursuing Just* Peace, 133–44.

Conclusion: The Special Responsibility of Catholics in the United States

Underlying the exchange between Cardinal Laghi and President Bush over Iraq was a very different view of what "the rest of the world" means to the United States and what the United States means to the rest of the world. The Bush administration's preventive war doctrine was premised on a U.S. exceptionalism and the maintenance of U.S. military, political, and economic dominance through a policy of what some have called "muscular unilateralism."[43] The Obama administration's stated policies are generally less muscular and unilateral, but they, too, reflect how deeply ingrained these tendencies are in U.S. foreign policy.

Cardinal Laghi's vision of the U.S. role in the world could not have been more different. With power comes responsibility, so Laghi assumed that the United States, by virtue of its unique power, not its unique virtue, bears a heavy moral burden to know what the rest of the world means and what U.S. actions mean to the rest of the world. These actions include promoting the global common good, building a system of cooperative security that will ultimately make war obsolete, and reaching out in solidarity to other nations, especially those most in need.

U.S. power and influence notwithstanding, it is not always obvious to ordinary Americans—or to most students—what they can do to promote peace in places like Iraq, Uganda, and South Sudan. The student mobilization on college campuses in support of a peaceful independence referendum in South Sudan is a good example of what can be done. One initiative stood out because it went beyond typical student social justice activities and harnessed the national visibility enjoyed by athletics in the name of peace.

The University of Notre Dame, St. Mary's College, and Holy Cross College undertook a major educational and advocacy campaign that was led by student government and a not-so-usual-suspect: the nationally ranked Notre Dame men's lacrosse team. The catalyst was a visit from Sudanese bishops to Notre Dame in October 2010, which inspired Notre Dame's student senate to issue a resolution in support of the church's

43. Stephen Brooks and William Wohlforth, "American Primacy in Perspective," *Foreign Affairs* 81, no. 4 (July/August 2002): 20.

peacebuilding efforts. The student senate resolution in turn prompted the lacrosse team to do something different. Instead of the usual participation in charity events, they decided to take up Sudan as their social issue for the year. They educated themselves through briefings by faculty and Sudanese students. They then teamed up with the men's basketball team, student government, and other groups at Notre Dame, St. Mary's, and Holy Cross, and, with sponsorship by Adidas, hosted a major rally for peace in Sudan and a Playing for Peace basketball tournament.

In addition to the rally, more than one thousand students signed a petition to President Barak Obama urging his administration to do more to support peace in Sudan. That petition was followed by a delegation of Notre Dame students, led by the assistant lacrosse coach, to Washington, D.C. The delegation met with senior leaders at the White House, State Department, and Congress, as well as with executives at Catholic Relief Services, the largest development agency in South Sudan. That delegation was followed by student blogs on Sudan that were distributed by major NGOs working on the issue. The Playing for Peace in Sudan campaign culminated in an April 10, 2011, nationally televised broadcast of the Notre Dame-Georgetown lacrosse game, in which ESPN devoted its halftime show to a video and discussion of Playing for Peace in Sudan.

Playing for Peace in South Sudan could be a model for similar initiatives on college campuses around the country on other issues. It shows what can be done when Catholics creatively deploy the church's rich spiritual and ethical tradition, people power, and institutional assets to help build peace. It also shows what can happen when students have an understanding, consistent with CST, of what "the rest of the world" means to them.

Discussion Questions

1. Is peacebuilding integral to the faith of individual Catholics and the mission of the church? What is the basis for your answer (for example, Scripture, theology, CST)?

2. Watch the clip from the movie, *Hotel Rwanda* (50:52-54:50—UN evacuates foreigners from hotel). Who is most able to be a peacebuilder in that situation—the UN General or the priest?

3. Think of specific examples of Catholic peacebuilding. What "assets" did the Catholic community bring, and was there anything distinctively Catholic about the peacebuilding?

4. Are just war and pacifism really two complementary parts of the Catholic tradition, as the bishops' presumption against war suggests, or are they fundamentally incompatible?

5. Is the just-war tradition a form of conflict prevention, conflict mitigation, and post-conflict reconciliation, or is it mainly a way to legitimize war?

Chapter 8

Ron Pagnucco and
Mark Ensalaco

Human Rights, Catholic Social Teaching, and the Liberal Rights Tradition

The United Nations' adoption of the Universal Declaration of Human Rights (UDHR) in December 1948 laid the foundation for a global human rights movement and made the secular language of human rights the dominant idiom of struggles against injustice in the modern world.[1] While many agree with the basic rights enumerated in the UDHR, there is no one underlying philosophy or theology of rights given for it by the drafters, who came from a variety of political, philosophical, and religious backgrounds. They chose not to try to articulate any specific philosophical or theological justification for human rights because a variety of justifications existed, and they wanted to avoid controversies that would impede the United Nations' adoption of the UDHR. The experience of the Holocaust and other shocking atrocities of World War II provided a practical and immediate motivation for agreement on the human rights to be protected.[2] There was, and continues to be, a tension among the various

1. Universal Declaration of Human Rights G.A. Res. 217A (III) U.N. Doc. A/810 (1948). Hereafter, the Declaration or UDHR.
2. See Mary Ann Glendon, *A World Made New: Eleanor Roosevelt and the Universal Declaration of Human Rights* (New York: Random House, 2001). Commenting on the Declaration's drafting process, Johannes Morsink wrote: "The motif running throughout their adoptions and rejections is that the war and the ideology

philosophical and religious conceptualizations and justifications of rights. As one prominent Catholic philosopher of Rights in the period, Jacques Maritain, wrote of the UDHR, "we agree on these rights, *providing we are not asked why.*" Maritain goes on to note that agreement was reached "not on the basis of common speculative notions, but on common practical notions."[3] Thus we can see that from the very beginning, Catholic Rights Theory could be, and is, a part of a practical convergence on rights, illustrated in the UHDR, but that it has an implicit conflict with aspects of other philosophical and religious theories of rights, including Liberal Rights Theory, concerning the foundations for those rights and what qualifies as rights.

The *Compendium of Catholic Social Doctrine*, published in 2004, indicates the strong degree of support in Catholic Social Teaching (CST) and in the church generally for the UDHR and the modern human rights movement.

> *The Church [is] aware that her essentially religious mission includes the defence and promotion of human rights. . . .* For greater ef-

---

as practiced by Hitler were in themselves enough to convince them of the truth of the rights of the Declaration. They did not need a philosophical argument in addition to the experience of the Holocaust." See Morsink, "World War Two and the Universal Declaration," *Human Rights Quarterly* 15, no. 2 (May 1993): 358. See also Morsink, *The Universal Declaration of Human Rights: Origins, Drafting & Intent* (Philadelphia, PA: University of Pennsylvania Press, 1999); and Hans Joas, *The Sacredness of the Person: A New Genealogy of Human Rights*, trans. Alex Skinner (Washington, DC: Georgetown University Press, 2013).

3. Jacques Maritain, *Man and the State* (Chicago: University of Chicago Press, 1951), 77; while Maritain did think that the "practical convergence of extremely different theoretical ideologies and spiritual traditions" was based on "a sort of unwritten common law" among diverse peoples, providing a basis for common action, he did think that knowing which philosophical basis of rights is right "is essentially important" (ibid., 78). Drawing from John Rawls, Jack Donnelly refers to this practical agreement on international human rights as an "overlapping consensus" among "comprehensive doctrines" and that the lack of agreement concerning the "why" noted by Maritain "is not because there is no good answer but because there are many different good answers (and each [philosophical and religious] tradition remains committed to its own)." See Donnelly, *Universal Human Rights: Theory and Practice*, 3rd ed. (Ithaca, NY: Cornell University Press, 2013), 59.

> fectiveness, [the Church's] commitment is open to ecumenical
> cooperation, to dialogue with other religions, to all appropriate
> contacts with other organizations, governmental and non-
> governmental, at the national and international levels.[4]

Indeed the church has become a leading advocate of human rights since the late 1960s and has played an important role in many of the often-times deadly struggles against authoritarian regimes up to the present day.[5] As indicated earlier, however, in spite of the church's strong advocacy for human rights, there is in fact a basic tension between underlying assumptions of CST and underlying assumptions of the secular, Liberal Rights Theory (LRT) that informs much of the secular human rights movement. The church's support of human rights is not an adoption or sharing of

---

4. *Compendium of the Social Doctrine of the Church*, 159. Regarding "all appropriate contacts with all other organizations, governmental and non-governmental," in a letter dated July 2, 2007, to Amnesty International by Bishop William S. Skylstad, then-president of the U.S. Conference of Catholic Bishops (USCCB), he wrote: "It is deeply disappointing that the Executive Council of Amnesty International (AI) recently abandoned Amnesty International's neutral stance on abortion to take a pro-abortion position. As Cardinal Renato Martino, president of the Pontifical Council for Justice and Peace, recently said, 'if in fact Amnesty International persists in this course of action, individuals and Catholic organizations must withdraw their support, because, in deciding to promote abortion rights, AI has betrayed its mission.'" See Bishop William S. Skylstad, "A Plea to Amnesty International Members" (Washington, DC: United States Conference of Catholic Bishops, July 2, 2007). Amnesty International has kept its pro-abortion policy, and the USCCB and other Catholic organizations, including Catholic high schools, colleges, and universities, no longer support Amnesty International. As we note in this essay, many secular human rights groups, especially in the global north, have taken a pro-abortion rights position even though the right to abortion is not recognized by international human rights law. A recent survey of U.S.-based human rights groups listed in Yahoo Groups as Human Rights Organizations, conducted by Ward Ricker in 2011, however, found that a large number of the groups had no position or were neutral on the abortion issue, as Amnesty International had been when USCCB was cooperating with it. See http://www.abortionreason.com/humanrightsorgsoriginal.php.

5. See Monica Duffy Toft, Daniel Philpott, and Timothy Samuel Shah, *God's Century: Resurgent Religion and Global Politics* (New York: W.W. Norton, 2011); and Paolo G. Carozza and Daniel Philpott, "The Catholic Church, Human Rights, and Democracy," *Logos* 15, no. 3 (Summer 2012).

the assumptions of secular Liberal Rights Theory but rather a practical convergence, or agreement on most, though as we will see not all, international human rights norms.[6] Historically, after the Catholic Church's fierce critique, for a variety of reasons, of secular Liberal Rights Theory in the eighteenth and nineteenth centuries, the movement toward convergence began in 1891 with modern CST on workers' rights in Pope Leo XIII's social encyclical *Rerum Novarum*. This convergence was consolidated in the 1960s in documents of Vatican II and Pope John XXIII's encyclical *Pacem in Terris*. And while *Pacem in Terris* was the most supportive statement regarding human rights by any pope by that point in time (1963), it was not the dramatically new statement that some have claimed; indeed, Thomas D. Williams notes, "of the 25 discrete rights enumerated . . . all but three are referenced to earlier popes."[7]

In fact, modern CST on human rights is part of a tradition of thought that predates and is distinct from the secular Liberal Rights Tradition traced back to Thomas Hobbes and the British Enlightenment in the seventeenth century. The Catholic Rights Tradition dates back to the defense of Native Americans' rights against the Spanish in the sixteenth century by Bartolomé de las Casas, Francisco de Vitoria, and the scholars of the Salamanca School.[8] Drawing from natural law philosophy and thought about rights in canon law, they "vigorously and systematically defended the rights of the American Indians to ownership of their lands, to equality, and to sovereignty, principally on the basis that the natural rights of the Indians were grounded in their creation as rational beings in God's image."[9] These advocates for Indian rights also argued that there

---

6. See Carozza and Philpott, "The Catholic Church"; Thomas D. Williams, "Francisco de Vitoria and the Pre-Hobbesian Roots of Natural Rights Theory," *Alpha Omega* 7, n. 1 (2004): 47–59; Roger Ruston, *Human Rights and the Image of God* (London, UK: SCM Press, 2004), 18; Zachary R. Calo, "Catholic Social Thought, Political Liberalism and the Idea of Human Rights," *Journal of Christian Legal Thought* (Fall 2011): 1–13.

7. Williams, "Francisco de Vitoria," 58, n40. See also Ruston, *Human Rights*, 18.

8. See Carozza and Philpott, "The Catholic Church"; Williams, "Francisco de Vitoria"; Ruston, *Human Rights*; and Paolo G. Carozza, "From Conquest to Constitutions: Retrieving a Latin American Tradition of the Idea of Human Rights," *Human Rights Quarterly* 25 (2003): 281–313.

9. Carozza and Philpott, "The Catholic Church," 17–18.

is one natural global human community that shares a common destiny and a common good, laying a foundation for modern international human rights thinking generally[10] and for CST on global issues such as immigration and the global economy, which do not give state sovereignty as much significance as does international human rights law.[11]

Assumptions of Catholic and Liberal Theories of Rights

While there are exceptions, we can make some generalizations about the assumptions of secular Liberal Rights Theory and CST on human rights and make some comparisons. We begin with a look at secular Liberal Rights Theory, which is notable for its commitment to individual freedom, autonomy, and equality.[12] Roger Ruston quotes Kenneth Grasso's excellent summary of the assumptions of Liberal Rights Theory:

> First, a *radical individualism*: all social institutions and relations must be understood as nothing more than the purely conventional products of free choice and on the part of naturally autonomous individuals. Social relations are conceived as something artificial, external and contractual, rather than as being rooted in man's nature as a social being. Secondly, a thoroughgoing *subjectivism*: the liberal individualist theory of man culminates in . . . a dogmatic doubt that we can ever know what is good for

10. Ibid., 17.

11. In this volume, for an exploration of CST and immigration, see chapter 5 by Daniel Groody, CSC, and Colleen Cross; for a discussion of the global economy, see chapter 4 by Linda Plitt Donaldson and Susan Crawford Sullivan.

12. We agree with Donnelly that "'Liberalism' is a complex and contested set of orientations and values" but that it does have a basic commitment to individual freedom, autonomy, and equality. Donnelly discusses different liberal theories of rights ranging from the Classical to the social democratic. See Donnelly, *Universal Human Rights*, 65, 66. Because CST does have the basic liberal respect for individual autonomy, freedom, and equality but sees the human person as a social being located in communal relations with responsibilities to the common good, we label the CST position as "solidarity" (see Pagnucco and Gichure, chapter 9 in this volume), or "communitarian liberalism," following John A. Coleman, "The Future of Catholic Social Thought," in Kenneth R. Himes, et al, *Modern Catholic Social Teaching: Commentaries and Interpretations* (Washington, DC: Georgetown University Press, 2005), 522–44.

man and woman or that there even is such a thing as the human good. Thirdly, the elevation, in the absence of a substantive theory of the good life, of *individual autonomy*, individual choice, to the status of the highest good. . . . Fourthly, that the protection of autonomy of the individual demands the construction of an economic and political order will be *neutral* [regarding the definition of the good life]. . . . Finally, on the *privatization of religion,* the systemic exclusion of religion and religiously-based values from public life.[13]

Not all secular human rights scholars and activists would hold all of these views, especially the skepticism about knowing what objective rights are and how they are rooted in the good of the person. Indeed, Marie-Bénédicte Dembour discussed four different contemporary schools of thought on human rights, one of which she calls the "Natural School," which contends that human rights "are based on 'nature,' a short cut which can stand for God, the Universe, reason, or another transcendent source. The universality of human rights is derived from their natural character. Natural scholars believe that human rights exist independently of social recognition"[14] because they are an objective reality, not a social construction. There are a number of secular scholars and activists in this school. Dembour also claims that many in another school that she calls the "Protest School" also hold a "natural" view but are more focused on the struggle for the implementation of rights than on foundational issues.[15] The assumptions of secular Liberal Rights Theory, however, which we see in what Dembour calls the "Deliberative School," have become the most widespread view in the secular human rights movement, especially in the global north; this view rejects the "natural" basis of human rights, and contends instead that "human rights come into existence through societal agreements"[16] and are essentially socially constructed. The Catholic Theory of Rights falls

13. Grasso quoted in Ruston, *Human Rights*, 10.

14. Marie-Bénédicte Dembour, "What Are Human Rights? Four Schools of Thought," *Human Rights Quarterly* 32 (2010): 3.

15. Ibid.

16. Ibid.

squarely in the "Natural School," with natural-law reasoning as a central feature of CST on rights.[17]

Ruston also provides an excellent summary of CST on human rights; these are all natural law assumptions:

> The Catholic paradigm of rights begins not from the sovereign individual, but with the social person, made in God's image, endowed with reason and freedom of choice, able to tell the difference between an objective good and evil. Personality is bestowed by relationships, the primordial one being that between the human person and God, and human nature is essentially relational. Persons are endowed with some inbuilt goals and needs that must be respected if lives are not to be ruined or degraded. These give rise to rights and duties that are two sides of

---

17. Maritain gave the classic Catholic definition of natural law, beginning with the foundational statement that all human beings share the same human nature and "that we also admit that man is a being gifted with intelligence, and who, as such, acts with understanding of what he is doing, and therefore with the power to determine for himself the ends which he pursues. On the other hand, possessed of a nature . . . which is a locus of intelligible necessities, man possesses ends which necessarily correspond to his essential constitution and which are the same for all—as all pianos, for instance, whatever their particular type and in whatever spot they may be, have as their end the production of certain attuned sounds. If they do not produce these sounds they must be tuned. . . . But since man is endowed with intelligence and determines his own ends, it is up to him to put himself in tune with the ends necessarily demanded by his nature. This means that there is, by the very virtue of human nature, an order or a disposition which human reason can discover and according to which the human will must act in order to attune itself to the essential and necessary ends of the human being. The unwritten law, or natural law, is nothing more than that." Maritain then provides an example: "[T]he prohibition of murder is grounded on or required by the essence of man. The precept: thou shalt do no murder, is a precept of natural law. Because a primordial and most general end of human nature is to preserve being . . . man insofar as he is man has a right to live" (Maritain, *Man and the State*, 88). A classic natural law argument is that friendship is something that all humans can recognize as a good in itself; see Robert P. Georges, *Conscience and Its Enemies: Confronting the Dogmas of Liberal Secularism* (Wilmington, DE: ISI Books, 2013); and John Finnis, *Natural Law & Natural Rights*, 2nd ed. (New York: Oxford University Press, 2011). For a discussion of the varieties of natural law theories, see Coleman, "The Future of Catholic Social Thought."

the same coin: for example . . . a duty to speak the truth implies a right to be given it. Rights are derived from the essential conditions for human flourishing rather than from the single value of sovereign individual choice.[18]

As indicated earlier, in CST, human beings are not free to define human rights as they please, largely because they are based on natural law, the "inbuilt goals and needs" of the human as social being that Ruston noted above. Rights claims that conflict with the natural law and divine law have no real or objective validity. As Pope John XXIII emphasized, "Every basic human right draws its authoritative force from the natural law." And therefore the church must "reject the view that the will of the individual or the group is the primary and only source of a citizen's rights and duties."[19] According to natural law, racism, for example, violates natural and divine law; Martin Luther King, Jr., invoked natural and divine law to oppose legal racial segregation in his famous *Letter from a Birmingham Jail:* "An unjust law is a code that is out of harmony with the moral law. To put it in the terms of Saint Thomas Aquinas, an unjust law is a human law that is not rooted in eternal and natural law."[20] According to natural law philosophy, the inbuilt goals and needs of the human person are to love and to live in community, not to hate. Hatred has a negative impact on the individual who hates as well as on the community. These assumptions about the source of rights differ from the social construction assumptions in secular Liberal Rights Theory.

As indicated before, CST has a social perspective that emphasizes rights *and* duties. Looking at the UDHR through the lens of CST, one sees a very limited and vague mention of duties, namely only Article 29, one of thirty Articles: "Everyone has duties to the community in which alone the free and full development of his personality is possible." That is certainly a statement consistent with CST; however, one finds in the American Dec-

18. Ruston, *Human Rights*, 11. For a brief discussion of feminist and non-Western critiques of liberal individualism, see Heather Widdows, *Global Ethics: An Introduction* (Durham, UK: Acumen, 2011).

19. *Pacem in Terris*, paragraphs 30 and 78.

20. Martin Luther King, Jr., "Letter from a Birmingham Jail [1963]" in *Loving Your Enemies* (New York: A. J. Muste Memorial Institute, n.d.), 19.

laration of the Rights and Duties of Man, adopted at the Ninth International Conference of American States in Bogota, Colombia, months before the UDHR was adopted in 1948, a much stronger position on rights and duties. For example, in the Preamble, it states: "The fulfillment of duty by each individual is a prerequisite to the rights of all. Rights and duties are intertwined in every social and political activity of man. While rights exalt individual liberty, duties express the dignity of that liberty."[21]

That quote could come straight from the *Compendium of the Social Doctrine of the Church*. The body of the American Declaration is divided into two chapters: one on Rights and one on Duties. Of its thirty-eight Articles, nine (24 percent) enumerate duties. Again, this is consistent with CST. Paolo Carozza and others argue that one major reason for the strong statement of duties in the American Declaration is in fact the influence of the Latin American Catholic Rights tradition.[22] At the very least, we can say that the American Declaration's inclusion of responsibilities is certainly in keeping with the ethos of CST.

A related important difference between the two theories of rights is CST's rejection of the "social contract"; as the *Compendium* notes: "The natural social disposition of men and women . . . makes it evident that the origin of society is not a 'contract' or 'agreement,' but in human nature itself. . . . It must not be forgotten that the ideologies of the social contract are based on a false anthropology."[23] This view does not preclude the idea that people voluntarily enter into associations that serve the common good; rather it emphasizes the natural human proclivity to associate for the common good. Jeanne Heffernan Schindler explained the fundamental Catholic critique of the individualism of the social contract:

> The basic atomism underlying [Liberal Rights Theory] becomes clear when one considers its central heuristic device . . . the social contract. The parties to the contract are individuals—not couples, not families, not kinship groups—who, before making

21. *American Declaration of the Rights and Duties of Man*, Inter-American Commission on Human Rights, Organization of American States http://www.cidh.oas .org/Basicos/English/Basic2.american%20Declaration.htm.

22. See Carozza, "From Conquest to Constitutions."

23. *Compendium*, paragraph 149, footnote 297.

their self-interested compact, view one another suspiciously as threatening to their lives and property. . . . Human associations [were] considered secondary, derivative, and conventional. Those that were not the product of conscious agreement by contract were taken to be unnatural limitations upon human freedom. . . . [The book of] Genesis by contrast, portrays man as precisely designed for communion, both with God himself and with other human beings.[24]

The individual is born into relationships and is an irreducibly social being with rights and with duties to others that go beyond the mere reciprocal respect for freedom and autonomy. The idea of atomized, competitive, mutually suspicious individuals forming agreements is unthinkable. The individual needs others in order to flourish. Even the state, born of human sociability, is a natural community with a positive role besides keeping order.[25] Life together requires the cultivation of the virtue of solidarity, which is a "firm and persevering determination to commit oneself to the common good; that is to say to the good of all and of each individual because we are all really responsible for all."[26] The common good is "the sum of social conditions which allow people, either as groups or as indi-

24. Jeanne Heffernan Schindler, "Political Theory and Catholic Themes," in *Teaching the Tradition: Catholic Themes in Academic Disciplines*, ed. John J. Piderit and Melanie M. Morey (New York: Oxford University Press, 2012). Some pre-Hobbesian Catholic scholars espoused a non-individualistic version of social contract; see Frederick Copleston, *A History of Philosophy*, vol. 3: *Late Medieval and Renaissance Philosophy* (New York: Doubleday, 1993), 335–52. Interestingly, although John Locke believed that it was a historical fact that individuals came together to form social contracts, he was open to the possibility that historically it was families and tribes, not individuals, that formed social contracts. See Copleston, *A History of Philosophy*, vol. 5: *The British Philosophers: From Hobbes to Hume* (New York: Doubleday, 1994), 134.

25. See Kenneth R. Himes, *Christianity and the Political Order: Conflict, Cooptation, and Cooperation* (Maryknoll, NY: Orbis Books, 2013), 196–98; and chapter 3 in this volume by David Coleman, "The State and Civil Society in Catholic Social Teaching."

26. Pope John Paul II, "On Social Concern," paragraph 38. For a discussion of solidarity, see chapter 9 in this volume by Ron Pagnucco and Peter Gichure, "Solidarity: A Catholic Perspective."

viduals, to reach their fulfillment more fully and more easily."[27] This emphasis on humans as social beings, on solidarity and the common good leads CST to affirm strongly economic, social, and cultural rights along with civil and political rights, exemplified by *Pacem in Terris*, paragraphs 11–27. The social emphasis in CST leads us to ask of a rights claim: "Does this rights claim have any connection with an assumption of responsibility for others and a recognition of duty that goes beyond mere recognition of reciprocal freedom?"[28]

However, CST does not espouse collectivism; as Kenneth Himes noted:

> Without denying the communal nature of the person there is also the emphasis on the dignity and uniqueness of the person. . . . Because of this aspect the Catholic vision is not easily reconciled with any collectivism that reduces the person to a cog in the wheel of the political community. Treating humankind as one great mass of people, without attention to the uniqueness of personal existence, is not an acceptable alternative to the failings of liberal theory. The communitarianism of Catholicism requires that the individual person be given attention within his or her concrete situation.[29]

While Himes and others call CST "communitarian," we follow John A. Coleman, SJ, and label it "communitarian liberalism" because of its respect for individual freedom, autonomy, and equality and its emphasis on community.[30] One example of communitarian liberalism is the individual's

---

27. Pastoral Constitution on the Church in the Modern World, paragraph 26 quoted in paragraph 1906, *Catechism of the Catholic Church* (New York: Doubleday, 1995). For a discussion of different aspects of the common good as a concept, see Coleman, "The Future of Catholic Social Thought"; and David Hollenbach, *The Common Good and Christian Ethics* (New York: Cambridge University Press, 2002).

28. Paul W. McNellis, "'Rights' vs. Common Good," *The Human Life Review* (Winter 1997): 87.

29. Himes, *Christianity and the Political Order*, 198.

30. Coleman, "The Future of Catholic Social Thought." As we noted in footnote 12, the concept of communal liberalism is essentially the same as the concept of solidarity; see chapter 9 in this volume by Pagnucco and Gichure.

freedom to oppose government laws and policies, which can both honor the autonomy and dignity of the person's conscience and serve the common good. As Cardinal Karol Wojtyla, the future Pope John Paul II, wrote: "opposition is not inconsistent with solidarity. The one who voices his opposition to the general or particular rules or regulations of the community does not thereby reject his membership. . . . It would be too easy to quote endless examples of people who contest—and thus adopt the attitude of opposition—because of their deep concern for the common good."[31] Again we are reminded of Martin Luther King, Jr., whose opposition to government laws and policies was an act of solidarity for the sake of the common good and led to the ultimate sacrifice.

International Human Rights Law and CST

Faintly resembling CST on solidarity, Article 1 of the UDHR states that human beings should "act towards one another in a spirit of brotherhood." But the principle of solidarity places duties on individuals that are not found in the UDHR. Other principles such as the universal destination of goods and the preferential option for the poor influence the Catholic Church's view of specific human rights claims in a manner that is very different from the secular orientation of the UDHR.

The church reserves the right, indeed it considers it a duty, to offer a constructive critique of the secular human rights movement. This critique manifests itself in several ways. In some instances, CST strongly affirms a specific right set forth in the UDHR but interprets that right in a very different manner. In other instances, CST challenges the validity of specific human rights claims that many in the secular human rights movement are inclined to endorse. In still other instances, the CST has a much broader interpretation of a right in comparison to the consensus norms of international human rights law. Some brief illustrations are in order.

Catholic Social Teaching on the sanctity of life and sexual morality challenge the validity of emerging rights claims that many in the secular human rights movement are increasingly inclined to endorse. There is no human rights convention that specifically recognizes the right to

31. Cardinal Karol Wojtyla, *The Acting Person* (Dordrecht, Netherlands: D. Reidel Publishing Company, 1979), 286.

abortion or to same-sex marriage. While there is no such convention, however, many in the secular human rights movement, especially in the global north, tend to interpret provisions of some conventions in a manner that supports a woman's right to terminate a pregnancy or the right of a gay or a lesbian couple to marry. With respect to abortion, many secular organizations point to Article 12 of the UN Convention to Eliminate All Forms of Discrimination against Women, which demands that states ensure to women equal access to healthcare services, including "family planning" services. The word abortion appears nowhere in this Convention; indeed, Article 12 is concerned primarily with a healthy, full-term pregnancy. In direct criticism of the pro-abortion rights view, Pope John Paul II wrote a lengthy encyclical in which he argued that abortion is another example of the human rights of the innocent, weak, and marginalized being violated.[32] Nonetheless, many in the secular human rights movement tend to construe a right to terminate a pregnancy from the overall thrust of the Convention to ensure the full development and advancement of women.

Similarly with regard to same-sex marriage, many in the secular human rights movement object to any governmental restrictions on the right to marriage as undue interference with fundamental human rights. Advocates of same-sex marriage claim to find support in Article 16 of the UDHR, which declares that "men and women of full age, without any limitation due to race, nationality or religion, have the right to marry and found a family." Article 16 does not specifically prohibit discrimination due to sexual orientation. But advocates of same-sex marriage point to Article 2

---

32. Pope John Paul II, *Evangelium Vitae* (The Gospel of Life) (Washington, DC: United States Conference of Catholic Bishops, 1995). In this encyclical, John Paul noted that human life "is sacred and inviolable at every stage and every situation; it is an indivisible good" (para. 87) and that there are many different threats to human life that must be addressed (para. 87). Abortion is an especially serious human rights violation because it is the taking of an innocent human life that is the most defenseless. To those who claim that it is not clear when life actually begins, he replied using a basic moral principle: "what is at stake is so important that, from the standpoint of moral obligation, the mere probability that a human person is involved would suffice to justify an absolutely clear prohibition of any intervention aimed at killing a human embryo." (para. 60). From the moment of conception, the unborn human being has human dignity and the right to life (para. 60).

of the UDHR which affirms that "everyone" has all the rights and freedoms set forth in the Declaration, "without distinction of any kind," a statement which would presumably encompass sexual orientation.

The church's rejection of the validity of the claim to a right to abortion and same-sex marriage obviously derives from its insistence that the natural law provides the only authoritative force for human rights. So, to paraphrase Pope John XXIII, the church cannot regard the claims that there is a right to abortion or same-sex marriage as a legitimate rights claims. Here the church's critical posture in the dialogue with those who make these claims in the secular human rights movement translates into a clear admonition: we must not trespass the moral boundaries of the natural law, the basis of rights.

By contrast, CST's position on immigrant rights is much broader than the rights guaranteed in international human rights law. Secular human rights organizations strongly favor immigrant rights, including the rights of undocumented migrants. However, the UN Convention on the Protection of the Rights of All Migrant Workers and Members of Their Families,[33] the principal human rights convention on migrant rights, generally does not afford the rights and protections to undocumented migrant workers. There may be important economic and humanitarian arguments for allowing undocumented migrants to work in a country that they have entered without authorization. The critical point here, however, is that human rights law, as it currently stands, simply does not recognize a right of anyone to enter another country in search of work.

In this instance, however, the church's insistence on the supremacy of the natural law directs the church to assert a nearly absolute right of workers, including undocumented workers, to cross national frontiers. Pope John XXIII unequivocally asserted that right in *Pacem in Terris*: "Every human being has the right to freedom of movement within the confines of his own country; and, when there are just reasons for it, the right to emigrate to other countries and take up residence there."[34] Pope John Paul II repeated this claim, and extended it to undocumented work-

---

33. *International Convention on the Protection on the Rights of All Migrant Workers and Members of Their Families*, 18 December 1990, A/RES/45/158.

34. *Pacem in Terris*, 25.

ers, as well.[35] The U.S. Conference of Catholic Bishops adopted this position and went so far as to assert that, although sovereign nations have a right to control their borders, that right is not absolute; thus, wealthy nations actually have an obligation to accommodate migration flows.[36] The human rights idea has considerably weakened the claim that states have absolute sovereignty. But CST's position about the rights of undocumented migrants and the obligations of wealthy states to accommodate migration flows virtually undermines the legal principle of state sovereignty. Here the church has adopted a position that few secular human rights organizations, which take international human rights law as their sole mandate, have dared to adopt.

The contrast between human rights law and CST is also apparent in regard to the church's teaching on personal duties to society, particularly duties toward the poor. Article 23 of the UN UDHR affirms that everyone is entitled to a standard of life that is worthy of human dignity. Article 11 of the UN Covenant on Economic, Social and Cultural Rights, which has not been ratified by the individualistic United States, demands that the state devote the maximum available resources to ensure to everyone "an adequate standard of living." This is a demand with varying interpretations that is difficult to monitor. The important point here is that the UDHR and the Covenant speak to state duties, which, even if states agreed to them, may or may not perform very well; the UDHR and the Covenant do not require an individual, or personal, duty toward the poor. To be sure, Article 1 of the UDHR affirms that human beings should act toward one another "in a spirit of brotherhood," and Article 29 states "everyone has duties to the community in which alone the free and full development of his personality is possible"; both statements fit well with CST. But Article 29 makes it clear that the only fundamental duty an individual owes to society is to refrain from infringing on the rights of others, which is

---

35. *Ecclesia in America*, 65. In defense of this position, the church cites the principle of the universal destination of goods: "all the goods belong to all people."

36. United States Conference of Catholic Bishops and the Conferencia Episcopado de Mexico, *Strangers No Longer: Together on a Journey of Hope* (2003), 36; See Mark Ensalaco, "The Catholic Church and the Immigration Crisis in the Americas," in *Ecclesiology and Exclusion: Boundaries of Being and Belonging in Postmodern Times*, ed. Dennis Doyle et al. (Maryknoll, NY: Orbis Books, 2012), 65–70.

the fundamental right posited by secular Liberal Rights Theory. The UDHR never affirms that rational and moral human beings should be charitable toward other human beings, much less that the CST principle that the "human person cannot achieve authentic selfhood except through a sincere gift of the self to the other."[37] If individuals show concern for the poor, donate to charitable organizations, or volunteer their services to those organizations, so much the better. But human rights law does not establish any personal duty to the poor. The spirit of brotherhood in the UDHR is a far cry from the gospel's call to love one's neighbor or CST's emphasis on the virtue and practice of solidarity.

From the perspective of CST, the problem with the UDHR and the conventions is not what these say but what they fail to say. In CST, duty to the poor is not only a duty that falls upon the state; it is equally a duty that falls directly on all human beings whom God endowed with reason and conscience. Herein lies the supreme importance of the principles of solidarity and preferential option for the poor. These attitudes are not optional. Pope John XXIII was forthright about this in *Pacem in Terris*: "Human society, as we here picture it, demands that men be guided by justice, respect the rights of others and do their duty. It demands, too, that they be animated by such love as will make them feel the needs of others as their own."[38] As these examples illustrate, the principles of CST offers a perspective on human rights that often challenges the axioms of the secular human rights movement. But it is important to note that in its dialogue with the modern world, the church is open to collaboration with secular NGOs in pursuit of a common goal to promote human dignity. That openness prompted the Catholic and Marianist University of Dayton to establish a human rights program curriculum and to collaborate with secular NGOs in the campaign to abolish modern-day slavery.

The Human Rights Program at the University of Dayton

In 1998, on the fiftieth anniversary of the adoption of the UDHR, the University of Dayton established one of the very first undergraduate

---

37. Himes, *Christianity and the Political Order*, 19.
38. *Pacem in Terris*, 35.

human rights studies programs in the United States. The program draws its inspiration from the university's commitment to promote respect for the inherent dignity of the human person created in the likeness and image of God. But in reality, the creation of the program was driven by the intense interest among students, especially those who had been active in the university's Campus Ministry and the Center for Social Concern, in pursuing careers with predominantly secular human rights and humanitarian organizations after graduation.

Accordingly, the Human Rights Studies (HRS) program provides students with the knowledge, skills, and values that are critical to careers with NGOs. Consequently, HRS students' engagement with social justice issues differs markedly from the experiences they may have had through their involvement in the service learning and social justice immersion activities of the Campus Ministry and Center for Social Concern. Those important activities are fundamentally oriented toward deepening students' Catholic faith; accordingly, prayer, meditations on Scripture, the celebration of Eucharist, and other religious activities are at the core of the Campus Ministry's and the Center for Social Concern's initiatives to inculcate concern for social justice among students. The primary mission of the HRS program is not to deepen student's religious faith by way of engagement in social justice activities; its mission is to educate and train future human rights professionals.

So, engagement in the HRS program is really engagement in a dialogue. HRS students must master the norms and methods of the secular human rights movement. Moreover, students must be intellectually open to understanding secular human rights NGOs' perspectives on human dignity and rights. For example, students must be prepared to understand secular positions regarding women's rights (including reproductive rights such as the right to use contraceptives for family planning or to prevent the spread of HIV/AIDs), the right to same-sex marriage, and a host of other human rights issues. These positions may be controversial to many Catholics, but they are the positions of many secular human rights NGOs.

The dialogue is not one-sided. The HRS program does not ask students to dismiss the validity of CST on human rights in order to prepare them for careers in the secular world. Instead, CST is intentionally integrated into the curriculum in a way that invites students to reflect on the vitally important contributions of CST to a deeper appreciation of human dignity and rights. This is especially important for HRS students who come to the program without knowledge of CST. Thus, students graduate from the program with deep knowledge of the principles of international human rights law and the advocacy strategies of human rights NGOs like Human Rights Watch. They also emerge with knowledge of the principles of CST and the humanitarian work of Catholic entities like Catholic Relief Services, and the U.S. Conference of Catholic Bishops Migration and Refugee Services. In this regard, the HRS program advances the mission of the Peace and Justice Committee of the Association of Catholic Colleges and Universities to promote CST in Catholic Higher Education.[39]

The ability of HRS students to apply secular human rights norms as well as the principles of CST to specific human rights issues has been put to the test in the real world. The experience of HRS students in the movement to abolish human trafficking provides a clear example of this.

In December 2011 the governor of Ohio signed Senate Bill 235 (SB 235) into law, making human trafficking a criminal offense in the state. In her public remarks at the ceremony, the state senator who had sponsored the legislation publicly acknowledged the role that the University of Dayton, and, above all, HRS students, played in securing the law's enactment. The story of SB 235 began several years earlier.

In 2009 the HRS program convened a major conference on human trafficking for the purpose of "stirring society's conscience to take action against human trafficking."[40] In 2010 the University of Dayton hosted a meeting of the Coalition of Catholic Organizations against Human Trafficking, a coalition sponsored by the U.S. Conference of Catholic Bishops Migration and Refugee Services (MRS). These conferences ignited intense interest in the problem of human trafficking among HRS students, who promptly formed a new student organization, the New Abolitionist Movement (NAM). The NAM adopted the basic advocacy principles of the Campaign to Rescue and Restore Victims of Human Trafficking and began working closely with area anti-trafficking groups. But the NAM

---

39. See Association of Catholic Colleges and Universities, "Catholic Higher Education and Catholic Social Teaching: A Vision Statement."

40. The HRS program published the Dayton Human Trafficking Accords Declaration at the conclusion of the 2009 Conference, "Trafficking is Slavery."

was also attentive to the advocacy positions of MRS and other Catholic agencies.[41]

Beginning in 2010, the NAM began to lobby the Ohio state legislature to enact SB 235. At that time, SB 235 was stalled in the Senate's judiciary committee because of some senator's concerns about the effect that the bill's enactment would place on the state's criminal justice system. Throughout the year, students met with senators to work out compromise language to allay the senators' concerns. This was an impressive exercise in real-world legislative advocacy. Students had to study the provisions of the draft bill, compare those provisions to other state laws, and scrutinize amendments put forward during the negotiating process to ensure those amendments did not seriously weaken the bill or jeopardize its enactment. Student engagement was so important that the NAM's founder was invited to testify before the Senate judiciary committee prior to a final vote on SB 235. But just prior to the judiciary committee's hearing, a prominent anti-trafficking organization publicly criticized the final version of the bill and introduced a controversial amendment that would have defined solicitation of prostitution as a criminal human trafficking offense. The action angered senators who were on the verge of voting for the bill, because the amendment would compel the state to prosecute and imprison people for acts state law defines as misdemeanor offenses. The controversy created a formidable dilemma that compelled the NAM to weigh pragmatic policy considerations against deep moral principles. On the one hand, if the NAM endorsed the last-minute amendment defining solicitation of prostitution as human trafficking, the Senate judiciary committee would certainly not enact SB 235. On the other hand, if the NAM refused to endorse the amendment in order to gain enactment of the bill, it might appear that the NAM tacitly condoned prostitution.

In the end, the NAM took the position that criminal prosecution is not an effective way to address the complex problem of prostitution. Here the NAM was able to apply principles set forth at the conclusion of a Vatican conference on prostitution, which called for a multi-dimensional

41. The campaign was launched under the auspices of the U.S. Department of Health and Human Services (HHS), after the enactment of the federal Trafficking Victims Protection Act.

approach to "liberate women of the street."[42] This approach demands outreach to women trapped in the illicit sex industry by poverty and substance abuse, as well as the authentic conversion of men who purchase sex. To be sure, it is important that society enact laws protecting women against the scourge of prostitution and trafficking, but simply compelling those who solicit prostitution to "face the full rigours of the law" cannot end this scourge. It is more important to bring about real change in society to shift attention to the "client" as an element of the consumer system underlying the sex trade.[43] In the end, the NAM's rejection of the amendment about solicitation in their judiciary committee testimony, and its courage to take on a powerful Washington NGO, helped convince senators to vote for SB 235.

The episode offers a valuable lesson about the contribution that CST on social justice can make to policy debates about serious social problems. This is a lesson in the value of dialogue. There are limits, however, to dialogue and collaboration. In 2011 the U.S. Department of Health and Human Services (HHS), the sponsor of the Rescue and Restore Campaign, issued regulations requiring all agencies that received federal funding to provide victims of human trafficking with comprehensive reproductive health services, including access to contraception and possibly abortion. The Migration and Refugee Service of the U.S. Conference of Catholic Bishops, which had an exclusive contract with HHS for nearly a decade, raised important moral objections to this regulation. Apparently as a result of these public objections, HHS terminated its contract with MRS.[44] The loss of federal funding was a serious setback to MRS's anti-trafficking program. But MRS compliance with the HHS regulation would have required the church to compromise a fundamental tenet of Catholic moral teaching. The loss of HHS funding was less damaging than the loss of the moral high ground.

42. See the Pontifical Council for the Pastoral Care of Migrants and Itinerant People, "International Meeting of Pastor Care for the Liberation of Women of the Street: Final Document" (Rome, 21 June, 2005), para. 12.

43. Ibid., para. 5, 15 (c), 16 and 27.

44. Prior to the termination of the contract, the American Civil Liberties Union filed suit in federal court to block HSS funding for MRS's anti-trafficking programs on the grounds of separation of church and state.

Conclusion

The UDHR was largely a practical reaction to the horrors of World War II; there was no consensus among the delegates on a philosophical or religious basis for it. The underlying tensions among the different philosophical and theological understandings of human rights are seen in some of the differences between CST on human rights and the Liberal Rights Theory that is commonly held in the secular human rights movement. For Catholics, principal affirmation found in UN human rights agreements that recognition of the inherent dignity of the human person is the foundation for freedom, justice, and peace in the world, is an obvious truth the Catholic Church has taught for centuries.[45] While there are some tensions with Liberal Rights Theory, Catholics have become an important part of the human rights movement that has emerged since the 1960s because it advances a crucial objective that is closely connected to the church's mission to create "a new social, economic and political order, founded on the dignity and freedom of every human person, to be brought about in peace, justice and solidarity."[46]

Discussion Questions

1. Looking at the Preamble of the Universal Declaration of Human Rights, what are some reasons given for respecting human rights?

2. In the UDHR, Articles 22–27 are economic, social, and cultural rights, while the other Articles are largely considered to be civil and political rights. Which category of rights do you think is more important? Why?

3. What do you see as some of the strengths and weaknesses of Catholic Social Teaching on human rights?

4. What do you see as some of the strengths and weaknesses of Liberal Rights Theory?

---

45. UDHR, Preamble para.1.
46. *Compendium*, 19.

5. What points of convergence and difference do you see between these two approaches? How would you deal with the differences?

6. What do you think are some of the most important human rights issues facing the world today and what do you think the church can do to address them?

Chapter 9

Ron Pagnucco and
Peter Gichure

Solidarity: A Catholic Perspective

We come across many uses of the word "solidarity" today—ethnic solidarity, worker solidarity, solidarity with the poor, global solidarity—the list goes on. Some analysts discuss solidarity in a descriptive way, as the degree of unity in a group. Others focus on solidarity as a moral duty of support for those in need. As used in much of the scholarly literature, the concept of solidarity includes both a descriptive (empirical) dimension and moral (normative) dimension.

In this chapter we will explore the concept of solidarity in Catholic Social Teaching (CST) and locate that understanding in the broader discussion of solidarity by philosophers, political theorists, and social scientists. We will close the chapter with a concrete example of global solidarity between the University of Notre Dame and The Catholic University of Eastern Africa in Nairobi, Kenya.

The definition of solidarity we use in this chapter includes both empirical and moral dimensions. Drawing from the scholarly literature, we define solidarity as *a certain type of relationship that has the following components: the relationship is seen by its participants as being one of interdependence and unity; in which there is shared identity, interests, feelings of belonging (a "we feeling") and mutual moral obligations.*[1] One way

---

1. Our discussion of solidarity is general. For discussions of the three specific types of solidarity—social, civic, and political—see Kurt Bayertz, ed., *Solidarity*

to determine with whom we see ourselves in solidarity is to answer the questions: "Should we support them? Should we support us?"[2] The "us" is our solidary group, or "in-group." The "them" is an "out-group" with which we do not share solidarity. Exactly who and what "them" is, and what, if any, moral obligations we have to "them" is often a topic of much debate within solidary groups. As we will see, how exclusive or inclusive a solidary group is can also be a topic of debate among scholars who study solidarity.

The philosopher Sally Scholz notes that solidarity "is neither individualism nor communalism but blends elements of both. . . . [W]hile not losing the individual in the community, [solidarity] emphasizes the bonds with others or interdependence. . . . The good of the community is tied up with the good of the individual and vice versa in solidarity."[3] Catholic Social Teaching shares this view. Scholz also points out the unique nature of solidarity's moral obligations, noting that "perhaps the most distinguishing [characteristic of solidarity], is that solidarity entails positive moral obligations. Political philosophy has historically been preoccupied with articulating rights and privileges of citizens or describing negative duties."[4] Rights and negative duties usually entail "freedom from" something, noninterference, such as in the duty not to block free speech or assembly. The concept of solidarity includes respect for such rights and negative duties. The positive duties of solidarity, however, require action to improve a situation, such as action to feed the hungry or to otherwise actively contribute to the community's well-being. Respect for the individual's freedom and autonomy is combined with a recognition of inter-

---

(Dordrecht, Netherlands: Kluwer Academic Publishers, 1999); Dariusz Dobrzański, ed., *The Idea of Solidarity: Philosophical and Social Contexts* (Washington, DC: The Council for Research in Value and Philosophy, 2011); and Sally Scholz, *Political Solidarity* (University Park: Pennsylvania State University Press, 2008).

2. Stephen Reicher and S. Alexander Haslam, "Beyond Help: A Social Psychology of Collective Solidarity and Social Cohesion," in *The Psychology of Prosocial Behavior*, ed. Stefan Sturmer and Mark Snyder (Malden, MA: Wiley-Blackwell, 2010), 296. Later in their essay Reicher and Haslam go on to note that the second question will seem "superfluous even to ask, for giving and receiving support from each other would seem to be part-and-parcel of the very nature of being 'us' " (301).

3. Scholz, *Political Solidarity*, 18–19.

4. Ibid., 19.

dependence and its responsibilities. This understanding of the positive moral obligations of solidarity is shared by CST.

As indicated earlier, scholars debate whether or not we are psychologically capable of solidarity with individuals and groups beyond the boundaries of our solidary or in-groups. Scholars also debate the ethical issues involved: do we have the same moral obligations to people in distant lands as we have to people in our own families, groups, or countries? We will explore the two basic schools of thought, what we are calling the "Bounded Solidarity" and the "Cosmopolitan Solidarity" schools, on the descriptive/empirical and moral/normative issues, and show where CST fits in.

Theories of Solidarity: Bounded Solidarity and Cosmopolitan Solidarity Schools

Influenced by the work of philosopher Nigel Dower,[5] we identify two basic schools of thought on solidarity and call them the "Bounded Solidarity" school and the "Cosmopolitan Solidarity" school. Scholars in these two schools differ on various issues, most notably on the capabilities of humans for broad and far-reaching solidarity, and on whether or not there is one moral community with moral obligations of all to all.

5. Nigel Dower, *World Ethics*, 2nd ed. (Edinburgh: Edinburgh University Press, 2007), 25. We are using the label of "Bounded Solidarity" school for the theories Dower labels "communitarian." Since CST is sometimes called "communitarian" and does not fit Dower's description of communitarian, we decided to use a different term to avoid confusion. For a discussion of the theories Dower calls communitarian, see Dower, *World Ethics*, 25. We are using the term "Cosmopolitan Solidarity" school for the theories that Dower labels "cosmopolitan." While Dower does not include CST by name under his cosmopolitan label, he does include Natural Law and Thomas Aquinas. Several CST scholars have noted that CST has much in common with cosmopolitan theory; see, for example, Kenneth R. Himes, *Christianity and the Political Order: Conflict, Cooptation and Cooperation* (Maryknoll, NY: Orbis Books, 2013). Drew Christiansen, "Commentary on *Pacem in Terris* (Peace on Earth)," in *Modern Catholic Social Teaching: Commentaries & Interpretations*, ed. Kenneth R. Himes, Lisa Sowle Cahill, Charles E. Curran, and Thomas Shannon (Washington, DC: Georgetown University Press, 2005); and chapter 7 by Gerard Powers in this volume. We put CST in the Cosmopolitan Solidarity school.

We begin with a look at the "Bounded Solidarity" school, which holds that humans are not capable of a broad-reaching solidarity, and that there are no universal moral obligations or standards such as universal human rights—all solidary relationships and moral obligations are local and limited or "bounded."

Conversely, the "Cosmopolitan Solidarity" school holds that humans are capable of global solidarity, and that humans are one moral community with obligations to each other, including distant, unknown others. In the Cosmopolitan Solidarity school there are two different models of how local and national groups fit (or don't fit) into global solidarity. Drawing from the philosopher Kwame Anthony Appiah,[6] we call these the "Impartial" solidarity model and the "Partial" (or "Rooted") solidarity model. Catholic Social Teaching falls into the Cosmopolitan Solidarity school and uses a Partial solidarity model.

Bounded Solidarity

Philosopher Kurt Bayertz discusses the views of the Bounded Solidarity school, which includes historically well-known scholars. Bayertz cites the work of the prominent eighteenth-century philosopher David Hume, who "emphasized that sympathy and benevolence do not usually extend beyond the intimate sphere: we evince them undividedly for the members of our family and our friends, less for our neighbors and acquaintances, hardly at all for the inhabitants of our town or our compatriots, and towards the inhabitants of distant continents we are ultimately indifferent."[7] Solidarity and moral obligations are limited because of human capabilities. The philosopher Simon Derpmann observed that some scholars consider transnational solidarity "a desirable, but nonetheless unrealistic vision overestimating. . .the capacities for human affiliation with the distant [other]."[8] Bayertz provides a good summary of what he and other scholars in the Bounded Solidarity school see as the empirical reality: "One is not 'solidary' with just anybody, but only with the other members

6. Kwame Anthony Appiah, *Cosmopolitanism: Ethics in a World of Strangers* (New York: W.W. Norton, 2006).

7. Bayertz, "Four Uses of Solidarity" in *Solidarity*, 8.

8. Simon Derpmann, "Solidarity as a Moral Idea and Cosmopolitan Obligations," in Dobrzański, *The Idea of Solidarity*, 105.

of the particular community to which one believes oneself to belong. A differentiation between those belonging to 'us' and everybody else is thus prerequisite; in most cases, one is only solidary with the former."[9]

Moral obligations follow the (supposed) empirical reality that people have solidarity with some groups and no solidarity with other groups and that moral obligations are based on the degree of solidarity, or lack thereof. Solidary or in-group relationships usually have their own norms, customs, and mutual obligations. Bayertz makes an argument typical of the Bounded Solidarity school: the existence of attachments to particular relationships and groups leads him to reject any universalistic ethic or obligation that proposes that "each individual is morally obliged to help all other individuals without differentiation"[10] since, he claims, humans do not have a sense of solidarity with the human race as a whole, and morality "cannot be reduced to universal [and impartial] principles since [morality] includes particular reasons and obligations to act."[11] Bayertz does argue for the universal ethical obligation of refraining from doing harm,[12] but he does not see a universal obligation to prevent harm. One philosopher in this school made the notable claim that if one does not have a relationship with starving children in Africa, one does not have a moral obligation to help them.[13]

Nigel Dower summarizes the theories in what we call the Bounded Solidarity school by saying that generally these theories reject ethical universalism and limit "the domain of one's duty (or at least primary duty) to those to whom one stands in some meaningful relation, the relation being meaningful if it is informed by such diverse factors as sentiment, affection, shared traditions, convention, reciprocity or contract. . . . These theories may be called 'bounded' or 'closed' theories of ethics. . . . [They] have a tendency either to deny the existence of global obligations or, in terms of what the theory says, regard obligations at that level as

9. Bayertz, "Four Uses of Solidarity," in *Solidarity*, 4; see also Piotr Boltuc, "Solidarity and the Shape of Moral Space," in Dobrzański, *The Idea of Solidarity*, 83–96.

10. Bayertz, "Four Uses of Solidarity," in *Solidarity*, 8–9.

11. Ibid., 5. See also the essays in Dobrzański, *The Idea of Solidarity.*

12. Bayertz, "Four Uses of Solidarity," in *Solidarity*, 9.

13. Peter Singer, *One World: The Ethics of Globalization*, 2nd ed. (New Haven: Yale University Press, 2004), 159.

marginal and relatively unimportant."[14] In our terminology, bounded solidarity includes bounded ethics.

Cosmopolitan Solidarity

The empirical and ethical claims of the school of thought we are calling "Cosmopolitan Solidarity" are quite different from those of the Bounded Solidarity school. Proponents of Cosmopolitan Solidarity contend that humans are capable of broad, far-reaching solidarity, identifying with and caring for distant, unknown others and humanity as a whole. In other words, humans are capable of expanding their in-group boundaries. There is significant empirical evidence to support this claim. Political scientist Lawrence Wilde reports that in a 2005 World Values Survey conducted in fifty-seven countries, 77 percent of people replying either agreed or strongly agreed that they saw themselves as world citizens.[15] The respondents combined the world citizen identity with national and/or local identities. Research on political altruism and prosocial behavior has found that people have been willing to help people they don't know, near and far geographically, and can have very inclusive definitions of who is a member of their group.[16] In their review of studies on in-group and out-group helping, psychologists Stefan Sturmer and Mark Snyder note "the amazing potential of common group membership to foster the expansion of empathy and helping to people one has never seen before or who are geographically distant but to whom one feels psycho-

---

14. Dower, *World Ethics*, 25.

15. Lawrence Wilde, *Global Solidarity* (Edinburgh, Scotland: Edinburgh University Press, 2013), 156.

16. See Marco Giugni and Florence Passy, eds., *Political Altruism? Solidarity Movements in International Perspective* (Lanham, MD: Rowman & Littlefield, 2001); Sturmer and Snyder, *The Psychology of Prosocial Behavior*; Luis Cabrera, *The Practice of Global Citizenship* (New York: Cambridge University Press, 2010); Ulrich Wagner, Linda R. Tropp, Gillian Finchilescu, and Colin Tredoux, *Improving Intergroup Relations: Building on the Legacy of Thomas F. Pettigrew* (Malden, MA: Blackwell-Wiley, 2008); and Kai J. Jonas and Amélie Mummendey, "Positive Intergroup Relations: From Reduced Outgroup Rejection to Outgroup Support," in Wagner et al., *Improving Intergroup Relations*, 220.

logically connected through perceptions of similarities on the basis of a common 'we.'"[17]

The Cosmopolitan Solidarity school includes CST and other theories that "advocate some kind of world ethic for individuals, as belonging to one global moral community—where community is defined in terms of the claimed moral relations, not in terms of established traditions, felt relations and shared values in practice."[18] Unlike the Bounded Solidarity school, the Cosmopolitan Solidarity school contends that humans are psychologically capable of global solidarity and identifying as world citizens or members of the global human community. The Cosmopolitan Solidarity school holds that all human beings are of equal value and it espouses universal ethical standards and rights for all. The Universal Declaration of Human Rights is a good example of a universal standard of rights.

Since the Cosmopolitan Solidarity school claims there is one human moral community that transcends all local, bounded communities, what does this mean for relationships and moral obligations in local communities and the nation-state? What moral obligations, if any, do we have to them? There are two different models of Cosmopolitan Solidarity addressing these and related questions: the impartial solidarity model and the partial solidarity model.

Impartial Cosmopolitan Solidarity

For the most part, advocates of the impartial model of cosmopolitan solidarity, writes sociologist Craig Calhoun, "offer no new account of solidarity save the obligations of each human being to all others, they give little weight to 'belonging,' to the notion that social relationships

---

17. Stefan Sturmer and Mark Snyder, "Helping 'Us' versus 'Them': Towards a Group-Level Theory of Helping and Altruism with and across Group Boundaries," 33–58, in Sturmer and Snyder, *The Psychology of Prosocial Behavior*, 55.

18. Dower, *World Ethics*, 25. For a critique of Cosmopolitanism, see Gillian Brock, ed., *Cosmopolitanism Versus Non-Cosmopolitanism: Critiques, Defenses, Reconceptualization* (New York: Oxford University Press, 2013). One may accept the moral equality of all human beings and still believe members of one's family, group, or country deserve preferential treatment and that one has moral obligations to them that supercede all others.

might be as basic as individuals."[19] In fact, the impartial model is based largely on liberal individualism; advocates of the impartial model place emphasis on "justice among individuals. They tend to denigrate or at least marginalize national and more local loyalties, to ignore religious belonging, and in general to treat individuals as essentially discrete and equivalent."[20] For example, philosopher Peter Singer states: "The interests of all persons ought to count equally, and geographic location and citizenship make no intrinsic difference to the rights and obligations of individuals."[21] Singer does write that partial behaviors can have impartial justifications; for example, he would agree with other advocates of impartial solidarity that "it is right for parents to care most for their own children, but only because this will ensure the best possible global child-care arrangements."[22] Drawing from Calhoun's work, we can see that the impartial model, "minimizes attention to social solidarity in favor of analysis framed in terms of individuals and the universal."[23]

Partial Cosmopolitan Solidarity

The partial solidarity model has a positive view of local belonging and sees it as compatible with global solidarity. Simon Derpmann observed that being a member of the local community "may enable the satisfaction of morally legitimate desires. It may be important . . . to belong to such a community in order to lead a fulfilling life. If this is true . . . one needs good reasons to negate the communal obligations that go along with it."[24] Like we would find in the Bounded Solidarity school, this is a positive recognition of the importance of local belonging for human well-being.

---

19. Craig Calhoun, "'Belonging' in the Cosmopolitan Imaginary," *Ethnicities* 3, no. 4(2003): 535.

20. Craig Calhoun, "Cosmopolitan Liberalism and Its Limits," in *European Cosmopolitanism in Question*, ed. Roland Robertson and Anne Sophie Krossa (New York: Palgrave and Macmillan, 2012), 112.

21. Peter Singer, "Poverty, Facts, and Political Philosophies: A Debate with Andrew Kuper," in *Global Responsibilities: Who Must Deliver on Human Rights?*, ed. Andrew Kuper (New York: Routledge, 2005), 173.

22. Calhoun, "'Belonging,'" 538. See also Peter Singer, *The Life You Save: Acting Now to End World Poverty* (New York: Random House, 2009).

23. Calhoun, "Cosmopolitan Liberalism," 116.

24. Derpmann, "Solidarity as a Moral Idea," 111.

However, Derpmann goes on to argue that humans are capable of "mutually non-exclusive solidarities"[25] and that "cosmopolitanism can be understood to be compatible with the evolution of *multiple loyalties.* Those loyalties are neither exclusively universal, nor only national or local, but represent different layers of identification of a person. . . . A cosmopolitan community with cosmopolitan obligations allows for communal obligations within it."[26]

The preceding view expressed by Derpmann summarizes well the Cosmopolitan Solidarity school's partial solidarity model, the model used in CST. Indeed, what he wrote could have come from a CST text.

Catholic Social Teaching on Solidarity

We begin our discussion of CST on solidarity with a look at how CST combines local and national belonging with global solidarity. In CST, human beings are social beings that naturally form groups ranging from the family to the nation-state and that are capable of solidarity with the global human community. Local and national relationships can actually help people develop global solidarity. As Craig Calhoun observed, "thinking in terms of the abstract equivalence of human beings is helpful—in theories of justice and human rights, for example. . . . Cosmopolitanism becomes richer and stronger if approached in terms of connections rather than (or in addition to) equivalence."[27] Calhoun then points to the Catholic Church as an example of the successful combination of global identity and solidarity with local parish and national church identities and solidarities. Calhoun claims that the Catholic Church "offers a reminder of more general importance: the organizations, networks, and pathways by which we transcend locality are still particular, specific—to people, dimensions of human life, ways of bringing some human beings closer rather than others."[28] In the same line of thought, theologian Dorian Llywelyn observed that the church respects ethnic and national

25. Ibid., 110.

26. Ibid., 111. See also Appiah, *Cosmopolitanism*, xviii; and Calhoun, *Cosmopolitan Liberalism*, 118–22.

27. Calhoun, "Cosmopolitanism in the Modern Social Imaginary," 113.

28. Ibid., 113.

belonging: "since grace does not efface nature, Christianity does not wipe out ethnicity or nationality. It does, however, relativize it."[29]

Among the "organizations, networks and pathways by which we transcend locality" we find various church programs specifically designed to foster global solidarity, such as parish partnerships between parishes in the United States and in developing countries, and the Catholic Relief Services Global Solidarity Partnership program, through which dioceses in the United States and developing countries establish partnerships.[30] All of these programs celebrate, rather than downplay, ethnic and national belonging and cultures even as they transcend them.

A discussion of the nation-state shows us key differences between the impartial and partial models. Pope John Paul II wrote: "The term 'nation' designates a community based in a given territory and distinguished from other nations by its culture. Catholic social doctrine holds that the family and the nation are both natural societies, not the product of mere convention. . . . [T]he nation cannot be replaced by the State, even though the nation tends naturally to establish itself as a State."[31] Citizens have a duty to work for the common good of their nation-state while avoiding an unhealthy, exclusive nationalism.[32] Noting growing interdependence through globalization, John Paul called for a global solidarity that respected but looked beyond local and national loyalties and obligations: "New ethical choices are necessary; *a new world conscience must be created*; each of us, without denying his origin and the roots of his family, his people and his nation, or the obligations arising therefrom, must regard himself as a mem-

29. Dorian Llywelyn, *Toward a Catholic Theology of Nationality* (Lanham, MD: Lexington Books, 2010), 288.

30. See Catholic Relief Services, *Global Solidarity Partnership Conference Report, June 1–2, 2005, CRS Headquarters, Baltimore, Maryland* (Baltimore: Catholic Relief Services, 2005); William Vos, Agnes Kithikii, and Ron Pagnucco, "A Case Study in Global Solidarity: The St. Cloud-Homa Bay Partnership," *Journal for Peace & Justice Studies* 17, no. 1 (2008): 45–60; Janel Kragt Bakker, *Sister Churches: American Congregations and Their Partners Abroad* (New York: Oxford University Press, 2013).

31. Pope John Paul II, *Memory and Identity: Conversations at the Dawn of a Millennium* (New York: Rizzoli International Publications, 2005), 70.

32. Ibid., 67.

ber of this great family, the world community. . . . This means that the worldwide common good requires *a new solidarity without frontiers*."[33]

The differences between CST's view and the impartial solidarity model are illustrated by comparing Pope John Paul's and Peter Singer's views of the nation-state. Singer, taking the impartial view, wrote, "the modern idea that we owe special loyalty to our national community is not based on a community that exists independently of the way we think about ourselves. If . . . the modern idea of the nation rests on a community we imagine ourselves to be part of, rather than one that we really are part of, then it is also possible for us to imagine ourselves to be part of a different community. That fits well with the suggestion that the complex set of developments we refer to as globalization should lead us to reconsider the moral significance we currently place on national boundaries."[34] Singer then asks if it would be better if "we begin to consider ourselves as members of the world"[35] instead of the nation-state. The nation-state is socially constructed, not a "real" community, and individuals can re-imagine themselves as members of the global community; obligations are based on the needs of others, and national boundaries are morally irrelevant, imagined fictions. In his excellent discussion of Singer's work and impartial universal standards, theologian Charles Camosy notes that CST contends that we have real, not imagined, interdependent relations and moral obligations in the groups and nation-state of which we are members, and that global interdependence is real as well and globalization "simply highlights this already existing relationship."[36] Camosy continues: "The Church hardly needs to "imagine" the concept of a transnational community, because the Church *is* such a community."[37] One can experience this transnational reality in the local parish.

---

33. Pope John Paul II, *John Paul II in America: Talks Given on the Papal Tour September 1987* (Boston: Daughters of St. Paul, 1987), 294.

34. Singer, *One World*, 170–71.

35. Ibid., 171.

36. Charles C. Camosy, *Peter Singer and Christian Ethics: Beyond Polarization* (New York: Cambridge University Press, 2012), 166.

37. Ibid., 167.

Interdependence, Moral Virtue, and Solidarity

We have discussed the basic ideas of the Cosmopolitan Solidarity school and of its two models—the impartial solidarity model and the partial solidarity model—which CST holds. We have seen how CST integrates local and national solidarities into global solidarity and how the church itself is a concrete example of this integration. Now we look at other important aspects of CST on solidarity. We begin by recognizing the broad-reaching importance of the concept of solidarity in CST. As the *Compendium* notes: "Solidarity is one of the basic principles of the entire social teaching of the Church."[38] This principle has consistently appeared in modern CST under one guise or another since 1891.[39] Echoing the current understanding of solidarity noted by Scholz earlier in this chapter, Matthew Lamb writes that beginning in the late nineteenth century, the term "solidarity" "was adopted from labor-union movements by Catholic social theorists. . . . They used 'solidarity' to differentiate Catholic social theory from the modern theories of liberalism [liberal individualism] and communism."[40] The importance and broad applicability of the concept of solidarity in CST is illustrated by its use in many of the other chapters of our book.

In CST, solidarity includes an empirical dimension and a moral dimension. Empirically, the human is a social being that is born into interdependent relationships and needs others to be fully human, and globalization is increasing interdependence among peoples. Solidarity is also a moral principle to guide the conduct of our relationships with others. While all the components of solidarity we noted at the beginning of this chapter are included in the CST concept of solidarity, CST gives the greatest emphasis to the moral aspect—in particular, to solidarity as

---

38. Pontifical Council for Justice and Peace, *Compendium of the Social Doctrine of the Church* (Washington, DC: United States Conference of Catholic Bishops, 2005), para. 194, fn. 421.

39. *Compendium*, para. 194, fn. 421.

40. Matthew Lamb, "Solidarity," in *The New Dictionary of Catholic Social Thought*, ed. Judith A. Dwyer (Collegeville, MN: Liturgical Press, 1994), 909. See also Franz Mueller, "Solidarism," in the same volume.

a virtue.[41] John Paul II saw the empirical reality of growing interdependence through globalization as a key component of global solidarity, but his—and the CST—definition of solidarity emphasized its moral aspect: "a firm and persevering determination to commit oneself to the common good . . . to the good of all and of each individual, because we are all really responsible for all."[42] The "common good" is defined in CST as "the sum of social conditions which allow people, either as groups or as individuals, to reach their fulfillment more fully and easily."[43]

A concrete example of global solidarity can be found in the Catholic Relief Services' Parish Partnership Manual. The guidelines for solidarity-based partnerships between parishes in the developed and developing world are: (1) emphasize relationships over resources; (2) practice mutuality and equality; (3) seek to give and receive, learn and teach; (4) work to change unjust systems and structures; (5) deepen our faith by experiencing the universal Catholic Church.[44] Global solidarity is based on relationship-building, equality, and mutuality—we are to become friends, and each of us has gifts we can share with others for the good of all, whatever those gifts may be. Hopefully, such concrete transnational connections will help participants see themselves more clearly as members of the human family.

The principle that each of us belongs to the global human family and that we have moral obligations to one another has been a part of CST for many centuries. Today's increasing interdependence through globalization, however, creates an urgent need for solidarity. As the *Compendium* notes, this growing interdependence "is the determining factor for relations in the modern world in the economic, cultural, political and religious sense"[45] and provides an opportunity for negative moral acts such as exploitation and for the positive moral responses of solidarity. Solidarity is both a

41. *The Catechism of the Catholic Church* defines "virtue" in the following way: "The human virtues are suitable dispositions of the intellect and will that govern our acts, order our passions, and guide our conduct in accordance with reason and faith" (869). For a broad discussion of solidarity ethics, see Rebecca Todd Peters, *Solidarity Ethics: Transformation in a Globalized World* (Minneapolis, MN: Fortress Press, 2014).

42. *Compendium*, para. 193.

43. Ibid., para. 164.

44. Catholic Relief Services, *Parish Partnership Manual* (Baltimore: Catholic Relief Services, n.d.), 2.

45. *Compendium*, para. 443.

personal virtue that shapes an individual's actions, and a social virtue that shapes the actions of groups and nations; it includes the commitment to genuinely seek the good of the other, whomever and wherever they may be, to the point of being willing to sacrifice for the good of the other. As a social virtue, solidarity leads us to transform structures of sin, such as unjust trade policies favoring wealthy nations, into *"structures of solidarity* through the creation or appropriate modification of laws, market regulations, and juridical systems."[46]

While CST advocates solidarity with the entire human family, and affirms local and national belonging as legitimate and valuable in that broader context, it gives special attention to the poor and the oppressed. We have seen how CST justifies partial local and national solidarities in the context of a universal, global solidarity. How does it justify its partial preferential option for the poor and oppressed? Solidarity with the poor and oppressed is especially important in order to bring them into full community with everyone else. As theologian Marie Vianney Bilgrien writes: "Solidarity . . . searches out the poorest and the most oppressed because they are the clearest manifestation of where justice is lacking."[47] Indeed, poverty and oppression are manifestations of a lack of solidarity. Bilgrien, however, goes on to remind us of solidarity's broader meaning: "Solidarity also forces the virtuous person to see the victim and the executioner, the oppressed and the oppressor, the poorer and the one who causes the unjust poverty and to accept both as equal members of the same human family, worthy of dignity."[48] Solidarity always means love of everyone, including oppressors and enemies.

Similarly, everyone needs to collaborate in order for problems such as poverty to be resolved. The *Catechism* notes:

> Socio-economic problems can be resolved only with the help of all the forms of solidarity: solidarity of the poor among them-

---

46. Ibid., para. 193.

47. Marie Vianney Bilgrien, *Solidarity: A Principle, an Attitude, a Duty? or the Virtue for an Interdependent World?* (New York: Peter Lang, 1999), 254. See also Elias Omondi Opongo and Agbonkhianmeghe E. Orobator, *Faith Doing Justice: A Manual for Social Analysis, Catholic Social Teachings and Social Justice* (Nairobi, Kenya: Paulines Publications Africa, 2007).

48. Ibid., 254.

selves, between rich and poor, of workers among themselves, between employers and employees in a business, solidarity among nations and peoples. International solidarity is a requirement of the moral order; world peace depends in part on this.[49]

In some ways the above statement seems quite utopian: certainly we know of many cases in which the rich do not collaborate with the poor, and employers do not collaborate with employees, to achieve justice. CST, however, does not have a particularly naïve or utopian view of human nature. As the *Compendium* states, the "*social nature of humans does not automatically lead to communion among persons, to the gift of self. Because of pride and selfishness, man discovers in himself the seeds of asocial behavior, impulses leading him to close himself within his own individuality and to dominate his neighbor.*"[50] Also, we noted earlier that CST discusses structures of sin; these unjust social, political, and economic arrangements emerge from pride and selfishness, and need to be replaced with structures of solidarity, including just laws, market regulations, and juridical systems, among other things. Similarly, CST does recognize in its support for just war and humanitarian military intervention (Responsibility to Protect) that violence can legitimately be used for the sake of justice in certain kinds of conflicts, though CST has difficulty accepting the concept of "just revolution."[51] Nevertheless, in CST conflict is played down in favor of collaboration, dialogue, negotiation, and unity. Lamb notes that this is part of the general orientation of CST: "Where modern liberalism and collectivism viewed social reality as ultimately competitive and conflictive, [CST] emphasized society and economy as ontologically and ethically oriented toward cooperation and harmony."[52] We see a good example of this when Pope John Paul II wrote that a labor union should not be engaged in a "struggle 'against' others" or "to eliminate the opponent" but in a struggle "'for' the just good."[53] Pope John Paul II asserts the

---

49. *Catechism*, para. 1941.

50. *Compendium*, para. 150.

51. See the essay by Gerard Powers in chapter 7.

52. Lamb, "Solidarity," 909.

53. Pope John Paul II, *Laborem Exercens* (On Human Work, 1981), para. 20, in *Catholic Social Thought: The Documentary Heritage*, ed. David J. O'Brien and Thomas A. Shannon (Maryknoll, NY: Orbis, 1992), 380.

importance of unity, saying that in "the final analysis, both those who work and those who manage the means of production or who own them must in some way be united in . . . community."[54] Solidarity is never to be used against anyone, as in, for example, mobilizing a group to fight against another group. Rather solidarity is to encompass everyone and to be used for justice, the common good, and the betterment of the community as a whole. The end result of the struggle should be unity and reconciliation. As theologian Kristin Heyer has noted, "[l]iberation theologians and social ethicists have likewise noted magisterial Catholicism's tendency to prioritize unity, harmony and synthesis in ways that circumvent necessary conflict. . . . Without confronting issues of economic and political power and engaging grassroots mobilization, work toward and implementation of changes to the status quo will remain stunted."[55] Those who take a peacebuilding perspective, however, look at a range of possible stances for the church to take toward conflict, with a goal of promoting justice and peace—two goods that may be difficult to realize simultaneously.[56]

Whatever may be the limitations of the ways in which CST addresses conflict, undoubtedly many would agree with the well-known statement by Pope John Paul II that "peace is the fruit of solidarity."[57] Catholic Social Teaching's emphasis on solidarity has encouraged individuals and institutions to engage in relationship-building and collaboration for social justice and integral human development. One example of institutional involvement in a global solidarity project is the collaboration between the University of Notre Dame and the Nairobi-based Catholic University of Eastern Africa on the Dandora project in Kenya. This case study provides an example not only of global solidarity but of local solidarity as well.

54. Ibid., para. 20, 380–81.

55. Kristen E. Heyer, *Kinship across Borders: A Christian Ethic of Immigration* (Washington, DC: Georgetown University Press, 2012), 120.

56. See Robert J. Schreiter, R. Scott Appleby, and Gerard Powers, eds., *Peacebuilding: Catholic Theology, Ethics, and Praxis* (Maryknoll, NY: Orbis, 2010); and Cynthia Sampson, "Religion and Peacebuilding," in *Peacemaking in International Conflict*, ed. L. William Zartman, rev. ed. (Washington, DC: U.S. Institute of Peace, 2007), 273–323.

57. *Compendium*, John Paul II, quoted in para. 102.

Universities and Solidarity: The Dandora Project

Dandora is located on the eastern side of Nairobi, in the Embakasi Division. It has a population of almost half a million people. Part of Dandora is occupied by the Dandora Municipal Waste Dumping Site managed by the City Council of Nairobi.[58] The Dandora Municipal Waste Dumping Site was established by the City Council of Nairobi in the 1970s as a landfill over an unused quarry. It remains the only main site for disposal of solid waste from the entire Nairobi area, with an estimated two thousand tons of unsorted waste deposited there daily. The dumpsite is located on about thirty acres of land.

The site is an overfilled garbage heap surrounded by residential homes, businesses, schools, and churches. The dumpsite is a key livelihood-generating income for over six hundred people.[59] It provides economic opportunities for the youth groups involved in garbage collection and recycling, and a community of residents that work and live in the dumpsite area has emerged. They have built houses in the periphery of the dumpsite. The dumpsite continues to attract young children eager to make easy money at a very early age, contributing to school dropout rates in the area. It is estimated that more than two thousand children work in the dumpsite. The dumpsite has also been associated with numerous health issues: air quality is negatively impacted by the constant burning of waste and spontaneous methane fires that erupt at the dumpsite resulting in noxious smoke and fumes.

The establishment of local gangs pitted against each other for control of the dumpsite has led to general insecurity in the area. These gangs extort money from those who would like to scavenge the dumpsite. This has made it very hard to address the issue of relocating the dumpsite. However, as the *Integral Human Development Report for Dandura* notes: "The actual beneficiaries of the dumpsite . . . are the influential and politically connected individuals and private companies that are involved in the transportation and deposit of solid waste in the city."[60]

---

58. Kerubo Okioga, *Intergral Human Development Report for Dandora* (Draft) (Nairobi, Kenya: Dandora Law and Human Development Project, 2012), 10.

59. Ibid., 12.

60. Ibid.

In 2011, the University of Notre Dame, the Catholic University of Eastern Africa, located in Nairobi, and Holy Cross Catholic Parish in Dandora came together and formed the Dandora Law and Human Development Project (DLHDP) to try to solve this very critical problem in Dandora. The parish is served by Holy Cross priests, members of the religious order at the University of Notre Dame. Faced with the problem of the dumpsite, it was obvious that something had to be done. The priests approached the University of Notre Dame, who agreed to see whether they could do something. It was determined that the Ford Family Foundation at the University of Notre Dame could contribute resources and sue the Kenyan government but that this should not be done without the involvement of a local university in Nairobi.

They approached the Catholic University of Eastern Africa for partnership. At first everything seemed obvious: with Kenya's new constitution in place, it was possible to sue the government and other actors for this abuse of human rights.

Initially the problem was viewed as how to remove a dumpsite that was affecting the health of the people of Dandora, as it seemed clear that the people's health was being adversely affected. The Holy Cross parishioners of Dandora had always inquired how this dumpsite could be removed from Dandora, which would not be easy given the noncooperation of the government. With the new constitution, those in power could be taken to court and possibly compelled to remove the dumpsite. This task was to be undertaken by the law schools of both universities in collaboration with Dandora Parish.

Though it looked like a straightforward case, the reality was that this approach was misguided. There were more people who were affected by the dumpsite than was imagined. There were many people who were beneficiaries of the dumpsite, including the many poor residents who scavenged the dumpsite for their livelihood. This was a hard-hitting finding for people who wanted to address the issue of health and human rights. But human rights must address all human beings in an integral way. Those who literally lived on the dumpsite needed to be protected, and those who suffered because of the dumpsite also had to be protected.

The proposed relocation of the Dandora Dumpsite clearly generated two different views on what to do. One was that "the dumpsite must be relocated and closed for health, human rights, and developmental and environmental reasons."[61] The other was that "the dumpsite is an important source of livelihood and a coping strategy for extreme poverty and without proper alternatives, such as the extension of social security and protection or the employment of those dependent on the dumpsite for their livelihoods, the dumpsite cannot be closed or relocated, but perhaps better managed."[62]

Listening and learning was undertaken through a variety of activities with the main objective of collecting the information necessary to understand the needs of Dandora residents and the complexities of urban poverty. There was no choice but to listen to all and develop solutions.[63]

The Way Forward: Solidarity. The two universities and Dandora Parish saw that the only way out was to map the area under investigation and then do research to see the needs of the area and look for ways of addressing those needs. Through their project, the DLHDP, they commissioned research that resulted in the *Integral Human Development Report for Dandora*, which revealed how complex the issues were. The report demonstrated that one cannot solve problems partially. This will infringe on others' rights, thus defeating the purpose of the whole effort.

Lessons Learned. The lesson learned from this case is that solidarity with the marginalized must take into consideration many challenges that may not be obvious. Working together in solidarity, the University of Notre Dame, the Catholic University of Eastern Africa, and Dandora parish came to learn that there were many underlying issues not immediately apparent. Although the dumpsite was affecting the health of Dandora, it was also clear that Dandora was a beneficiary of the dumpsite. The *Integral Human Development Report for Dandora* found that it was not a simple matter of saying that the dumpsite should be removed. It was no longer a simple issue of human rights being abused by the government, but instead

61. Ibid., 13.

62. Ibid.

63. Ibid., 3. As Opongo and Orobator write: "Solidarity . . . means an awareness of the fact that *my life affects your life, and yours affects mine.* . . . From an African perspective solidarity is founded in the concept of *Uburtu* which is expressed differently in many African cultures but with a similar fundamental meaning. . . . *Uburtu* calls for an awareness of the needs of others and a full participation in the organization of the community" (Opongo and Orobator, *Faith Doing Justice*, 36).

an issue of urban poverty entangled with many factors that cannot be solved by one approach. The report ultimately recommended more dialogue with all the stakeholders and a continued search for a common solution, an exercise in inclusive solidarity.

Conclusion

We discussed various theories of solidarity and located CST on solidarity in the Cosmopolitan Solidarity school. Like other theories in this school that hold a partial solidarity model, CST affirms multiple group memberships with their moral obligations, from the local to the global. The Catholic Church exemplifies the integration of these levels of belonging in its own structure and has advocated for centuries the view that we are all members of one human family and all children of God. The church's spirituality, rituals, ethical teaching, and concrete social relations make a unique contribution to enacting Cosmopolitan Solidarity. Theory alone is not enough; we always must ask: what are the concrete ways solidarity can be learned, enacted, and sustained. In CST we can see that the beliefs, ethics, and practices of a particular religious community need not be exclusivist but in fact may lead its members to a global inclusiveness. The partial and particular can lead to the embrace of the universal. We close with a quote from Pope John Paul II that illustrates this important point by his application of an ancient Christian parable to a globalizing world:

> *God himself has created our basic interdependence and called us to solidarity with all.* This teaching is formulated in an incomparably effective manner in *the parable of the Good Samaritan,* who took care of the man who was left half dead along the road from Jerusalem to Jericho. We all travel that road and are tempted to pass by on the other side. Referring to the Samaritan who was moved by compassion, Jesus told his listeners: "Go and do the same." Today, Jesus repeats to all of us when we travel the road of our common humanity: "Go and do the same" [cf. Luke 10, 37].[64]

64. John Paul II, *John Paul II in America*, 94.

Questions for Discussion

1. How are individualism and collectivism different from solidarity?

2. Do you think people are capable of global solidarity, of seeing themselves as part of one human family and acting accordingly?

3. Give an example of what you think is a "structure of sin" and an example of a "structure of solidarity."

4. If we know that nongovernmental organizations have projects that succeed in saving lives, do we have a moral obligation to donate money to them? If so, how do we choose which ones, and how much? What does the parable of the Good Samaritan mean for us in this era of globalization?

Susan Crawford Sullivan and
Ron Pagnucco

Sharing the Vision of Justice

As we reach the end of this overview of Catholic Social Teaching (CST) and the college campus, what can we conclude? On the one hand, there is much room for optimism; the examples of CST as lived out on campuses across the county are rich and inspiring. Furthermore, these are but a few examples of the many ways in which our college campuses are putting CST into practice. On the other hand, CST is sometimes called the church's best-kept secret. One study of a nationally representative sample of parish council members in parishes across the United States found an extremely low level of knowledge about CST.[1] Also, it is quite possible for students in Catholic colleges and universities to complete their entire education without ever learning anything about CST. Some ways in which CST is ostensibly lived (such as service outreach to poor communities near our colleges), if done without reflection and awareness, can become divisive and condescending to our neighbors in poverty.

Peter-Hans Kolvenbach, SJ, the former superior general of the Jesuit order, spoke of Jesuit colleges and universities as places where students must learn to become adults who are in solidarity with the poor of the world. His words are applicable beyond Jesuit colleges to the broader body of Catholic colleges and universities. The measure of our universities, he

---

1. D. Sullins, "Catholic Social Teaching: What Do Catholics Know and What Do They Believe?," *Catholic Social Science Review* 7 (October 2003): 243–65.

said, "is not what our students do but who they become and the adult Christian responsibility they will exercise in the future toward their neighbor and their world."[2] For faculty, this means that "every discipline, beyond its necessary specialization, must engage with human society, human life, and the environment in appropriate ways, cultivating moral concern about how people ought to live together.[3] This must occur, he continued, from the point of view of the poor and others who suffer injustice, making sure their concerns find a place in research and teaching.[4]

For this to happen, CST needs to become a more widely used resource in teaching and research. Theologian Monika Hellwig, the former president of the Association of Catholic Colleges and University, discussed the reasons why CST is not more widespread in the curriculum: interdisciplinary demands, difficult style of the encyclicals and other official texts, lack of space in the curriculum, and lack of qualified faculty. She noted that theology or religious studies faculty may not feel prepared to delve into economic or political analysis beyond their areas of expertise, while social scientists often want to stay within their own disciplinary expertise and avoid the appearance of advocating for particular religious or partisan positions. Interdisciplinary work is not necessarily rewarded in the academy and its professional organizations.[5]

The contributors to this volume are faculty, most of whom are not theologians, thinking about how to integrate CST into their teaching and research interests. We recognize that non-theologians and some theologians may not be experts in CST. We believe, however, that more faculty members who might be interested in learning about the Catholic social

---

2. Peter-Hans Kolvenbach, "The Service of Faith and the Promotion of Justice in American Jesuit Higher Education," Keynote Address to "Commitment to Justice in Jesuit Higher Education," Santa Clara University, October 6, 2000, reprinted in *A Jesuit Education Reader: Contemporary Writings in the Jesuit Mission in Education, Principles, the Issue of Catholic Identity, Practical Applications of the Ignatian Way, and More*, ed. George W. Traub (Chicago: Loyola University Press, 2008), 144–62.

3. Ibid.

4. Ibid.

5. Monika Hellwig, "Curricular Contexts and Challenges for Catholic Social Thinking," in *Living the Catholic Social Tradition: Cases and Commentary*, ed. Kathleen Maas Weigert and Alexia K. Kelley (Lanham, MD: Sheed & Ward, 2005), xii–xxii.

tradition need to become familiar with it and where appropriate, incorporate it into their courses. This can be done in the interest of providing students information to bring to bear on their own analysis of societal issues and helping provide experiences or spaces where students can reflect on experiences relevant to themes in CST. In some disciplines, CST can be effectively combined with community-based learning pedagogy.[6] Catholic Social Teaching cannot be contained solely in theology or religious studies, as students may take only the few required courses, and these courses do not necessarily introduce CST. Catholic Social Teaching also cannot be confined to campus ministry and social service activities, although these are excellent places for deeper incorporation of CST to occur. Many areas of inquiry, particularly in the social sciences, can lend themselves to a deeper integration with the basic principles of CST.

In his recent book on Catholic social learning, Roger Bergman, director of the Justice and Peace Studies Program and a professor of sociology at Creighton University, points out that in hundreds of pages of Catholic social teaching texts, there is only about a page and a half written on Catholic social pedagogy.[7] Bergman goes on to discuss the only CST document to address Catholic social learning, a section in the 1971 Rome Synod of Bishops *Justice in the World*. This document notes that "individualism, materialism, and consumerism"[8] as well as the mass media and narrow concepts of schooling stand as cultural obstacles to bringing about a more just world. To bring about justice requires transformative education, whereby learners both engage in social analysis and come in direct contact with those who are suffering. As *Justice in the World* states and Bergman cites, "[E]ducation demands a renewal of heart, a renewal based on the recognition of sin in its individual and social manifestations . . . a practical education: it comes through action, participation, and vital contact with the reality of injustice."[9] This means that one role of

6. See Susan Crawford Sullivan and Margaret A. Post, "Combining Community-Based Learning and Catholic Social Teaching in Educating for Democratic Citizenship," *Journal of Catholic Higher Education* 30, no. 1 (2011): 113–31.

7. Roger Bergman, *Catholic Social Learning: Educating the Faith That Does Justice* (New York: Fordham University Press, 2011).

8. Ibid., 16.

9. Ibid., 16–17.

education is to help us recognize our individual and collective responsibility for contributing to the common good.

In our experience, many students at Catholic colleges are clearly hungry for more knowledge of Catholic social teaching. For faculty teaching about poverty, immigration, the environment, human rights, or a whole host of other issues, CST provides a rich theoretical and theological lens for students to explore these issues. Catholic Social Teaching also provides principles which can apply whether or not students or faculty members are themselves Catholic. Although scholars of Catholic higher education such as David O'Brien and Monika Hellwig have discussed reasons why it is difficult to provide more courses which incorporate CST, it is important to keep trying to find new ways to do so. Faculty from a variety of disciplines and/or faith backgrounds (including none) may be willing to come together as a study group exploring a theme central to CST. This happened in the early 1990s at the College of the Holy Cross, where faculty from biology, religious studies, sociology, history, classics, mathematics, chemistry, and economics spent nearly a year exploring the implications of the preferential option for the poor. The papers they prepared for a symposium on the anniversary of the murdered Jesuit educators at Catholic University in El Salvador resulted in the volume *Love of Learning: Desire for Justice: Undergraduate Education and the Option for the Poor.*[10]

One new initiative of the Association of Catholic Colleges and Universities is a Catholic Social Teaching Fellowship Program for interested faculty to learn more about CST. The purpose of the one-year fellowship is to develop high levels of competency in CST among interested faculty who teach at Catholic institutes of higher education. The fellowship program will situate CST in the broader Catholic intellectual tradition and give faculty, from any academic discipline, a deeper understanding of the church's social teachings so they are prepared to meaningfully integrate the church's concepts on social justice and peace into their teaching and research.

As noted in the volume's foreword, the Association of Catholic Colleges and Universities has produced a vision statement on CST and Catholic higher education. This document is updated annually with input

---

10. *Love of Learning: Desire for Justice; Undergraduate Education and the Option for the Poor*, ed. William Reiser (Scranton, PA: University of Scranton Press, 1995).

from faculty and administrators of Catholic colleges and universities across the United States. The Vision Statement makes clear that CST should be an integral part of our institutions in a number of ways:

- CST should be employed in teaching and incorporated in disciplines across the curriculum where relevant, not just in theology or religious studies. The Statement identifies community-based learning as one particularly fruitful pedagogy for engaging the intellectual resources of CST in bringing students into solidarity with the community around them.
- CST should also be employed in assessing the education that graduates of Catholic colleges and universities receive. The Statement asks, "Do graduates approach their careers as vocations in service to the common good? Do students understand higher education as a privilege that brings a corresponding responsibility to contribute to society with special attentiveness to the vulnerable, less fortunate, and powerless?"[11]
- CST principles should also be present in some of the research conducted at Catholic colleges and universities, with research questions animated by understandings of the common good and the benefit of society.
- The Vision Statement also highlights the importance of CST principles in the institutional culture of our colleges and universities. "Catholic Social Teaching has been used to evaluate Catholic higher education's employment, labor, and contracting policies with regard to respecting the basic rights of workers; following sound environmental practices, such as energy consumption, recycling, and food service sourcing; and nurturing collaborative neighborhood relationships. While much more needs to be done, practicing the ideals taught in the classroom regarding finances, justice, and neighborliness provides a living witness of CST."[12]

11. The full text of the vision statement appears in appendix 1 of this volume. Association of Catholic Colleges and Universities, "Catholic Social Teaching and Catholic Higher Education: A Vision Statement," 2012, http://www.accunet.org /VisionStatement.

12. Ibid.

Future Directions

Catholic Social Teaching is often called "the church's best-kept secret." What is no secret is the fact that younger Americans increasingly are turning away from organized religion. In a 2012 poll that received significant media attention, the Pew Research Center reported that 20 percent of all Americans, and a third of Americans under the age of thirty, are religiously unaffiliated. This is the highest percentage ever reported and a dramatic increase from earlier decades.[13] It's not that such people are not spiritual or personally religious—over two-thirds of religiously unaffiliated people say they believe in God and twenty percent even pray every day—but they do not participate in organized religion. Saying that churches focus too much on money, power, or politics, a large number of people are opting out. As noted, this is particularly true for the younger generation—while over a third of adults under age thirty are religiously unaffiliated, only 10 percent of those over age sixty-five are.[14] Another Pew Forum report states that while the overall population of Catholics in the United States has remained relatively stable over the years, this is mainly due to Catholic immigrants coming to the country. One-third of Americans raised Catholic no longer consider themselves Catholic, and former Catholics now make up 10 percent of all American adults.[15] The percentage of Catholics who describe themselves as "strong" Catholics has declined sharply in recent decades.[16] Furthermore, young adult Catholics, whether practicing Catholics or not, often have little knowledge of the Catholic faith.[17] The word "Catholic" itself can be a stumbling block to some young people, even those raised Catholic and who populate our

13. "'Nones' on the Rise," Pew Research Religion & Public Life Project, http://www.pewforum.org/2012/10/09/nones-on-the-rise/; October 9, 2012.

14. Ibid.

15. "Religious Landscape Survey," Pew Research Religion & Public Life Project, http://religions.pewforum.org/reports; August 30, 2013.

16. "'Strong' Catholic identity at a four-decade low in U.S.," Pew Research Religion & Public Life Project, http://www.pewforum.org/2013/03/13/strong-catholic -identity-at-a-four-decade-low-in-us/; March 13, 2013.

17. See, for example, Christian Smith with Patricia Snell, *Souls in Transition: The Religious and Spiritual Lives of Emerging Adults* (New York: Oxford University Press, 2009).

Catholic colleges and universities, as they may associate Catholicism with things like intolerance or partisan politics. The fallout of the pedophile scandal also continues to negatively affect people's attitudes towards the Catholic Church.

Yet, college students hunger and thirst for meaning in their lives and justice in the world around them. One only needs to look at the proliferation of campus service programs, immersion programs, community-based learning courses, and student organizations which exist now in large numbers in comparison to a few short decades ago. The essays in this volume show the intellectually rich conceptualizations in CST and what students and others at Catholic colleges are doing about issues such as poverty, peace, the environment, and human rights. Many students do not know CST and probably misperceive what the Catholic Church has to say about such issues. By exploring the theory and practice of CST, students will be able to expand their points of view and engage a powerful, if imperfect, vision of justice. And as the most systematically developed body of Christian social thought, CST deserves its place in the study of social theories and practices, by Catholics and non-Catholics alike. For example, CST concepts of solidarity, human rights, and the preferential option for the poor can be fruitfully studied and discussed by people of all backgrounds, as we hope these chapters have shown.

With few exceptions, Catholic higher education does not yet have rigorous survey data demonstrating the impact of CST on student moral and civic development. From the perspective of our own classes, we see significant evidence of student growth and development, through students' writing, classroom discussions, and as expressed in end-of-semester evaluations, from which we present a couple of excerpts:

- "It has been more than just an academic experience for me. This course has personally challenged me and has directly impacted my decisions about what I will be doing once I graduate."
- "The most meaningful aspect of the community-based learning project was integrating faith and religious background into the project—getting to see my faith in action. It has given me a new perspective on options for the future—has shown me something else I am interested in and now have skills in."

The website of the University of Notre Dame's Catholic Social Tradition minor shows similar comments from Notre Dame students who have chosen the CST minor:

- "Minoring in CST has opened my heart and mind to what it means to put my faith into action."
- "The CST minor has opened me to many experiences that now shape my relationships with people and my relationship with God. It has taken the idea of service from an occasional and superficial 'doing your duty' to a continual real and rich relationship with the global community."
- "I believe it is important to be concerned about the marginalized in our society, to understand the problems they face, and to take action for change. Every person, of any age, deserves a dignity that can only be achieved through access to the basic human rights such as healthcare. As a future pediatrician, I plan to apply what I have learned through my Catholic Social Tradition minor to provide health care to children in poverty."[18]

Beyond such anecdotal evidence, we need rigorous analysis of how CST is transmitted and the impact of learning about CST on student moral and civic development, both short-term and after graduation. Scholars have begun to study service-learning or community-based learning, as well as volunteer experience in college. For example, one longitudinal study of students in forty-two institutions found that student involvement in service during college enhanced their academic achievement (more time spent studying, better grades, degree attainment) life skills development (such as leadership and conflict resolution skills), and sense of civic responsibility (commitment to one's community, social values, racial understanding).[19] Other research shows that community service involvement helps college students clarify their identities, better understand others from diverse backgrounds, and see themselves as more intimately

18. cstminor.nd.edu.

19. Alexander W. Astin and Linda J. Sax, "How Undergraduates Are Affected by Service Participation," *Journal of College Student Development* 39 (1998): 251–63.

connected with others.[20] Research also points to the long-term benefits of volunteering. A longitudinal study of over twelve thousand students nine years after graduation found that controlling for variables affecting student predisposition to volunteer in college, those who volunteered in college were more likely to attend graduate school, be involved in their communities, feel empowered to effect social change, and feel that college had prepared them well for work.[21] We need more study of the teaching and impact of CST. A new long-term multi-institutional research initiative is underway to identify the conditions and experiences that enhance student understanding of and commitment to CST principles and to assess how institutions can better pass on the knowledge and practice of the Catholic social tradition.

Conclusion

Catholic Social Teaching is a rich resource to assist faculty in helping to develop moral and ethical citizens who use CST principles as the lens through which they see, judge, and act in the world. In this volume we have seen several Catholic campuses that offer powerful examples of how to use CST to deepen students' understanding of the structural dimensions of social problems, and to give them opportunities to act on that analysis. The Association of Catholic Colleges and Universities is developing an initiative to help interested faculty members develop competency in CST, and research is underway to help faculty empirically examine the impact of CST-enriched courses on student development and citizenship activities beyond the classroom. The comparison of CST concepts with concepts of justice and peace in secular and other religious traditions can lead to fruitful insights. Now is the time to move forward in integrating CST and putting it into action on our campuses.

20. Robert A. Rhoads, "In the Service of Citizenship: A Study of Student Involvement in Community Service," *The Journal of Higher Education* 69 (1998): 277–97.

21. Alexander W. Astin, Linda J. Sax, and J. Juan Avalos, "Long-Term Effects of Volunteerism during the Undergraduate Years," *The Review of Higher Education* 22 (1999): 187–202.

Appendix 1

Catholic Higher Education and Catholic Social Teaching: A Vision Statement

Association of Catholic Colleges and Universities, 2012

In 1998, the United States Conference of Catholic Bishops issued "Sharing Catholic Social Teaching" to clarify and proclaim the essential place of the social teaching of the Church in the Catholic faith and in Catholic education. Catholic colleges and universities have fruitfully enacted many of the document's recommendations for higher education. In light of those successes and in recognition that much has changed in our world in the decade since the document was written, Catholic higher education continues to assess its context, commit to the principles of Catholic Social Teaching (CST) and to advance a vision that includes new reflections and creative responses.

Catholic Social Teaching is the tradition of thought in which the Church seeks to advance justice in the world by engaging social, cultural, political, and economic realities in our day. Thus, CST is both fitting and essential to the Catholic university's mission: the education and formation of its students, the research it undertakes, and the conduct of its corporate and institutional life. See the "Catholic Social Teaching" portion of the USCCB website for a CST overview (visit www.usccb.org and search for "Catholic Social Teaching").

Education and Formation

Catholic Social Teaching assumes that participation in societal life, local and global, public and economic, is an inherently moral undertaking.

To that end, CST can be a powerful tool in preparing students for the ethical and moral dimensions of professional practice and good citizenship.

Many Catholic colleges and universities strive to incorporate CST across the curriculum. While this can be a challenging responsibility, it can be done in a manner consistent with the educational and accreditation standards of each academic discipline.

The goal of incorporating CST across the curriculum can serve as one way of deepening the dialogue between the disciplines in which each makes its own "distinct contribution in the search for solutions" (*Ex corde Ecclesiae*, 32).

Catholic Social Teaching should also be employed as a lens through which to assess the education we offer. Do graduates approach their careers as vocations in service to the common good? Do students understand higher education as a privilege that brings a corresponding responsibility to contribute to society with special attentiveness to those who are vulnerable, less fortunate, and powerless?

Community-based learning illuminated by CST provides a profound opportunity for students to connect higher education with active participation in society. Community-based learning that integrates the intellectual framework of CST can help students understand the commitment of the Church to issues of social and economic justice, bring students into deeper solidarity with their communities, incorporate the mission of the institution and its Catholic identity, and, through evaluation and reflection, provide a foundation for life-long reflection and service. Through ongoing dialogue with on-campus groups (faculty, campus ministers, and administrators), as well as off-campus groups (such as neighborhood organizations, non profits, and businesses), engaged learning opportunities can find root in the academic and spiritual life of the campus and, at the same time, meet an authentic need of the local community.

Research

Devoted to seeking justice and serving the world, Catholic higher education commits itself to academic research grounded in CST. Research is central to the university's service to the Church and society (*Ex corde Ecclesiae*, 32). Catholic Social Teaching depends upon an ongoing analysis of changing societal conditions in light of its moral and ethical principles. Faculty of any faith disposition or none are encouraged to frame research questions and conduct research using the principles of CST (for example, concern for the common good, solidarity, preferential option for the poor) for the good of society. Universities are particularly encouraged to promote research based on principles of CST through university sponsored fellowships and research grants. Universities are similarly encouraged to support engaged research done in partnership with community organizations, including Catholic social ministry agencies.

Institutional Culture

Catholic higher education offers a living context that calls the educational community into a deeper understanding and practice of CST. For that reason, schools continue to strive to incorporate CST into all aspects of their institutional life. Catholic Social Teaching has been used to evaluate Catholic higher education's employment, labor and contracting policies with regard to respecting the basic rights of workers; following sound environmental practices, such as energy consumption, recycling, and food service sourcing; and nurturing collaborative neighborhood relationships. While much more needs to be done, practicing the ideals taught in the classroom regarding finances, justice, and neighborliness provides a living witness of CST.

Toward a World Made New . . .

According to the *Compendium of the Social Doctrine of the Church*, the dignity of the human person and our inherent social nature are the foundation of CST. The *Compendium* states that the dignity of the human person, the sanctity of human life, and life and justice issues must be addressed in fostering the common good of all, from conception to natural death. Too often, justice and life issues are seen as the concerns of competing constituencies. We envision a time when our graduates and the world community will understand and engage the whole spectrum of concerns that constitute what John Paul II termed a "culture of life."

We live in a global society made increasingly complex through ongoing revolutions in transportation options, communication technologies, economic exchanges, religious convictions, cultural diversity, and political developments. While globalization holds the threat of greater conflict, it also presents opportunities for the advancement of human dignity and the common good through global institutions such as the United Nations and, therefore, progress toward a "culture of life," replacing the dominant competitive paradigm with cooperation. The following issues profoundly impact the "culture of life" for people around the globe and command the careful attention of our colleges and universities.

Economy and the Dignity of Work

Catholic Social Teaching offers a moral vision for the economy where "the dignity and complete vocation of the human person and the welfare of society as a whole are to be respected and promoted" (# 331). Catholic Social Teaching asserts that the economy should serve the person, and that "everyone has the right to participate in economic life and the duty to contribute, each according to his own capacity" (# 333). Work is the essential way people develop their capacities, provide for the material needs of their families, contribute to the common good, and participate in God's creation. The new economic realities of our time call for a deeper engagement between economics and CST. Concepts such as the dignity of labor, the common good, the preferential option for the poor, and human solidarity are essential to forge a more just, merciful, and sustainable global economy. Students formed in a CST vision and methodology learn that economic responsibility is not reduced to competitiveness and the maximization of profit.

Environment

Global climate change and environmental degradation pose fundamental challenges to our contemporary form of life. Just as care for the sick and respect for the sanctity of life have made Catholic universities centers of research on bioethics, our era desperately needs a similar combination of ethical reflection and scientific research grounded in care for God's creation. To address these global moral challenges, students need education in the complex science of climate change and resource consumption in tandem with a rich moral formation. Research and course work on the science and morality of environment and climate change can be reinforced and grounded by making our campuses practical laboratories in sustainable living. Furthermore, Catholic higher education is called upon to help the world see and justly respond to the fact that environmental degradation will adversely affect the world's poor in profound ways.

Migration

Extreme poverty, violent conflicts, natural disasters, human rights violations, and imbalanced international trade agreements remain the primary reasons people uproot from their homelands and risk their lives and search for better lives. Guided by CST, institutions of Catholic higher education work against the forces of injustice in society in order to stand in solidarity with migrants, regardless of their immigration status. Through education, advocacy, and direct service, and through providing scholarships and educational opportunities that open doors to the marginalized and excluded, we seek to foster right relationship that promote diversity in the human family and promote human dignity among those who are most vulnerable in our society.

Gender, Ethnic, and Racial Discrimination

Societal injustices based on gender, race, ethnicity, economic status, and other factors persist and remain beyond an individual's control. Catholic higher education continues to examine such factors and educate university communities on the role that CST principles have in enabling the full realization of human potential. Catholic Social Teaching themes provide a framework for addressing discrimination as an issue of social injustice that requires interdisciplinary collaboration among the natural and social sciences and the humanities on our campuses.

Peace

Catholic Social Teaching incorporates a rich tradition of reflection on peace. This tradition includes both the ethics of war and peace (just war and nonviolence) as well as the spirituality, theology, ethics, and praxis of peacebuilding (conflict prevention, conflict management, and post-conflict reconciliation). Since peace is not just the absence of war, but the result of justice motivated by love, peace calls for the development of just institutions at all levels of society, including international institutions that can address questions that individual nations cannot address alone. Catholic colleges and universities are uniquely positioned both to educate about, reflect on, and contribute to the development of this tradition, as well as to serve as a resource to the many "artisans of peace" in the Church who are transforming conflict around the world.

Human Rights

The Church has extolled the United Nations Universal Declaration of Human rights as "a milestone on mankind's moral progress," because the Church shares the belief that respect for the inherent dignity of the human person is the foundation for freedom, justice, and peace in the world. The Church actively promotes human dignity and rights throughout the world in dialogue with secular human rights organizations.

Catholic Social Teaching offers vital contributions to the promotion of human dignity and rights. It teaches that all human beings are free and equal in dignity and rights because God created them in his likeness and image; that God endowed human beings with reason and conscience and commanded them to act in solidarity towards one another in a spirit of love; that personal rights must be balanced with duties to the common good; and that demands for justice must be tempered with appeals for reconciliation in the search for peace.

Human Rights Studies at Catholic colleges and universities, like peace and social justice studies, engages students in a dialogue between CST and the modern human rights idea, invites them to reflect on the vitally important contributions CST makes to in global efforts to promote human dignity and rights, and prepares them for careers in service to the common good.

Conclusion

Catholic colleges and universities have made steady progress engaging CST during the past decade. Looking forward, there is hope for further integration of CST in the curricula, research, and institutional operations of Catholic higher educational institutions. We have much to offer the human community as it embraces profound challenges in the coming years. Catholic colleges and universities will continue to be at the forefront of ensuring that the Church's social teaching contributes to addressing these challenges. To that end, Catholic colleges and universities will strive to develop institutional plans and secure the necessary funding to support faculty and administration in the integration of CST in educational activities, research, and corporate endeavors. By matching determination with conviction, justice can become ever more a reality in our time.

> Only in charity, illuminated by the light of reason and faith, is it possible to pursue development goals that possess a more humane and humanizing value. (*Caritas in Veritate*, 8)

Association of Catholic Colleges and Universities
One Dupont Circle, Suite 650
Washington, DC 20036
www.accunet.org

Appendix 2

Catholic Social Teaching Documents: Papal Social Encyclicals and U.S. Bishops' Pastorals[1]

Papal and Vatican Documents

- *Rerum Novarum* (On the Condition of Labor)—Pope Leo XIII, 1891
- *Quadragesimo Anno* (After Forty Years)—Pope Pius XI, 1931
- *Mater et Magistra* (Christianity and Social Progress)—Pope John XXIII, 1961
- *Pacem in Terris* (Peace on Earth)—Pope John XXIII, 1963
- *Gaudium et Spes* (Pastoral Constitution on the Church in the Modern World)—Second Vatican Council, 1965
- *Dignitatis Humanae* (Declaration on Religious Freedom)—Second Vatican Council, 1965
- *Populorum Progressio* (On the Development of Peoples)—Pope Paul VI, 1967
- *Octogesima Adveniens* (A Call to Action)—Pope Paul VI, 1971
- *Evangelii Nuntiandi* (Evangelization in the Modern World)—Paul VI, 1975
- *Laborem Exercens* (On Human Work)—Pope John Paul II, 1981
- *Sollicitudo Rei Socialis* (On Social Concern)—Pope John Paul II, 1987
- *The Church and Racism: Towards a more fraternal society*—Pontifical Council for Justice and Peace, 1989
- *Centesimus Annus* (The Hundredth Year)—Pope John Paul II, 1991

1. United States Catholic Conference of Bishops http://www.usccb.org/beliefs-and-teachings/what-we-believe/catholic-social-teaching/foundational-documents.cfm.

- *Veritatis splendor* (The Splendor of Truth)—Pope John Paul II, 1993
- *Evangelium Vitae* (The Gospel of Life)—Pope John Paul II, 1995
- *Dignitas Personae* (The Dignity of a Person)—Congregation for the Doctrine of the Faith, 1998
- *Ecclesia in America* (The Church in America)—Pope John Paul II, 1999
- *Fides et Ratio* (Faith and Reason)—Pope John Paul II, 1998
- *Doctrinal Note on Some Questions Regarding the Participation of Catholics in Political Life*—Congregation for the Doctrine of the Faith, 2002
- *Compendium of the Social Doctrine of the Church*—Pontifical Council for Justice and Peace, 2004
- *Deus Caritas Est* (God Is Love)—Pope Benedict XVI, 2005
- *Sacramentum Caritatis* (The Eucharist as the Source and Summit of the Church's Life and Mission)—Pope Benedict XVI, 2007 (especially paragraphs 47, 49, 82-84, and 88-92)
- *Caritas in Veritate* (Charity in Truth)—Pope Benedict XVI, 2009
- *Lumen Fidei* (The Light of Faith)—Pope Francis, 2013

U.S. Bishops' Pastorals

- Labor Day Statements
- Respecting the Just Rights of Workers, June 2009
- Forming Consciences for Faithful Citizenship, November 2007
- A Culture of Life and the Penalty of Death, November 2005
- Catholics in Political Life, June 2004
- "For I Was Hungry and You Gave Me Food" Catholic Reflections on Food, Farmers, and Farmworkers, December 2003
- Strangers No Longer, January 2003, Joint Statement from Bishops of the United States and Mexico
- A Place at the Table: A Catholic Recommitment to Overcome Poverty and to Respect the Dignity of All God's Children, December 2002
- Statement on Israeli-Palestinian Violence, March 2002
- A Call to Solidarity with Africa, November 2001
- A Pastoral Message: Living with Faith and Hope After September 11, November 2001

- Resolution on the Israeli-Palestinian Crisis, June 2001
- Global Climate Change: A Plea for Dialogue, Prudence, and the Common Good, June 2001
- Responsibility, Rehabilitation, and Restoration: A Catholic Perspective on Crime and Criminal Justice, November 2000
- Everyday Christianity: To Hunger and Thirst for Justice, November 1999
- In All Things Charity: A Pastoral Challenge for the New Millennium, November 1999
- Sharing Catholic Social Teaching: Challenges and Directions, June 1999
- A Good Friday Appeal to End the Death Penalty, April 1999
- A Commitment to All Generations: Social Security and the Common Good, May 1999
- A Jubilee Call for Debt Forgiveness, April 1999
- Living the Gospel of Life, November 1998
- Called to Global Solidarity, November 1997
- A Catholic Framework for Economic Life, November 1996
- A Decade After Economic Justice for All, November 1995
- Sowing Weapons of War, June 1995
- Confronting a Culture of Violence, November 1994
- Communities of Salt and Light, November 1993
- The Harvest of Justice is Sown in Peace, November 1993
- When I Call for Help: A Pastoral Response to Domestic Violence Against Women, September 1992
- A Matter of the Heart, November 1992
- Renewing the Earth, 1991
- Economic Justice for All, November 1986
- The Challenge of Peace, 1983
- Statement on Capital Punishment, November 1980
- Brothers and Sisters to Us, 1979
- Declaration on Conscientious Objection and Selective Conscientious Objection, October 1971

Contributors

David Coleman, professor of religious studies, Chaminade University of Honolulu. David has been at Chaminade for twenty-nine years, where he has taught World Religions, Buddhist Christian Dialogue, Catholic Social Teaching, Holocaust Studies, and a new course on nursing: Spirituality and Ethics. His research is focused on the politics of the sacred in which he explores religious institutions as social and political actors within civil societies. He currently is the dean of humanities and fine arts at Chaminade. David is a member of the ACCU Peace and Justice Education Advisory Committee and serves on the Hawaii Catholic Conference and the Board of Education for the Diocese of Honolulu. He works with the diocesan Office for Social Ministries as the diocesan director for Catholic Relief Service. He directs the Associate of Arts program in Chuuk, Federated States of Micronesia at the Caroline College and Pastoral Institute, established in 2010.

Colleen Cross, project coordinator of the Immigration Initiative, Institute for Latino Studies, University of Notre Dame. Colleen is a recent graduate of Notre Dame with a master's of theological studies and has previously worked with the U.S. Conference of Catholic Bishops. Her interests include theology, education, and migration.

Linda Plitt Donaldson, MSW, PhD, associate professor. Dr. Donaldson has been on the faculty of the National Catholic School of Social service since 2004, bringing extensive experience in nonprofit social service management and public policy advocacy. Prior to teaching at NCSSS, Dr. Donaldson worked for ten years in a community-based homeless services agency in Washington, DC, providing direct service; directing programs in advocacy, social justice, and family services; and developing affordable housing. Prior to her nonprofit experience, Dr. Donaldson was a legislative fellow for the late Senator Paul Wellstone. Her research interests are in the areas of advocacy, community organizing, social change practice, and strategies to end homelessness. She has also written about the integration of Catholic Social Teaching in graduate social work education, and co-edited a special issue of the journal *Social Work and Christianity* on Catholic Social Teaching and social work that was published in the summer of 2012.

Mark Ensalaco, associate professor of political science, founding director, Human Rights Program, University of Dayton. As member of the University of Dayton faculty since 1989, Mark regularly teaches courses in the Politics of Human Rights, Comparative Politics: Latin America, United States–Latin America Relations, and Political Violence. His research interests include human rights and human trafficking, Middle Eastern terrorism, and U.S. and Latin America relations, and he speaks and writes regularly on the intersections of these topics. Mark is a member of the ACCU Peace and Justice Education Advisory Committee.

Bernard Evans, associate dean for faculty, School of Theology; Virgil Michael Ecumenical Chair in Rural Social Ministries; associate professor of theology, College of Saint Benedict and Saint John's University, Collegeville, Minnesota. Bernie regularly teaches courses on the Environment in Christian Theology, Rural Social Issues, and Christian Social Ethics. His recent publications include *Vote Catholic: Beyond the Political Din* (2008) and *Lazarus at the Table: Catholics and Social Justice* (2006).

Fr. Peter Gichure, associate professor of theology, academic liaison, The Catholic University of Eastern Africa; lecturer in peace studies, Tangaza College; theological advisor, Peace and Justice Commission, Kenyan Episcopal Conference of Catholic Bishops; executive secretary of the Association of Catholic Universities and Higher Institutes of Africa and Madagascar. Fr. Peter's most recent publications include *Contextual Theology: Its Scope and Meaning* (2008); *Religion and Politics in Africa*, co-edited with Dianne Stinton (2008); and *Modelling a Catholic University to Meet 21st Century Challenges*, co-edited with A. L. Lando and J. B. Kanakulya (2011).

Fr. Daniel Groody, associate professor of theology, director of the Immigration Initiative, Institute for Latino Studies, University of Notre

Dame. Fr. Dan, a Holy Cross priest, draws on years of work in Latin America, particularly along the U.S.–Mexico border, and has authored and edited various books and articles that have been translated into five languages, including *The Preferential Option for the Poor Beyond Theology* (2013), *Globalization, Spirituality, and Justice: Navigating the Path to Peace* (2007), and *Border of Death, Valley of Life: An Immigrant Journey of Heart and Spirit* (2002). He has worked with the U.S. Congress, the U.S. Conference of Catholic Bishops, the World Council of Churches, and the Vatican on issues of theology, globalization, and migration. He is also the executive producer of various films and documentaries, including *Dying to Live: A Migrant's Journey* and *One Border, One Body: Immigration and the Eucharist*, which have received international acclaim and aired on various television stations, including PBS. Fr. Dan is a member of the ACCU Peace and Justice Education Committee.

Thomas M. Landy is director of the Rev. Michael C. McFarland, S.J. Center for Religion, Ethics and Culture at the College of the Holy Cross. His primary research is in global Catholicism, and he will soon launch an international project, Catholics & Cultures, at Holy Cross. In 1992 he founded Collegium, a colloquy on faith and intellectual life. A consortium of sixty-five Catholic colleges and universities in the U.S. and Canada, Collegium sponsors highly regarded summer faculty development programs around the country. Collegium is sponsored by the Association of Catholic Colleges and Universities, and Landy continues to serve as Collegium's executive director. He is editor of *As Leaven for the World: Catholic Reflections on Faith, Vocation, and the Intellectual Life* (Franklin, WI: Sheed and Ward, 2001), and, with Karen Eifler, the forthcoming *Becoming Beholders: Cultivating a Sacramental Imagination in the Classroom* (Collegeville, MN: Liturgical Press, 2014). He is the 2009 recipient of the John Henry Newman Medal, which honors exemplars of Jesuit Catholic education, from Loyola College in Maryland.

David O'Brien is emeritus professor of history and Loyola Professor of Catholic Studies at the College of the Holy Cross. From 2009 to 2012 he served as University Professor of Faith and Culture at the University of Dayton. A founding member of the ACCU Task Force on Justice and Peace Education, he was a member of the committee that assisted in preparation of the Report of the Task Force on Catholic Social Teaching and Catholic Education. He has written extensively on American Catholic history, and he was awarded the Theodore M. Hesburgh Award for Distinguished Service to Catholic Higher Education.

Ronald Pagnucco, associate professor of peace studies, chair, Department of Peace Studies, College of Saint Benedict and Saint John's University, Collegeville, Minnesota. Ron has authored or co-authored essays that have appeared in *Human Rights Quarterly*; *Research in Social Movements, Conflict and Change*; *The Journal of Intergroup Relations*; *Research on Democracy and Society*; the *Journal for Peace and Justice Studies*, and *Disruptive Religion* (C. Smith, ed. Routledge, 1995). With Jackie Smith and Charles Chatfield, he co-edited *Transnational Social Movements and Global Politics* (1997) and he co-edited with Chris Hausmann a special issue of the *Journal for Peace and Justice Studies* on "Peacebuilding in Africa" (20, no. 2, 2011). Ron is a member of the Peace and Justice Education Advisory Committee of the ACCU.

Gerard Powers, director of Catholic Peacebuilding Studies, University of Notre Dame. Jerry is professor of the practice of Catholic peacebuilding at the University of Notre Dame's Kroc Institute. He also coordinates the Catholic Peacebuilding Network, which links scholars with Catholic leaders from war-torn countries in an effort to enhance the study and practice of conflict prevention, conflict resolution, and post-conflict reconciliation. Before he joined the Kroc faculty in 2004, Powers was director of the Office of International Justice and Peace of the U.S. Conference of Catholic Bishops, and from 1987 to 1998 he was a foreign policy advisor in the same office. He is co-editor (with Schreiter and Appleby) of *Peacebuilding: Catholic Theology, Ethics and Praxis* (2010) and co-editor (with Philpott) of *Strategies of Peace: Transforming Conflict in a Violent World* (2010).

Susan Crawford Sullivan, associate professor of sociology, College of the Holy Cross. Susan's research interests lie at the intersection of sociology of religion, family, and poverty and public policy. Her book, *Living Faith: Everyday Religion and Mothers in Poverty* (University of Chicago Press 2011), won the 2012 Distinguished Book Award from both the Society for the Scientific Study of Religion and the American Sociological Association sociology of religion section. She has also written on Catholic Social Teaching and community-based learning, as well as on the role of college mission statements in promoting student community engagement.

She has published articles in journals such as *Sociology of Religion*; *Review of Religious Research*; *Journal of Catholic Higher Education*; and *Journal of College Student Development*. Prior to entering academia, Dr. Sullivan held a number of nonprofit positions, including working for Catholic Charities with homeless mothers and consulting overseas for UNICEF on child labor, former child soldiers, and orphans. Early in her career, she served as a U.S. Air Force officer. She has been a member of the ACCU Peace and Justice Advisory Committee since 2009.